NEW TOOLS FOR URBAN MANAGEMENT

HARVARD STUDIES
IN TECHNOLOGY AND SOCIETY

The volumes in this series present the results of studies by the Harvard University Program on Technology and Society. The Program was established in 1964 by a grant from the International Business Machines Corporation to undertake an inquiry in depth into the effects of technological change on the economy, on public policies, and on the character of the society, as well as into the reciprocal effects of social progress on the nature, dimensions, and directions of scientific and technological developments.

OTHER VOLUMES IN THE SERIES

Anthony G. Oettinger with Sema Marks, *Run, Computer, Run: The Mythology of Educational Innovation* (Harvard University Press, 1969).

Emmanuel G. Mesthene, *Technological Change: Its Impact on Man and Society* (Harvard University Press, 1970).

Anne P. Carter, *Structural Change in the American Economy* (Harvard University Press, 1970).

Robin Marris and Adrian Wood, eds., *The Corporate Economy: Growth, Competition, and Innovative Potential* (Harvard University Press, 1971).

Alan F. Westin, ed., *Information Technology in a Democracy* (Harvard University Press, 1971).

Everett I. Mendelsohn, Judith P. Swazey, and Irene Taviss, eds., *Human Aspects of Biomedical Innovation* (Harvard University Press, 1971).

NEW TOOLS FOR URBAN MANAGEMENT:
Studies in Systems and Organizational Analysis

RICHARD S. ROSENBLOOM
Professor of Business Administration
Harvard University

JOHN R. RUSSELL
Lecturer on Business Administration
Harvard University

With Contributions by:

Carter F. Bales
Robert P. O'Block
Mahlon Apgar, IV

DIVISION OF RESEARCH
GRADUATE SCHOOL OF BUSINESS ADMINISTRATION
HARVARD UNIVERSITY
BOSTON · 1971

Library of Congress Catalog Card No. 73–168850
ISBN 0–87584–093–0

PRINTED IN THE UNITED STATES OF AMERICA

TABLE OF CONTENTS

LIST OF FIGURES

LIST OF TABLES

PREFACE

IN THIS BOOK we are concerned with the interaction between an evolving body of intellectual tools, namely, methods of analysis, and an increasingly important sector of American life, the management of urban affairs.

Reference to technology ordinarily evokes images of the artifacts of an industrial society—aircraft, reactors, communication devices, production machinery, and the like—or of the "hard" sciences that shape and stimulate change in man's modern tools. There is a class of technology, however, that is intellectual in character, comprising the intangible tools of work in a complex society, rooted now in abstract disciplines such as philosophy and mathematics. Although the "hard" tools dominate the headlines and public consciousness, the "soft" ones shape much of the conduct of affairs and reshape the institutions within which decisions are made.

Several years ago, a flood of speculative commentary arose concerning the applicability of modern methods of analysis in the solution of contemporary urban problems. Much of this discussion centered on the so-called "systems" approach. Early efforts to apply systems techniques to urban problems dealt primarily with whether or not analysis and analysts could cope successfully with the intricacies and obstinacies of the urban environment. In other words, they addressed the problem of doing analytic work that would be considered adequate from a technical viewpoint. While the early "demonstrations" did serve to answer questions of technical proficiency, they were not designed to examine or deal with the problems of integrating a new approach, such as systems analysis, into the on-going management process of cities.

More recently others have sought to bring analysis into the urban environment in such a way that its results can and will be used by city administrators to improve the basis on which they make resource allocation and policy commitments. This book reports on exploratory studies of a small number of these recent efforts. Our focus, throughout, is on the interaction between new approaches to analysis and the organization and management of urban affairs. Matters of analytic technique or of the substance of urban problems are treated only incidentally. We believe that better methods can be used for analysis of urban issues, yielding beneficial results for city administrators and citizens alike. But for useful results to be attained, the problems of linking analysis effectively to action must be dealt with directly, thoroughly, and with sensitivity by both administrators and analysts.

New technology often creates new and uncertain opportunities for man and society. The extent to which those opportunities will be utilized and the consequences of their use are not determined by inherent technical factors; they emerge from the interaction of man and technology. A major new development may shatter an old equilibrium, but it remains difficult to discern in the early stages of change just what new equilibrium is being approached, and at what rate. Our strategy has been to conduct a few careful probes rather than to attempt a comprehensive mapping.[1] Thus Chapters 2–5 report case studies of efforts to effect innovations in analysis for urban decisions in a variety of settings. These are neither exhaustive nor necessarily representative of such efforts as they occurred in the United States during recent years. As

---

[1] Irene Taviss, in a recent survey of this literature, writes that the use of new technological devices (computers, etc.) in public decision making has "not been very widespread and studies of their actual functioning have been few."

targets of opportunity in a new field, they were chosen because of their intrinsic interest, the lessons they seemed to hold, and the availability of an informed participant observer who could report and analyze events for us.

We chose to have each study written by a participant in the situation being described. While we sacrificed, thereby, the cool detachment of the observer, we gained, hopefully, the fuller awareness and heightened sensibilities of the man who has lived the more involved role. As a balancing factor, each author's account has been subjected to careful critique by the principal authors and other colleagues, and the cases published here are the outcome of a process of evaluation and review.

The individual contributors were encouraged to approach each case on its own terms, to pose those questions that seemed most germane to the situation, and to reach those findings that could rest comfortably on the evidence at hand. Some may detect a lack of rigor in this method of research. Our intent was to be suggestive, rather than definitive, to discern and illuminate unifying characteristics amidst the idiosyncrasies of otherwise diverse situations. Thus these studies of urban management, strictly speaking, are a set of essays, in the several senses of that word.

The more general findings of our study, growing out of the four cases and other evidence, are given in Chapter 6. Here we speak only to the direct effects of a new technology and to one of its immediate indirect consequences, the reshaping of the host organization. Questions having to do with the effect of analysis on the process and values of democratic government are manifestly more important, but not answerable in the same sense as the more limited questions we have posed. It seems probable, however, that an understanding of the nature and immediate consequences of these innovations in analysis can improve the level of discourse about more global issues.

Many and diverse contributions by others must be acknowledged. Our greatest debt is to the numerous people whose thoughts and deeds brought about the undertakings in analysis and management described in this book. Financial support for this work came initially from the PPG Industries Foundation, under a grant to the Harvard Business School for a study of "Management and the City of the Future." Subsequent support, intellectual as well as financial, was provided by the Harvard Program on Technology and Society. Messrs. Apgar and O'Block prepared drafts of their studies while serving as Research Associates of our project at Harvard, but the revision of their cases, and the entire preparation of the chapter by Mr. Bales, were accomplished while the authors were on the staff of McKinsey & Company. We are deeply grateful for the freedom to participate in academic research that was granted to these authors by their firm. We also wish to acknowledge with much appreciation the financial support which came from the allocation of funds from gifts to the School by The Associates of the Harvard Business School.

In November 1969 the Program on Technology and Society sponsored a meeting on Systems Analysis in the Urban Sector. Many of the ideas in this book were shaped by the valuable discussion of the 20 invited participants at that meeting. Raymond Bauer read several of the case studies in early drafts and offered many useful comments. The entire manuscript was read by Emmanuel Mesthene, Juergen Schmandt, and Irene Taviss, whose comments and encouragement helped immeasurably. Jane Draper attended intelligently and effectively to the myriad administrative requirements of the project. Most important of all, Betty Fuchs assisted in the preparation of the entire mansucript. Her clear eye and sound judgment contributed to almost every page. Hilma Holton supervised the final editing and production of the book, easing our task at many points.

Though much credit is due to those named, and others unnamed, responsibility for what follows rests with the authors. Each case is the work of the author so identified, while responsibility for the work as a whole and its principal conclusions rests with the undersigned.

RICHARD S. ROSENBLOOM
JOHN R. RUSSELL

Soldiers Field
Boston, Massachusetts
June 1971

CHAPTER 1

INTRODUCTION

AMERICA'S CITIES ARE BESET BY PROBLEMS, but there is little agreement about the nature of these problems or what caused them. Some people have used dramatic terms, claiming that the cities are "in crisis" or "approaching the brink," and that "a total commitment is necessary to save them." Others recognize the urgency of certain specific needs, but point to the long-standing existence of most urban problems. Despite the absence of consensus on the precise nature of our cities' problems, their seriousness, or the most appropriate remedies, there is widespread agreement on one point: the cities are in trouble.

The sustained economic expansion and rapid technological change of recent decades have wrought radical physical and social change in the cities. Only urban government remains substantially the same. Institutions of the nineteenth century still govern the cities' preparation for the twenty-first. This institutional lag, aggravated by the pressures of rapidly rising urban populations and the irony of persistent poverty amidst evident aggregate economic growth, has helped to thrust the cities to the forefront of our national consciousness.

The shortcomings of contemporary urban life seem especially severe in relation to the seemingly unbounded technological power of American society. Some protagonists have proposed that the nation produce deliberate innovation in the cities by directing the capabilities of the space and defense industries (or of new enterprises created on the same model) to the design, development, and management of large-scale urban systems. Governors, congressmen, scientists and engineers, industrialists, and many others have given considerable public currency to the notion that "systems analysis" and the "systems approach," in particular, are capabilities developed and refined in the aerospace industry that have considerable relevance to urban needs.[1]

There is an obvious appeal to the suggestion that the technological and managerial capability that produced Apollo might be able to "solve" some of our urban ills. Moreover, the analogy has a certain plausibility — urban systems, like space systems, are complex and they are both matters of public responsibility. But there are differences to be noted also. The performance of urban systems is affected by choices made and action taken independently by many individuals and organizations. Moreover, the city is a system in which the consequences of those choices interact. Thus, the forces that will make the difference between beauty and blight, between freedom and frustration, and between order and sprawl, emerge from an unknowable web of interrelationships.

Nevertheless, a significant and evolving base of *intellectual technology* — a technology of analysis, planning and control — for understanding and shaping complex systems has been developed, largely from efforts in space and defense activities. These conceptual tools, buttressed by tangible improvements in devices for data processing and communications, seem to create opportunities for innovation in urban management. There is no consensus, however, on the nature and significance of these opportunities and on the extent to which they are being realized in practice.

---

[1] Footnotes appear at the end of each chapter.

So far, few cities have made any real commitment to the use of systems analysis or related methods to assist in solving their problems. Only a minute fraction of the nation's 81,000 local governments, the 10 million people they employ, or the 140 million urban residents that they govern, have been directly affected by any change of this sort. But those few municipalities that have done so present us with a wide range of kinds of use in varying types of government. There are instructive examples in large and small municipalities, state and county governments, and special agencies. There are examples in housing, transportation, and the physical and economic development of cities; in police, fire, sanitation, and the control of environmental quality; and even in health, education, and welfare. Some of these efforts have failed completely and some have achieved a high degree of success, but the majority fall somewhere in between.

The purpose of this book is to look in depth at some of these specific efforts in a descriptive and exploratory way. We can hope to learn something about the kinds of urban problems for which analysis is most effective, which analytical tools or methods are best suited to tackling these problems, what the potential is for adapting the present tools for *new* uses in the urban environment, what kinds of obstacles have been encountered, which obstacles can be overcome, and how. By answering these questions, we hope that we may help to "de-mystify" a field shrouded in rhetorical fog and contribute to a better understanding of the nature and limits of the technological potential. In addition, by evaluation of case studies and other evidence drawn from practical experience we can develop provisional answers to questions pertaining to methods and strategies that might be employed to utilize new techniques of analysis more effectively.

The efforts in urban analysis which we have chosen to examine are described in four case studies reflecting the prevalent diversity in the kind of problems tackled, the analytical tools employed to solve them, and the kind and size of government involved. The diversity of the cases extends also to the degree of success achieved. The cases highlight the relationship between the professional analysts and the city administrators as they work together during both the analysis of problems and the implementation of change.

The four case studies are presented in subsequent chapters. The first reviews two projects aimed at demonstrating the practicality and value in a number of medium-sized cities of conducting systems analyses to support major decisions in diverse problem areas. The "demonstration project" is a common way of promoting the use of new methods. This case examines the actual effectiveness of this approach in two cities, Dayton, Ohio, and East Lansing, Michigan. The Dayton case recounts the failure of an analytic approach to contribute to resolution of unemployment problems in that city's ghetto areas. The case illustrates clearly the importance of proper timing and of the participation and interest of administrative authorities in using the analysis in the city. The East Lansing demonstration was based on a straightforward analysis of fire station location. In this case the demonstration was successful. The problem was high on the list of priorities of the city manager, easily quantifiable, and the alternative solutions readily implementable.

Chapter 3 is a case set in the nation's largest city, reporting the experience of New York's Bureau of the Budget and operating agencies in the development of new analytic capabilities. The emphasis in this case is on the process of introducing analytic methods in a government composed of a vast number of agencies and administrators. The experiences illustrated in New York encompass the entire range of results from total failure to considerable success. The case examines a strategy for introducing analysis for varying kinds of problems under the jurisdiction of administrators with a diversity of views and needs.

For the other two studies, the setting shifts from municipalities to more novel organizational forms. The third case takes a look at an agency of state government, The New Jersey Housing Finance Agency, charged with administering a technically complex housing program for a number of cities. The case reviews the experience of a young "businesslike" public agency in developing and using a computer-based model for analysis of a key agency function. This example of analysis suggests the far-reaching organizational consequences of the introduction of a new technique. Finally, in a review of the uses of system analysis in a new city, we present a case study of innovations in analysis employed by the Rouse Company to plan and build the new town of Columbia, Maryland. More a matter of "systematic" analysis than of "systems" analysis, the experience in Columbia does show the value of such an approach and also offers a glimpse of how things may be in the city of the future.

Much discussion of the application of analysis in urban problems tends either to advocate it without reservation or to reject its significance outright. We believe that a considered review of the evidence in the case studies would establish that both conclusions are inadequate. Analysis is not a cure for chaos, but neither is it without value for hard-pressed urban administrators. Thus, a more difficult series of questions must be answered. Under what circumstances can the introduction of analysis be effective in urban management? In other words, what is the *domain of innovation*? How can the potential for innovation be realized in practice and its domain enlarged? Or, how should governments *manage* this sort of innovation? These are the questions we undertake to answer in Chapter 6. Obviously four cases are small samples of experience, with important limitations as a basis for broad generalizations. Moreover, in any field, the early use of new methods is an imperfect guide to their ultimate use and significance. But we believe that insight can be gained and provisional answers formulated from even this limited and unsystematic sample. Finally, in a brief epilogue in Chapter 7, we try to assess the worth of the new technology and the means by which its use could be promoted on a national scale. Taking into account both the demonstrated potential and the realistic obstacles to great utilization, we conclude with a proposal for a national program of incentives for the use of new tools of analysis in local government.

Defining the Topic

The notion of analysis implies the separation of an intellectual or substantial whole into constituents for individual study. Basically, analysis is a common sense, rational approach to problem solving. It means breaking a problem down into its components, trying to understand each component's relation to the problem as a whole and proposing alternative solutions from which to choose. Analysis is a *logical* thought process made explicit. The emphasis today on quantification of the problem's component parts has been made possible by the availability of computers, operations research, and a host of other "hard" and "soft" tools. Obviously, analysis, per se, is not a new ingredient in decision making in cities. What is new is the opportunity to do it in better ways.

Our study is limited to those opportunities for analysis of a sort that can affect the *actions* of urban administrators and policy makers. Principally, these are of two kinds: *systems analysis* and *operational analysis*. The differences between the two are important and can be defined in relation to three principal factors in a situation: The purpose of analysis; the definition of the problem; and the scope of the system.

In most cases, the *purpose of analysis* is to provide "scientific" *advice* about alternative actions confronting a decision maker. Two other results may occur either as by-products or as alternatives when prescriptive conclusions cannot be reached. One is a better *understanding* of the nature of a complex problem or system; the other is a *method,* or tool, for coping with a limited part of the problem or system.

Each analysis addresses a specific problem. An important part of the *problem definition* is the determination of what is given and what may be varied. The most tractable problems for analysis are those that pose questions of pure efficiency. In such problems a specified goal is given and the analyst seeks to identify the "best" way to attain it. If 500 people are to be trained in a certain skill, he asks "how," not "why." As Wildavsky has pointed out, public problems often imply considerations of "mixed efficiency" [2] in which both ends and means may vary. Would it be "better" to train 300 or 1,000? From the analyst's viewpoint, this poses a different kind of problem. Furthermore, in some problems the analyst may consider a third dimension of change — the institutions in which problems are to be implemented. A problem in which all three factors, means, ends, and institutions are fair game is one of total efficiency.

The essence of analysis lies in the explicit delineation of the *scope of the system* to be analyzed. Definitions of a problem and of the intended result of analysis are subjective and abstract, but the system always has an objective and concrete reality, an interrelated aggregation of people and things in flux. Taking into account his problem and his purpose, the analyst creates an abstraction to represent the real system. It is in the nature of things that he narrows the scope and simplifies the structure of the real system. The possible scope varies from limited operating subsystems, such as ambulance services or manpower training programs, to very broad community systems, such as residential and economic development for a metropolitan area. Since a system defined at any level can always be said to be "only" a subsystem within a higher-level definition, the urban analyst always deals with only a part of the "total" system.

The focus of this book is on two kinds of analysis whose differences in purpose, problem definitions, and scope are readily distinguishable. These are systems analysis and operational analysis.

Systems analysis is intended to produce advice rather than "studies." The analyst takes neither ends nor means as fixed; he is engaged in a creative process in which there is a continuing interaction between them. The systems analyst usually deals with problems of mixed efficiency; he questions the decision maker's goals and his definition of the problem, and may produce a new definition of goals, a new method of achieving them, or both. Because of his concern with producing usable advice, the systems analyst deals with limited systems and a limited time horizon. He tends to emphasize decisions that will be made in the near term (although they may have long-term consequences) and will define the boundaries of his system within the limits necessary to stay within the state of the analytic art or to meet decision-making timetables.

Operational analysis, in contrast, is concerned with choosing the best of a specific set of means for accomplishing a specified purpose. In practice, the operational analyst tends to be concerned with pure efficiency; he works within a given institutional structure with given operational purposes; his work offers tools more often than "advice," providing the administrator with a procedure — often automated — that will help him (1) reach his own conclusions about what ought to be done in specific situations, or (2) exercise better routine control over operations.

Within a city, for example, operational analysis might be used to assist officials who must decide how to treat numerous substandard dwellings as they come to the attention of the municipality. A typical analysis would be one that produced a set of computer routines to predict the effect on tenants' rents of alternative methods of rehabilitating such a structure. In contrast, a systems analysis directed at the same general problem would be likely to deal with the entire housing stock of a geographic area, rather than with single structures, and to encompass multiple criteria and objectives. For example, a systems analyst might undertake to determine the emphasis that should be given to various municipal programs (tax abatement, code enforcement, low interest loans, and so forth) aimed at bringing the housing stock up to code. The systems analyst still deals with a limited system. He may acknowledge the influence of other components of the "whole system" — such as population migration, increasing per capita income levels, and so forth — but if he is to provide a decision maker with useful results, he will treat these variables as environmental factors, outside his definition of the system, and will not pretend to have dealt explicitly with the forces that lie behind them.

There is a third type of analysis in which a much broader view of system scope is commonly employed. Urban planners, for example, have traditionally attempted to deal with the community as a comprehensive unit, first in physical and economic terms, more recently to reflect its social dimensions also. New technology has given rise to a new genre in urban planning models. A comprehensive analysis by Kilbridge, et al., of these models' conception and use is optimistic about their future, but cautious about near-term practical use. As they put it:

Urban models are so new that, to a considerable extent, *all* are research and training exercises. Even those put up for the most practical and immediate needs are frequently seen in retrospect to have served their greatest purpose in educating their makers about the nature and relationships of urban phenomena. Scarcely is a planning model operational before it is recognized as a clumsy effort, and its successor begun. The elegant original of today is the aboriginal of tomorrow.[3]

Our investigation has excluded analytical undertakings of this sort because of their limited practical application at present. In this sort of urban analysis the result, at best, is a contribution to *understanding* urban systems, broadly defined, rather than specific policy advice pertaining to problems of practical significance. In such an analysis, housing would be viewed as one part of a broader city system that must be understood in relation to other aspects of urban development such as industrial growth, changes in the family as an institution, and so forth. In the strict sense, this too is "systems analysis," but it seems more useful to reserve that term for analysis specifically intended to and capable of providing *advice* to responsible decision makers.

Obviously, the distinctions specified above define ideal types which in practice exhibit certain common characteristics. Similar models and conceptual tools are used in analysis of all three types. Yet there are important differences as well. The operational analyst usually deals with situations in which there is a relatively high degree of predictability. When the analyst deals with the community as a comprehensive unit, however, he must operate at so high a level of abstraction and so low a degree of predictability that his results have little, if any, direct application to contemporary decision making. The systems analyst operates in the sphere between these two. He ventures out into uncharted areas in which intuition and the judgment of experienced practitioners must be built into his analysis. At the same time he works assiduously to reduce the judgmental component of his analysis by artfully drawing the boundaries of his system and developing new and more systematic methods for understanding its behavior.

A Little History

The development of an innovative concept backed by novel and more powerful techniques has, at other times, and in other settings, brought about substantial changes in the methods used for planning and decision making in major social institutions. Taylor's *scientific management* had its greatest impact on industry. The subsequent development of *operations research* made its first mark on the military, as did the related emergence of the practice of *systems analysis* itself. We shall sketch briefly the historical development of these prior instances of management innovation because they represent the intellectual heritage on which is based the present advocacy of greater use of analysis in cities.

The idea that industrial organizations constitute "systems" that ought to be treated systematically and as a whole, using quantitative measures wherever possible, can be found in the work of Charles Babbage (1832),[4] and Frederick W. Taylor (1894).[5] Babbage was too far ahead of his time, and his ideas lay fallow. Taylor, on the other hand, gave new shape to his times, as his approach to scientific management became almost a religion in parts of industry. He applied common sense and basic techniques of engineering analysis to the behavior of men and their interactions with machines in industrial processes. He put himself, literally, next to the processes he was studying and trying to change, instructing mill hands and machinists in the patterns of work they were to follow, and devising methods of supervision and wage payment to insure that they would remain true to the "one best way." Scientific management gave birth to the "efficiency expert" whose special outlook and particular skills would affect American industry for two generations.

The 1940s saw the birth of *Operations Research* (OR), initially as an adjunct of military operations and subsequently as the beginning of a new wave of change in industrial management technique. The discipline now known as OR grew out of a redeployment of personnel in the British war effort, specifically the assignment of scientists to the operational commands. The profoundly simple rationale for that practice was expressed as follows by the distinguished British physicist, P. M. S. Blackett in a memorandum circulated in 1941 under the title, "Scientists at the Operational Level":

> Operational staffs provide the scientists with the operational outlook and data. The scientists apply scientific methods of analysis to these data, and are thus able to give useful advice.[6]

From its inception, OR combined both technical and social innovations. It introduced significant changes both in the tools employed for analysis and the people who put them to use. Its earliest practitioners were scientists who brought to their work a set of attitudes and habits of mind, as well as a kit of sophisticated mathematical tools, not shared by the men with operational responsibility for the problems under study.

The most recent development in this evolutionary chain is the emergence of *systems analysis* as a distinct field of practice. In a basic text on the subject, one of its foremost exponents, E. S. Quade of the Rand Corporation, defines systems analysis as:

> . . . inquiry to aid a decision maker choose a course of action by systematically investigating his proper objectives, comparing quantitatively where possible the costs, effective-

ness, and risks associated with the alternative policies or strategies for achieving them, *and formulating additional alternatives if those examined are found wanting.* Systems analysis represents an approach to, or way of looking at, complex problems of choice under uncertainty, such as those associated with national security. In such problems, objectives are usually multiple, and possibly conflicting, and analysis designed to assist the decision maker must necessarily involve a large element of judgment.[7]

While also originating within the military, systems analysis has been differentiated from OR because its practitioners have concentrated on strategic aspects of the design and acquisition of major systems. The principal impulse for systems analysis came from special groups — employed either in "think tanks" like the Rand Corporation or in special branches of the Defense Department. They developed a distinctive view of military problems which freed them from the previous conventional wisdom (although committing them — inevitably one supposes — to a new one). In the practice of OR, great emphasis had come to be placed on refinement of technique — finding rigorous and precise methods to optimize problems that necessarily came to be defined in increasingly narrow and abstract terms. In contrast, as Quade points out, systems analysis came to be associated

with that class of problems where the difficulty lies in deciding what ought to be done — not simply how to do it — and honors go to people who have the ability or good fortune simply to find out what the problem is.[8]

What element of novelty characterized these prior instances of innovation in analysis? Specifically, what changes took place in the concepts of analysis, the techniques employed, or the people who applied them?

The basic philosophy of analysis, its unifying idea, seems

to have been remarkably constant throughout this series of innovations. Although each pioneer, from Taylor onward, has given a new thrust to the idea of a synoptic, systematic, and quantitative approach, that core idea antedated their efforts and was not changed by them. In other words, there was no new *concept* in OR or systems analysis. Furthermore, none of the pioneers in these early developments invented important *tools* of analysis. The essence of each innovation was the application in a new setting of tools already in common practice elsewhere. That change, in each case, led to the introduction of different kinds of people to perform the analytic function in the new setting.

Taylor, for example, used no methods more sophisticated than common sense and some basic engineering techniques. But he applied them to an area of endeavor — the design and control of man-machine processes — that had hitherto been governed by tradition and idiosyncratic practice. The comparative advantage of the "new" tools was great, and the way was paved for the "efficiency expert," trained and committed to the diligent application of these techniques. As Blackett makes clear, the first OR applications involved conventional analytic techniques of probability and optimization. Although they were conventional in pure science, their use in military operations was novel; hence, the British scientists at the operational level were able to accomplish great things. Once again, a new specialization was born as people subsequently were trained specifically for operations research, as well as new tools invented to further its progress. A similar story emerges in connection with the development of systems analysis for the American defense establishment. The military systems analysts, such as Quade, emphasize that their distinctive competence comes from a willingness to tackle a new class of problems, rather than from their mastery of new techniques for problem solving.

New methods of analysis must be coupled to the choices that shape an institution's behavior if they are to have a real effect. This problem had to be solved by each innovator. Its solution was greatly facilitated in the development of both scientific management and OR by the fact that the new analysts worked at the operating level. This had two benefits. First, the analysts had an immediate exposure to the practical conditions of operations and were less likely to suggest impractical courses of action. Second, they knew and were known by decision makers whose acceptance was necessary to the implementation of their ideas. In contrast, the problem of implementation is intrinsically more complex for the systems analyst, who tends to deal with more aggregate systems and to be more remote from the practical level of operations.

Additional innovations have been necessary to improve the coupling between systems analysis and operations. Some simple innovations, like PERT and related computer-based methods for project scheduling and control have made it possible to insure a closer approximation between plans and action. We have also seen the development of this kind of innovation in the use by government of the technique known as Planning-Programming-Budgeting (PPB). PPB differs from traditional government financial management systems in several important respects. First, resource commitments are planned and budgeted in the framework of programs that reflect the objectives rather than the structure of a governmental unit. Thus, expenditures by several departments that relate to the accomplishment of a common objective would be collected in one program. Second, with PPB all costs associated with a program are included in the budget for that program.[9] Separate budgets are no longer established, for example, for capital and operating expenses, and the future implications of various budget decisions are ex-

plicitly stated. While either PPB or systems analysis can be
employed independently in government, the two reinforce
each other. As Charles Schultze puts it:

> One way of defining PPB is simply as a system for bring-
> ing analysis to bear on program decisions. Analytic efforts
> that stay outside of the stream of decisions remain just that
> — analytic efforts, not instruments for shaping decisions.
> The crucial element of PPB is that it operates through the
> budget process. It seeks to bring analysis to bear on decisions
> by merging analysis, planning, and budgetary allocation. It
> is a decision structure, and therefore must relate to other
> elements of the decision process.[10]

There is little novelty in the basic idea that systematic,
synoptic analysis could be used in the setting of the city. In
the early decades of the twentieth century, the then nascent
city planning movement became enthused, partly as a consequence of some industrialists' enthusiasm for Taylorism,
with the idea of greater "system" in analysis and attention
to the city as a system. In May 1910, Frederick L. Olmsted,
a leading figure in planning, told the second national conference of city planners that they must learn to cope with
"the complex unity, the appalling breadth and ramification,
of real city planning," in order to intervene in ". . . the play
of enormously complex forces which no one clearly understands." [11] The methods of city planning taught at the in-
troductory level today embrace the broad principles espoused
by the systems analysts: the clarification of purposes, development of specific criteria, identification of alternatives,
their rigorous evaluation by systematic methods, all carried
on within a recursive and dynamic intellectual process.

The earlier tools of the city planner, such as the master
plan, were simple and commonsensical. But the planners
seldom solved successfully the problem of translating their
plans into action. The aspiring urban analyst now invades

the same turf with broader ambitions and a more powerful set of tools, but he often lacks any more definite idea of how to change the nature of operations and affect the outcome of important decisions. Will he have any greater impact?

A Basic Dilemma

To urge that cities should make widespread use of systems analysis and operational analysis is to advocate the adoption of a unique kind of technological innovation. The possibility of such innovation does not insure its occurrence, nor does advocacy necessarily improve the odds. Prescriptions for the application of these tools in urban affairs are inevitably weakened by the fact that we seem to understand little of the process of technological innovation in the urban setting.

In contrast, knowledge of the way in which technological change takes place in other settings is much more complete. In the United States, until recent years, industry and agriculture have provided the locus for the introduction of most new technology. The contrast between the conditions affecting innovation in the private sector and those that would control its occurrence in urban management will help to clarify some of the obstacles to greater use of systems analysis and related techniques.[12]

The overall character of technological change in industry is determined by the conjunction of myriad diverse innovations, each one of which is shaped by forces embedded deep in our social and economic institutions. Private decisions affecting technology are highly decentralized. The economic pressures of the market determine the rate and direction of change.

Changes in materials and processes — a stronger material, a cheaper fertilizer, a faster mechanism, a more reliable product, and innumerable similar innovations — are introduced almost daily in factories, offices, farms, and households. Taken alone, any one change is of small moment; but the effects of these changes are cumulative. For example, James Bright, in one of the earliest studies of automation based on careful examination of industrial experience, found that evolutionary development of materials, production processes, factory layouts, and product designs, as well as the development of more automated machinery were all involved in what was commonly termed "automation." [13] Advances proceeded unevenly, sometimes in materials, at other times in design or equipment, with each advance affecting the possibility of changes on other fronts.

The prevailing mechanism for change in materials and processes is *organic,* in the sense that it is intimately connected to the structures and functions of the entire economic system. The major consequences of the process are not deliberately chosen; they tend to be "accidental" rather than "intentional." The nature of the process complicates attempts to mobilize action either to impede or facilitate the progress of such change on a national scale. For example, John F. Kennedy could decide whether or not to proceed with the Apollo Program, but he could do little to affect the pace of "automation," an important contemporary technological issue. Yet the aggregate effect of evolutionary technological change can lead to dramatic social change. For example, while there has been no single dramatic innovation in agriculture, there has been enormous change. One in four workers in the United States was employed in agriculture in 1929; by 1975, within the span of one man's working life, that number will be one in 25.

Apollo — like its military predecessors beginning with the Manhattan Project — exemplifies a different mechanism, one in which major changes are introduced by projects that create entire new technological systems. These are examples of *managed* innovation. Managed innovation is used to create large-scale complex systems intentionally by a process of step-by-step technological development. Most development of this sort, so far, has been guided by decision-making and control procedures created by the federal government. Managed innovation, in contrast to the more prevalent organic innovation, is specific, rather than diffuse, focused on the introduction of new systems, rather than the evolutionary adaptation of old, and often directed toward political, rather than merely economic goals.

Perhaps because the welfare of cities is a function of government, many advocates of technological solutions to urban problems implicitly accept the model of managed innovation as the framework for their realization. For example, one early attempt at innovation in dealing with urban problems was cast in that mold exactly. In 1964, the State of California commissioned four large aerospace firms to perform systems analyses of solid waste management, information systems, transportation, and criminal justice.[14] All four studies resulted in recommendations that called for the huge infusions of funds and centralized administrative control that are the modus operandi of the aerospace industry. These studies and their recommendations were given wide national publicity and are often cited as examples of the feasibility of using systems technology to deal with social problems. None, however, has been implemented on a scale even close to what was suggested.

We believe that, in fact, this model for the managed introduction of new technology has little, if any, relevance to urban needs. To begin with, the scale and complexity of many urban problems, particularly social problems, are substantially greater than those customarily encountered by the defense and space industries. The urban system is a "natural" system of great complexity; to replace significant parts of it by deliberate action would require a leap of invention far greater than that involved in Apollo. Moreover, there is no comparable base of theory or even of controlled observation of experience to facilitate the guidance of technical work. From a purely technological standpoint, then, the possibility of managed innovation for the deliberate introduction of large-scale changes in urban systems seems remote.

Second, the institutions responsible for coping with urban problems are not well suited for the management of change on such a scale. Existing institutions do not permit either mobilization of the broad consensus necessary to the public expenditure of funds on a large scale nor the centralized administrative structure necessary to its wise application. For these reasons, we see little profit in asking how the nation can apply the familiar model of managed innovation to the solution of urban problems.

There is some similarity between the characteristics of attainable innovations in the urban environment and the organic process by which innovation usually occurs in the private sector. In both environments, individual innovations tend to be small in scale and to appear primarily as evolutionary adaptations within a larger system. In both, it is difficult or impossible to design and develop large-scale systems under the direction of a central management. But it is risky to draw too close an analogy between the two. Innovation in the city cannot be governed by the incentive of private gain that has motivated and shaped continuing innovation in industry and agriculture. This difference poses a central dilemma: Urban needs and urban institutions may not allow for either the "managed" or the "organic" processes by which important change now takes place in other sectors of our society.

SUMMARY

This is a study of experience in and projects for innovation in a particular setting. The city is the setting; the innovation involves the use of methods of operational and systems analysis. In an exploratory and descriptive study, the case studies, themselves, are an important part of the findings. The four studies in Chapters 2 through 5 offer the reader a series of perspectives on how the tools of analysis are really being used in the city. In addition, using evidence from the cases and other sources, we shall develop provisional answers to more general questions. To what extent is analysis useful for dealing with the problems of cities? How can efforts to use it be made more effective? Our findings — and some "educated guesses" — on these and related questions are given in Chapter 6. An important concern — based on the historical analysis given above — as we look at this will be the effectiveness of the link between analysis and action, and not just the "success" of analysis, per se. Finally, in Chapter 7 we shall offer a few tentative thoughts on ways in which more widespread effective use of analysis can be promoted in cities. An Appendix offers a more detailed exposition of analytical methods, for those unfamiliar with general practice.

FOOTNOTES

CHAPTER 1

1. Distinguished journals and authors have been enthusiastic about the idea. *Fortune* headlined one article by stating that "the systematic planning that built missiles and space (sic) can be used with telling effect to attack urban complexities." In a frequently quoted article, John Eberhard, then Director of the Institute for Applied Technology in the Department of Commerce, asserted that "only by taking a systems approach can our technological resources be coupled to the work of creating the sort of city in which people can lead the 'good' life." And, in 1969, Simon Ramo, Vice Chairman of the Board of TRW, Inc., concluded the preface of his book on systems analysis by stating:

. . . allowing for all the factors that we know are there, granted man's shortcomings and a ceiling on his resources and on his understanding of himself it [systems approach] will lead us to designs and operations that will at least not be chaotic. The systems approach, if it is used widely, is, at the least, a cure for chaos. Simon Ramo, *Cure for Chaos* (New York, David McKay Co., Inc., 1969), p. x.

2. Aaron Wildavsky, "The Political Economy of Efficiency: Cost-Benefit Analysis, Systems Analysis and Program Budgeting," *Public Administration Review*, December 1966, pp. 292–310.

3. Maurice D. Kilbridge, Robert P. O'Block, and Paul V. Teplitz, "A Conceptual Framework for Urban Planning Models," *Management Science*, Vol. 15, No. 6, February 1969.

4. Charles Babbage, *On the Economy of Machinery and Manufactures* (Philadelphia, Carey & Lea, 1832).

5. Frederick W. Taylor, *Scientific Management* (New York, © Harper and Bros., 1947).

6. P. M. S. Blackett, *Studies of War* (New York, Hill and Wang, 1962), pp. 171–176. (Quote from p. 171.)

7. E. S. Quade, *Analysis for Military Decisions* (Chicago, Rand McNally, 1964), p. 4.

8. *Ibid.*, p. 7.

9. For example, under a traditional system, a city's budget would state separately the resources to be spent by the police department, fire department, and other city agencies. Under a PPB system there might be a "Personal Safety program" (reflecting the city's objective of protecting the personal safety of its citizens). Expenditures by *all* the city's departments

(police, fire, and others) that relate to the accomplishment of that objective would be collected in that program. Only that part of those departments' budgets that pertained to personal safety, however, would be put in that program.

10. Charles L. Schultze, *The Politics and Economics of Public Spending* (Washington, D.C., The Brookings Institution, 1968), p. 77.

11. Mel Scott, *American City Planning Since 1890* (Berkeley, University of California Press, 1969), pp. 117–118. It should be noted that planners at that time restricted their concern to the "physical" city, choosing not to embrace its complex human dimensions in their notion of the "system."

12. There are, of course, important interactions between the two sectors. Without the technological capital of generations of market-directed innovation, the contemporary achievements in managed innovation would have been vastly more difficult. Publicly sponsored technology, in turn, contributes to the base of innovation in the private sector. The development of computers, jet transports, electronic communication and control devices, and others on the leading edge of change in the private economy have been facilitated, if not made possible, by public investment.

13. James R. Bright, *Automation and Management* (Boston, Harvard Business School, Division of Research, 1958).

14. For a description and assessment of the California studies, see Harold R. Walt, "The Four Aerospace Contracts: A Review of the California Experience," in *Applying Technology to Unmet Needs, Appendix Volume V, Technology and American Economy.* Studies prepared for the National Commission on Technology, Automation and Economic Progress (Washington, D. C., Government Printing Office, 1966).

DEMONSTRATIONS OF SYSTEMS ANALYSIS IN TWO URBAN JURISDICTIONS

JOHN R. RUSSELL

JOHN R. RUSSELL

John Russell is a Lecturer on Business Administration and a Member of the Faculty of the Graduate School of Business Administration, Harvard University. Dr. Russell teaches a course entitled *Technology, Business, and the City* in the M.B.A. Program at the Harvard Business School. He holds a Bachelor of Science degree in Mechanical Engineering, and received his Masters and Doctoral degrees from the Graduate School of Business Administration, Harvard University.

CHAPTER 2

DEMONSTRATIONS OF SYSTEMS ANALYSIS IN TWO URBAN JURISDICTIONS
(*John R. Russell*)

IN RESPONSE TO CLAIMS THAT ANALYTIC APPROACHES could be usefully applied to the problems of American cities, several demonstration programs have been undertaken covering a variety of urban issues and locations. This case study examines two of these programs. Both were built on the premise that analysis could be made an effective component of urban management through the application of outside initiative, funds, and technical expertise. Thus, our purpose, like that of the project sponsors, will be to examine the extent to which such demonstrations are, in fact, an effective means of bringing analysis to bear in the urban sector. Did these programs produce potentially useful analytic work, that is, were the results acceptable as a basis for decision making? If indeed some or all of them were potentially useful, were they actually used? What institutional and administrative factors determined whether or not they were used? And what actions on the part of urban administrators and analysts seem likely to ensure the success of future analytic work in the cities?

One program, the State-Local Finances Project of the George Washington University (SLFP), financed by the Ford Foundation, was organized to assist 15 state, county, and city jurisdictions to develop and install Planning-Programming-Budgeting (PPB) systems. As a key element in building competence in PPB, each jurisdiction was expected to do some analytic work that would support one or more resource allocation decisions. Both the PPB development work and the analysis were to be carried out in-house by members of the jurisdiction's staff; representatives of SLFP would act only as consultants to and critics of this in-house activity. The project, which ran for approximately one year, was scheduled to end in July 1968. After that, the jurisdictions were expected to continue on their own to expand and refine both their PPB structures and their systems analysis capabilities.[1]

The other project was organized under the auspices of the International City Management Association (ICMA), with the co-operation of the American Society of Planning Officials and the National Bureau of Standards (NBS). Funds were supplied by the Department of Housing and Urban Development (HUD) for the purpose of carrying out systems analyses in three cities (Charlotte, Poughkeepsie, and East Lansing). As was the case with SLFP, these analyses were to be done primarily by the cities' own personnel. NBS, however, would provide strong technical assistance, particularly with regard to planning each analysis and writing any computer programs that might be needed. Work was to start in early spring 1968, and be finished by the end of July (the same ending time as SLFP).

When July arrived, however, the SLFP and ICMA programs, combined, had produced analytic results in only three of the intended eighteen governments. In the ICMA program, East Lansing was almost finished with a firehouse location study. Of the SLFP jurisdictions, Dade County, Florida, had completed an analysis of police protection, and Dayton was nearing the end of an analysis of subemployment problems in its model city. Most SLFP jurisdictions had found it necessary to devote all available resources to the development and implementation of a basic PPB structure and to postpone any substantial analytic effort. As for the other ICMA cities, interest had declined in Poughkeepsie when the city manager and his planning director both took positions elsewhere; and Charlotte had been unable to accumulate the information needed for its study of the location of community service centers. Only Dayton, East Lansing, and Dade County, therefore, presented opportunities for case research and, unfortunately, Dade had to be eliminated from this research project because the political sensitivity of its analytic results made publication impossible. Thus, in the pages that follow, primary emphasis will be on Dayton, where the writer was a member of the three-man project team. Much briefer treatment will be given to the analysis done in East Lansing.

BACKGROUND TO THE DAYTON ANALYSIS

Dayton's selection of an issue for analysis grew out of its involvement in the federally sponsored model cities program. In early 1967, the city, like many urban communities, had elected to compete for planning funds under the Demonstration Cities and Metropolitan Development Act of 1966. A model city area was delineated in the city's core and a proposal prepared and submitted to HUD requesting funds to develop detailed plans for the physical and social rehabilitation of this area. These funds were granted and, in the latter part of 1967, the city began in earnest the planning phase of its model cities program. The target area encompassed 2,200 acres, 32,500 Black residents, and about 10,000 dwelling units. Poor employment conditions were thought to be a critical problem and, in early 1968 when the city was planning its project with SLFP, the city manager chose subemployment as the subject for analysis.

In March, a project group was formed consisting of the city's PPB director, who would serve as chairman, a city planner from the local Plan Board, and the writer. The PPB director's overall responsibility was to oversee the city's participation in SLFP. He was part of the city manager's staff and had responsibility for coordinating with all departments the development of a citywide program structure and the step-by-step conversion of existing budget procedures into a PPB format. Neither he nor the city planner had previous analytic experience. The writer's involvement developed as part of a program of research at the Harvard Business School. His background included some analytic experience in the defense/aerospace sector but none in the urban environment. The group was asked by the city manager to complete its work by the end of July, to coincide with the official ending of the State-Local Finances Project.

In early April, the project group began its activities by developing a conceptual model of the subemployment system. The model was expected to point out how well the group understood the nature of the system and what kinds of research would be necessary to increase that understanding.

A Conceptual Model of the Subemployment System

The model that evolved depicted the subemployment system quite simply as consisting of three major components — the sub-employed population, the subemployment agencies, and the job market (see Figure 2-1). The *total* subemployed population included all persons who were either unemployed or who, even though employed full-time or part-time, were unable to earn sufficient wages to keep themselves and their families above the federally-defined poverty level. (The latter were classified as "under-employed.") Not all underemployed or unemployed persons are chronically subemployed. The real, or hard-core, subemployed are those for whom unemployment or underemployment is the usual rather than the exceptional condition. They are persons whose racial, educational, attitudinal, job experience, or other characteristics have excluded them from normal patterns of employment — persons who will rarely find permanent and rewarding jobs unless they receive some kind of effective special attention. It was this hard-core group that the analysts believed were of prime concern to the city and should be emphasized in the analysis.

The second system component was the subemployment agencies, those organizations designed to provide special services for the subemployed. Fifteen such agencies in the model city were identified and investigated. (Thirteen were already functioning and two very large new ones were being organized.) In combination, they offered a wide variety of services, reflecting both

FIGURE 2-1. DIAGRAM OF THE SUBEMPLOYMENT SYSTEM

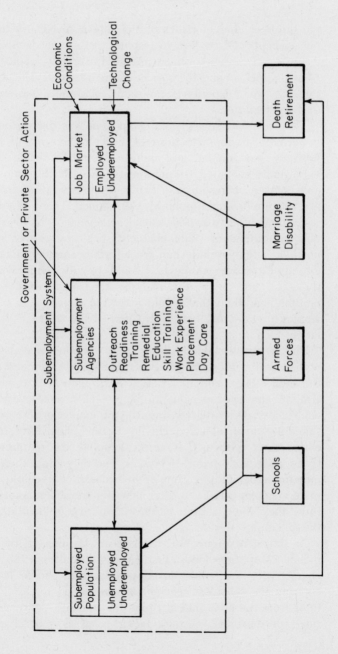

the different characteristics of the subemployed and the evolving concepts of how best to respond to their needs. Some agencies specialized while others provided a broader choice to their clients. Chief among the services were remedial education, skill training, work experience programs, placement assistance, and day-care facilities.

The third and final system component was the job market. In it were the job opportunities that reflected the needs of the area's business, government, and industrial establishments. Each job opportunity included "requirements" — reasonable or unreasonable, spoken or unspoken — that a prospective candidate had to meet before he could be hired and retained. These might include restrictions as to sex, educational achievement, experience, age, race, attitudinal or other characteristics, any one of which, if not met, might exclude him from further consideration. Not all job opportunities, moreover, would provide "employment" in the sense required by the analysis; some might have wage rate or time conditions that would leave the employee in an underemployed state and, hence, still part of the subemployed population.

The system formed by these three components was dynamic, with constant interaction between the components and between the total system and its external environment. Within the system, subemployed persons might remain subemployed, or they could move either directly into the job market or into one of the subemployment agencies. Having availed themselves of a subemployment service, they could complete the requirements of that service or drop out. In either event, they might then go back into the subemployed population because of unemployment or underemployment. Even after entering the job market successfully, they could return, either voluntarily, or involuntarily, to the subemployed state.

As shown in Figure 2-1, the system was affected by external influences of three kinds: first, factors that altered the size and character of the subemployed population — people leaving or entering the school system and/or the armed forces; migration to or from the area; and attrition due to death, retirement, marriage, or disability. Second, factors such as general economic conditions and long-term technological change. Third, private and governmental action (at local, state, or federal levels) that affected the number, character, and size of the various sub-employment agencies.

Initially, the analysts hoped that a relatively detailed computer simulation of this system could be developed. The subemployed population would be represented by a "reservoir" of people classified by the type of subemployment services that they needed. The computer would simulate the "processing" of this reservoir through an actual or hypothetical subemployment agencies component. Then each individual in the reservoir would be matched with a suitable position in the job market or returned to the subemployed population if no job were available. If adequate information could be obtained, assessments would be introduced of the probability that a candidate would complete each step of the path between the subemployed state and permanent employment, thus making the process stochastic. A model like this would permit local decision makers to test the impact of changes in their assumptions about the system or in the services allocated to it. Before proceeding very far in beginning this phase of the work, however, the project group wanted to sharpen its perspective by determining just what use city management expected to make of the completed analysis. What, in other words, was the purpose of the effort?

DEVELOPING A PURPOSE FOR THE ANALYSIS

The task of developing a purpose for the analysis proved considerably more difficult than anticipated. Profound and rapid change was taking place in the subemployment system at the very time that analysis was undertaken, and this change tended to obscure any clear-cut analytic objectives. In effect, the analysts were confronted with *two* subemployment systems. The first (which was labeled the "old" system) was in being through the late spring of 1968. The second, or "new" system was in the formative stages and consisted of the old system augmented by two very large new subemployment programs, the Concentrated Employment Program (CEP) and the National Alliance of Businessmen's effort, NAB-JOBS. (These programs will be discussed in greater detail later.)

In the analysts' view, the evolving presence of NAB and CEP seemed to make obsolete the initial statement of purpose issued earlier by the city manager. In March 1968, he had described that purpose as follows:

> . . . [the analysis] focuses upon vocational training, and will seek the optimum mix of vocational training programs which will bring an estimated 3,500 (tentative figure) unemployed residents of Dayton's Model Cities target area into the labor market with productive jobs. The project will also seek improvements in job development strategy.[2]

This implied that the primary objective of the analysis was to ensure that the work skills being taught in the city's "institutional" (as contrasted with "on-the-job") skill training programs were suitably matched to the known and forecasted needs of the local job market. By mid-April, however, when the analysis project was started, it appeared to the project group that the concept of an "optimum mix of vocational training programs" was no longer pertinent. The developing CEP and NAB programs would be so large as to overwhelm the small institutional vocational training activities already under way at existing subemployment agencies. In addition, these two new programs would emphasize, not pre-job vocational training, but on-the-job training. Thus, the "optimum mix of vocational training" would be a natural fallout from placing people in the various on-the-job training slots offered by NAB and other employers rather than a result of specifying various course offerings in a "schoolroom" setting.

NAB and CEP also tended to obscure the purposes of analysis in another way. Their presence meant that analysis was being done after, rather than before, major policy and resource allocation decisions had been made, thereby seeming to rob the work of any sense of immediacy.

In an effort to resolve these inconsistencies and to re-establish a clear-cut goal for the analysis, the project group spoke with those city administrators who were most concerned with the issue of subemployment. The diverse viewpoints which these managers expressed reflected not only widely differing needs, but also a spectrum of opinion regarding the power of "systems analysis." For example, both the PPB director and the model city project director viewed analysis as a means of making resource trade-offs between basic city activities. Both needed to justify the division of funds among functional areas such as subemployment programs, police protection, street lighting, education, and recreational facilities; and both wanted "system scope" and "analytic purpose" defined in these terms.

The Concentrated Employment Program director, in contrast to these first two administrators, took the position that an analytic approach probably could not be applied under any circumstances to problems that involved people. On the other hand, he expressed a real need for data regarding the subemployed population, the existing subemployment agencies, and the job market — that is, for an *understanding* of the subemployment system in the model city. He evinced no interest, however, in receiving advice about alternative courses of action for dealing with subemployment problems, only a justifiable concern with the implementation of CEP in accordance with federal guidelines and timetables. It was clear to the project group that what he wanted most was to be left alone to pursue his considerable workload.

A fourth view was expressed by the city manager, who agreed with the analysts that the question of an optimum mix of vocational training programs was no longer relevant. Instead he seemed now to want advice on how the two new subemployment programs (CEP and NAB) should be structured and how they should relate to the existing subemployment agencies and the subemployed population (a position quite at odds with that of the CEP director). It was important to him that CEP and NAB — particularly the former, to which substantial local and federal funds were being committed and over which the city had direct administrative control — should be successful. The analysts were requested, explicitly, to do whatever they could to ensure that success. They were instructed, as well, to produce not just "another academic study," but something that would be useful "for decision-making purposes."

Unfortunately, none of these discussions provided the analysts with an entirely satisfactory answer to the question of objectives for the analysis. The group worked on its own, therefore, to develop a format for what it believed would be a potentially "useful" analytic effort. The initial step would be to establish, if possible, a set of politically practicable and acceptable objectives for the subemployment system. Then, to deal with the problem of rapid change in that system, quantitative descriptions of both the old and new subemployment systems would be undertaken. (Early research efforts had already shown that the information required to support a detailed simulation model would not be available in time to meet project schedules. Whatever was done quantitatively would have to rely on fairly aggregate data, particularly regarding the job market.) The description of the old system would define the subemployment problem in detail as it existed in the spring of 1968. Further, it would establish just how much progress was being made toward meeting stated system objectives. The new system, then, would be viewed as an alternative course of action taken to correct the deficiencies of the old system; and the analysis would attempt to determine the probability of the new system being able to do this. These findings would satisfy the CEP director's needs for information and the city manager's desire for an assessment of the NAB/CEP evolution. Then, to meet the manager's requirement for something that would be useful "for decision-making purposes," the question of alternatives for the future would be raised — that is, the analysis would look beyond the near-term operation of the new subemployment system and ask how it, too, might be modified beneficially should the city ever want to do so. No attempt would be made to deal with the broad, interfunctional questions raised by the model city project and PPB directors; limits on time and expertise simply would not permit it.

The group planned to spend the remainder of April and May accumulating background data about the three system components. For information regarding the subemployed population, there was a choice of several model city area surveys carried out by various groups including the Model City Planning Council. (The Council was in charge of the total model city project.) The local office of the Bureau of Employment Services (BES) agreed to act as the primary source of job market data. Research into the subemployment agencies would be done through interviews conducted by the project group. Following the acquisition phase, the month of June would be spent processing and analyzing the data and doing any necessary follow-up research. A written report would be prepared in August for submission to the city manager.

OBJECTIVES FOR THE SYSTEM

To develop a set of objectives for the subemployment system, the analysts relied on their earlier interviews with city administrators, subsequent dialogue with key people in the subemployment agencies, and statements made in the city's model city proposal as submitted to HUD. The various viewpoints seemed to the group to be well covered by the following list:

1. To equalize employment rates between the model city and the Dayton SMSA (Standard Metropolitan Statistical Area) as a whole, and to maintain this equality.
2. To place on jobs with incomes above the poverty level those model city residents who, because of race, personal attitude, skill or educational deficiencies, or other causes, are *chronically* subemployed.
3. To assist in the breakdown and elimination of disparate occupational patterns that affect model city residents adversely.
4. To insure that the jobs provided for accomplishment of the second objective, above, offer model city residents equal opportunity for financial and organizational advancement.

In the analysts' view, these objectives emerged rather naturally and easily from their research. The concept of parity between the model city and the greater Dayton area, evident in all but the second objective, proved particularly useful since it permitted everyone to sidestep, temporarily, such difficult issues as the "optimum" level of subemployment or the "best" occupational distribution pattern. Attention could focus, instead, on redressing the *disparity* between two population groups.

No one voiced opposition to the statement of objectives but this may have been the result of circumstance rather than unanimity. Employment conditions in the SMSA had been improving steadily. Unemployment rates were nearing historical lows. Thus, the road to parity could be a relatively smooth one with more and more model city residents simply moving in to fill newly created jobs in an expanding labor market. Quite a different situation might exist if an economic downturn took place, for the achievement of parity might be noticeably detrimental to many outside the model city. More opposition might also have emerged if the sources of subemployment funds had been different. Most programs were supported by the federal government or some other outside source, and the use of such "outside" money to benefit one special group was likely to be less controversial than using city tax revenues for the same purpose. Had Dayton been planning to use substantial sums from its own tax revenue, serious objections could have arisen.

THE ANALYSIS

Following the development of objectives, the analysts turned their attention to the accumulation and evaluation of information about the subemployment system and to the development of policy alternatives. The results of these efforts are set forth in a much condensed form, in the paragraphs that follow.

The Subemployed Population

Despite conditions in the SMSA, it was apparent that the subemployment problem in the model city was severe. In fact, it approached very closely the pattern of unemployment and underemployment uncovered by the U.S. Bureau of Labor Statistics in the cores of other, much larger, U.S. cities.[3] Of a potential work force of approximately 11,000, about 3,000 (27 percent) were subemployed. Of these 3,000 persons 2,400 (80 percent) were unskilled, and of the unskilled 1,700 had not completed high school. These 1,700 were considered to be the "hard-core" as defined earlier.

As to those model city residents who were *employed,* their occupational distribution pattern was markedly different from the SMSA as a whole. Relatively few were found in professional, managerial, technical, proprietor, clerical, or sales positions. The percentage in service positions, on the other hand, was very high (almost 60 percent for employed females). Indeed, to achieve parity of occupational distribution would require more than a program to hire the hard-core subemployed. Nothing short of a drastic reshuffling of the model city work force could reach that objective.

The Job Market

If forecasts held true, the demand for labor would be sufficient (in the next several years) to keep the total number of unemployed in the SMSA quite low. This forecasted demand was adequate to absorb all of those who were subemployed as well as those who might normally be expected to leave the school system and become subemployed. These predictions, however, were strongly dependent on general economic trends.

Despite this optimistic outlook for *overall* employment conditions, the expected distribution of demand by occupational category was not particularly favorable to the subemployed. It was concentrated in the very high skills (high enough to exclude most of the subemployed) and the very low skills. In the semi-skilled occupations there appeared to be less current demand and not so great an expectation of future expansion. Thus, if the subemployed took those jobs that were most readily available, existing patterns of occupational disparity would be aggravated. If they chose to compete for the better, semi-skilled positions, they could expect openings to be limited and competition keen.

The Old Subemployment Agencies

Prior to June 1968, the third component of the subemployment system consisted of about thirteen agencies with budgets totaling an estimated $1.9 million annually. Of this total, approximately 70 percent was provided by the federal government, while most of the remainder came from state government and private sources. City government made contributions to only two agencies totaling less than $40,000. Interviews with agency personnel indicated that, in total, 300 to 400 male and 100 to 300 female hard-core subemployed were being placed by the agencies annually *and* retained on the job.

Analysis of the Old System

It seemed obvious, then, that the old system — notwithstanding a growing job market — was incapable of making substantial progress toward the first two system objectives (parity of employment between the model city and the Dayton SMSA and placement of the hard-core subemployed).

An equally pessimistic conclusion was reached with regard to the third and fourth objectives (the breakdown and elimination of racially biased occupational patterns and placement of subemployed persons in jobs offering good advancement opportunities). For most of the agencies, legal restrictions permitted skill training programs to be established only if there was a demonstrable shortage of workers in that skill. Because current and projected demand was greatest for low skilled occupations, training programs had to focus on service jobs such as janitor, porter, baker, short order cook, nurses aide, and so forth. And, while these programs were moving (albeit slowly) toward accomplishment of the first two objectives, they were hindering accomplishment of the third and fourth objectives by increasing the number of model city residents in the low-skill, low-pay service jobs from which advancement is difficult.

Description and Analysis of the New System

The new subemployment system (intended, hopefully, to correct the deficiencies of the old) consisted of the old system augmented by the CEP and NAB projects. CEP was a federally funded effort built around relatively traditional means of placing disadvantaged persons in jobs and keeping them there. Its uniqueness lay not in new techniques but in the geographic and administrative concentration of its programs. Readiness training, remedial education, work experience programs, day care, placement, and other services were all to be drawn together within this single agency and — for maximum effectiveness and visibility — directed toward a single geographic area. (In Dayton this area was the model city.) Not all of CEP's functions would be performed by its own staff. Various activities, such as remedial education, for example, might be subcontracted to some other agency; but CEP was to retain funding control and ultimate responsibility for its clients. The program was built on the premise that hard-core subemployment can best be ameliorated by an approach that makes subemployed persons more acceptable and receptive candidates for the job market.

A private, unfunded, but Presidentially initiated and encouraged program, NAB-JOBS, worked on the concept that most subemployed persons already are suitable for employment. They are excluded from the more desirable, more lucrative jobs, however, by various arbitrary or unjust factors such as educational requirements that are needlessly high, testing procedures that are biased, or the exclusion of persons with police records. Thus, the reasoning went, if business would change its selection standards and its approaches to employee training many persons thought to be unemployable would prove employable. NAB, therefore, would enlist pledges from employers stating that a certain number of jobs would be set aside for persons who met specific criteria for classification as hard-core subemployed. The *basic* NAB concept was to change the character of the job market so that it would accommodate the subemployed person as he was, rather than rely on a change in him as a job prerequisite.[4]

Both the NAB and CEP programs were in the formative stages during the analysis project. Their organizational structures were in a state of flux as were the precise means by which the two would accommodate and assist each other's development and operation. It was almost impossible, therefore, to gauge the eventual extent of interdependence between the two, or the degree to which their individual plans would be additive. It was equally uncertain how they would alter the performance of existing agencies. Most troublesome of all, there was no way to estimate how effective either of the organizations would be relative to its stated goals. The analysts had little choice, therefore, but to key their work to these publicly declared goals and to the organizational structures and methods that *seemed* to be evolving during the research period — a tenuous approach at best. The following assessment of the new system emerged.

The new job market would differ from the old by the addition of about 2,000 NAB-sponsored jobs and 200 job pledges received by CEP from the area civil service. These jobs would be set aside exclusively for persons designated hard-core subemployed. With an estimated backlog of about 1,700 such people, there appeared, on the face of it, to be a job for all of them. Moreover, if NAB and CEP requirements were met, these jobs should provide above-poverty level wages and a reasonable chance for advancement, thus helping to achieve not only the first two system objectives (those regarding full employment) but also the two objectives concerned with occupational distribution and advancement opportunities. There were early indications that suggested these requirements were being satisfied. An examination of the first 500 NAB-JOBS pledges showed, for males, a notable absence of service jobs and a high percentage of machine operative slots. For females, pledges were almost exclusively in the clerical and operative categories.

The new subemployment agencies component offered greatly increased capacity for skill and readiness training, remedial education, placement, and day-care services. Annual budgets for the new agencies totaled almost $5 million, two and one-half times the rate of expenditures for the old agencies. Approximately 86 percent of this amount was covered by federal contributions, 8 percent by the city, and the remainder by other sources. If agency capacity were fully and successfully utilized, the system could, within two or three years, eliminate the backlog of sub-employed *and* handle an estimated yearly influx of 500 high school dropouts. (See Appendix 2-A for a description of the approach used to measure the adequacy of the new system.) One problem might arise, however, because of the planned division of this capacity between the sexes. CEP, as a matter of policy, would try to enroll twice as many men as women. The NAB had three times as many jobs for men as women. The subemployed population, on the other hand, included almost twice as many women as men.

Alternatives for the Future

Having developed information about the old and new sub-employment systems, and having assessed each system's capacity to progress toward its four objectives, the analysts turned their attention to the development of alternatives for the future. Three possibilities were examined. The first two would involve major resource commitments by the city. The third would focus on efforts to influence the long-term behavior of the Dayton business community and would not require large-scale expenditures. The three alternatives were by no means mutually exclusive; they could be carried out in some reasonable combination. And, of course, action by forces external to the subemployment system could substantially alter the desirability or feasibility of any of them.

Alternative #1

Under the first alternative, Dayton would make a continuing commitment to maintain some CEP-like program regardless of future funding decisions by the federal government. The city would endorse the CEP approach for dealing with subemployment and acknowledge that, even after CEP had reduced the existing backlog of subemployed, a smaller but continuing effort would be necessary to handle, at a minimum, the yearly influx of school dropouts and high school graduates who were unable to find work without help.

At predicted CEP rates, the cost for each person successfully placed by such a program would be about $1,700. Thus, if the city continued to contribute the same amount to an effort of its own as it contributed to CEP ($360,000), it could handle about 200 high school dropouts per year. To accommodate 500 (the probable maximum number) would require a yearly outlay of approximately $900,000. While this would be almost three times the 1968 expenditures on subemployment, it would be less than 2 percent of the city's annual operating budget. It seemed reasonable to suggest, therefore, that Dayton *could* mount a program, without federal assistance, that would deal on a continuing basis with the problem of placing most of the model city's disadvantaged young people in permanent job slots.

Alternative #2

The second alternative would attempt to modify the subemployed population itself. An underlying assumption about the subemployment system is that more schooling enhances the likelihood that a person will be able to find satisfactory employment without recourse to specialized services.[5] Therefore, decreasing the number of high school dropouts should also decrease the size of the subemployed population. There was already a federally sponsored program in Dayton whose primary objective was to keep teenagers from leaving high school. This was the Neighborhood Youth Corps — In-School activity, which provided work experience and tutoring services to those who, without the income and/or academic assistance, might drop out of school.

Follow-up statistics on the Dayton NYC-IN program were sparse and difficult to interpret; but, under almost any set of assumptions, its graduates seemed to have a better-than-average post-school employment record, a fact that was particularly noteworthy since the program concentrated on the more difficult cases where home environments were least conducive to keeping a young person in school. This suggested that Dayton funds might be used productively to enlarge the present NYC-IN program beyond its federally funded level of 350 students per year.

NYC-IN was not an inexpensive program. Depending somewhat on assumptions made about the program's enrollees, the cost of preventing one person from becoming subemployed appeared to be in excess of $5,000. This figure did not compare favorably with the *predicted* cost of using a CEP-like approach to remove someone from the subemployed population after he is in it. The word "predicted" is important, however, for if CEP failed to meet its placement quotas, or had a retention rate substantially below expected levels, then its costs would quickly surpass those of NYC-IN. Furthermore, there seemed to be important intangible benefits to the individual and perhaps to society in the NYC-IN approach; notably the avoidance of the emotional and economic problems that may accompany even a short stay in the subemployed population.

Alternative #3

The third, and final, alternative concerned the city's posture toward the activities of the Dayton business community. The NAB program represented a very real change in business response to the subemployment problem. Perhaps the most natural solution to that problem, certainly for government the least expensive, would be for business to assume responsibility for absorbing and training the disadvantaged. Clearly, if the objective of occupational parity was to be achieved, those segments of business and industry where Black employment had lagged had to be stimulated to reverse the pattern. NAB was the only program that had ever provided such a stimulus.

It seemed highly desirable, then, for Dayton to maintain and, if possible, increase the sense of involvement that NAB had already fostered in the city's business community. Steps taken by city management toward those ends could well have a substantial effect on subemployment. With this in mind (and looking ahead to the time when NAB's first burst of enthusiasm might fade), the following possibilities were suggested:

1. The city might offer to share the administrative costs of continuing the NAB offices and its job development activities.
2. The city might cooperate with NAB by making job pledges of its own that would be included in the total NAB effort.
3. The city could keep NAB closely informed of the needs of the model city area and keep the citizens *fully* informed of progress toward system objectives (or lack of progress).

From a systems standpoint, this third alternative was directed primarily at increasing the flow of people across the direct path from subemployment to employment. Secondarily, it might reduce the influx of young persons to the subemployed population by demonstrating that the attitudes of business have changed permanently — that there is, in fact, some point to remaining in the school system longer. (No attempt was made to estimate the probable cost or effectiveness of this alternative relative to the other two.)

A Critique of the Technical Aspects of the Analysis

The preceding sections are a vastly condensed version of the analysis actually presented to the city. Missing are many pages that outlined and supported assumptions regarding various aspects of the system and that invited the reader to question the findings if his own judgment and experience suggested the correctness of other assumptions or other conclusions. To anyone unfamiliar with subemployment problems and programs, the description set forth above must appear deceptively straightforward. To someone even moderately familiar with the area, it must seem that most of the major uncertainties and unknowns were largely ignored or, at best, glossed over.

It is important, therefore, to point out to the first group that the analysts were faced at almost every turn with the need to make critical, often tenuous assumptions about some aspect of the system. It is equally important to note for the second group that the project team was at the outset keenly aware of its own meagre understanding of subemployment, that it quickly became aware of the overwhelming task that had been set for it, and that the frustration of operating under a dictum to produce something useful in four months of part-time research was very great. Several times during the early weeks, the possibility of requesting a more tractable topic for this demonstration project was discussed, but — because of the city's deep, highly publicized commitment to the work — rejected. So the effort continued, and if the preceding sections convey an impression of confidence in the results, the complete analysis, quite to the contrary, indicated at several points the great difficulty of drawing almost any conclusions whatsoever. Good research demanded more before conclusions were reached; administrative fiat dictated that something "of use" be produced on schedule.

The purpose of this section, therefore, is to identify and evaluate the major analytical problems encountered in the project, taking into account the circumstances imposed by that fiat, and to reach some conclusion about the potential usefulness of the analysis in light of these problems. The difficulties fell under three broad headings: informational inadequacies about the state of the system, uncertainty regarding program effectiveness, and distortions caused by the selection of system boundaries.

Informational Inadequacies

Serious informational inadequacies and/or uncertainties were encountered throughout the subemployment analysis. Some of these problems, despite their severe impact, could have been corrected or avoided with relative ease and little additional cost. It is improbable that they would trouble a second analysis made in light of experience gained during the first. Others were more intractable; their elimination, while technically feasible, would require extensive additional data gathering. Still others seemed to stem from causes generic to the subemployment system, and would persist regardless of any corrective efforts. The following paragraphs identify and discuss some of the more critical ones.

Nearly all data regarding the subemployed population were developed from the Model City Survey, a family-by-family canvass begun in November 1967 (independent of the subemployment analysis), and carried on by five teams of one welfare mother and one city building inspector each. Reinforced as it was by the results of several other surveys, this canvass was unquestionably the most extensive body of information ever accumulated about the area's population. Nevertheless, there were several reasons to be skeptical about its contents.

As originally planned, for example, it was to have been a "100 percent" sample of the target area; but lack of control over the interview teams resulted in failure to reach almost half the population. Since the 50 percent sample obtained was completely uncontrolled, questions must be raised regarding the bias that was introduced. Even if the intended coverage of all residents had been achieved, the employment statistics still would have been suspect; for interviewing was permitted to stretch out for almost nine months — a period during which general employment conditions in the SMSA were improving steadily. Data gathered at the beginning of the survey, therefore, may have been obsolete by the time work was complete. Both these shortcomings could easily have been avoided if better survey control had been maintained and/or the goal of total population coverage had been abandoned in favor of some carefully devised sampling procedure. Even if these corrective actions had been taken, however, serious problems would have remained.

One would have been the question of male undercount. Surveys in a number of core city areas throughout the country have failed consistently to locate between a fifth and a third of the adult males expected to be part of the population. The Model City Survey indicated that this same "undercount" phenomenon existed in Dayton. And this meant that the total number of unemployed males estimated to be in the model city varied by

2,000 (from 500 to 2,500), depending on assumptions made about undercount. This level of uncertainty in such a basic system variable is so great as to reduce substantially the probability that program decisions, based on analysis, will prove to have been good ones. Moreover, our ability to reduce this uncertainty is limited. Some additional data regarding persons in the armed forces or in jail might have been obtained to help sharpen estimates of undercount; but it is difficult to picture any systematic, reliable way to confirm the existence, location, or size of this group. Moreover, if employment conditions in Dayton "improve," the number of undercount males is likely to increase, rather than decrease, because undercount males from other areas will be encouraged to migrate to Dayton. In other words, the actual presence and status of males who tend to be undercounted may be as much a function of employment conditions as the definition of "employment conditions" is a function of assumptions about the presence and status of undercount. A perplexing circle, to be sure.

An additional and quite different "data problem" arose because a number of highly subjective judgments underlay the interpretation of information about the model city population. The terms "subemployment" and "underemployment," for instance, are based on a subjective definition of "poverty." Any change in that definition would affect markedly the number of persons classified "subemployed" and, therefore, in need of assistance from the subemployment system. A similar judgment underlies conclusions about the minimum age at which it is appropriate to place children in day-care centers while their mothers work; and the number of female heads of household designated "unemployed"—and hence of concern to the subemployment system —is highly sensitive to this judgment. There would have been no problem, of course, in adjusting the subemployment analysis to reflect a spectrum either of definitions of "poverty" or of conclusions with regard to the minimum age at which day care is acceptable. The problem arises because—no matter how certain the data itself may be—different social values, held by different individuals, can lead in turn to different interpretations of these

data. People can be defined in or out of the subemployed population based on these differences. If the differences are very great
—particularly among those responsible for making program decisions—then the technical success of analysis, in terms of
pointing the way to feasible policy alternatives, will be in
jeopardy. It may be impossible to reach consensus even on the
scope or nature of the problem, much less on a course of action
to deal with it. And this may be true despite close agreement
by everyone on the objective, or objectives, for the total system.

Finally, in the context of doing research on the job market,
the question of access to data was encountered. Job market information was available from a wide variety of organizations—
from the firms where job vacancies existed, from employer
groups like NAB, and from such agencies as Ohio's Bureau of
Employment Security (BES). None of these sources was under
administrative control of the city, thus raising the possibility that
analysts working for city management would be refused access
to critical items of information. In this instance, nearly all sources
responded well to requests for information, but if the results of
analysis, no matter how dispassionate, have placed these organizations in a position that they view as unfavorable, then major data
sources for further analysis work may be gone.

To summarize, data problems of many kinds and at many levels
arose to impede the analytic process. Least troublesome in the
long run were those concerned with such items as the structure
and administration of population surveys and the failure to
gather enough data on particular components of the system.
These inadequacies can be easily corrected in the future. Far
more significant were the difficulties that stemmed from the fragmented control of data sources and the fact that differing subjective value structures could undermine the credibility of information and hence of analytic results. These difficulties are
largely uncontrollable by the proponents and practitioners of
analysis. And the more effective analysis becomes, in general—
that is, the more it impinges on traditional organizational arrangements and modes of operation—the more severe these difficulties are likely to be.

Uncertainty about Program Effectiveness

Much effort was expended by the analysis group in gathering and sifting information about the costs and effectiveness of the subemployment agencies. The number of data sources was as great as the number of agencies and, like the sources of job market data, most were under no obligation to provide information. No subemployment agency would permit an examination of its files by the research group, and several agencies refused to answer certain kinds of questions about their activities. There was, moreover, an obvious sense of competition between agencies, sometimes for funds from a common source, and nearly always for vindication of their particular approach to improving subemployment conditions. Thus, there was reason to be skeptical of the opinions voiced by these agencies about their own activities. Despite this handicap, there seemed to be no basis for great concern about the *cost* data developed. A considerable amount of estimation was required where specific information was either missing or in a form unsuitable for use in the analysis. Still, the results probably reflected quite well the approximate amounts being spent. The assessment of each agency's *effectiveness*, however, inspired far less confidence. Indeed, the inability to deal adequately with questions of effectiveness was one of the most disappointing and frustrating aspects of the entire project.

Most of the agencies could provide some rough approximation of their past performance in terms of the number of persons that they had placed on jobs. None, however, kept records of the long-term job history of its clients following initial placement. Only the annual survey of graduates undertaken by the In-School Neighborhood Youth Corps approached such post-placement data gathering and, since many of these graduates could not be located, even this evidence was highly uncertain. On the face of it, there was no inherent reason why this failure to accumulate data could not have been corrected. A little planning and persistence by an agency should produce rather complete employment histories of its clients, particularly as the agency's longevity in the community increases. In fact, both NAB and CEP proposed to accumulate extensive follow-up data. This is not meant to suggest that record keeping will result in complete information about program effectiveness for it will not. Historical performance data may be a good indication of how effective a particular agency is under particular circumstances, but it may not be a satisfactory guide to that same agency's performance under different circumstances. And systems analysis, seeking to estimate the effect of different program alternatives, needs at least some insight into the way different levels of input and changes in the external environment will alter agency performance.

The value of historical data is also questionable because of the speed with which it can become obsolete. Most subemployment programs were quite new or had recently undergone substantial redirection. No agency in Dayton's model city—with the exception of BES—was more than a few years old. Even the senior ones were being phased out or faced with reorganization and/or emasculation as a consequence of the CEP and NAB efforts. The analysts, therefore, were forced to estimate prospectively the probable effectiveness of completely new programs or of existing programs that had been changed to reflect new approaches or policies. Good historical data, had it been available, would not have been very helpful.

Hatry and Cotton suggest that one way of estimating the effectiveness of new programs is by the "examination of similar programs that have been conducted in other jurisdictions." [6] Viewed from the perspective of several months' hindsight, however, the application of this procedure to Dayton's CEP program would have been a mistake. Cleveland, a neighbor of Dayton, had one of the most mature and highly acclaimed CEP programs in the country and Dayton's own CEP was modeled closely after it. In October 1968, Cleveland reported that, since its inception in June 1967, CEP had placed 2,600 graduates with 534 companies. The retention rate for these placements was running at 63 percent.[7] Dayton's program, on the other hand, encountered severe difficulties following its official start in August 1968. Of

75 who entered the first training cycle, only 13 finished. In the second cycle, the number dropped to eight.

Eventually, of course, Dayton's CEP effort may equal or exceed the performance in Cleveland. Its start-up problems may have been caused by poor administration, by the particular persons who were enrolled in the initial training cycles, or by some entirely different cause or causes. The point to be made is that Cleveland's established performance record did not prove a reliable indicator of what could be expected from a similar program located only a few miles away.

These problems inherent in both retrospective measurement and prospective estimation of the effectiveness of subemployment programs are of great importance, for it seems reasonable to postulate that similar problems of equal severity will confront other efforts to apply analysis to social systems such as subemployment. If true, this means analysts may frequently make large errors in assessing either the expected effectiveness of a social program or even an appropriate range between the lowest and highest probable levels of effectiveness. Indeed, if the Dayton experience is typical, one may well ask if analysts can do any more than add their voices to those who are speculating about what the newest social program will accomplish. To the extent that the size, policies, and administration of the various programs within an area are stabilized, and that data are accumulated about program performance, we would expect this situation to improve. But insofar as subemployment (or other social) programs remain in a state of flux, the absence of reliable effectiveness measures is likely to be a continued impediment to the successful application of an analytic approach.

The Selection of System Boundaries

Setting system boundaries for the subemployment program required answers to two questions: First, what range of interdependent functions should be included? Second, how large a geographic area should be covered?

With regard to the number of functions, it will be recalled

that both the PPB and model city project directors wanted to have analysis deal with subemployment as just one aspect of a broader, more encompassing model city system. Such an approach, of course, would have required the analysts to assess against some common objective (or objectives) the costs and effectiveness not only of subemployment programs but also of such other activities as police operations, recreational facilities, welfare procedures, elementary and secondary education, and so forth. The task of making meaningful trade-offs between these activities would have made analysis hopeless within the constraints of available time. It was decided, therefore, to include in the system only those functions that bore directly on the relatively short-run job prospects for the hard-core subemployed.

Even with this restricted focus, there were important aspects of the subemployment system that could not be dealt with adequately — at least within the time allotted and probably not within any reasonable time framework. It was, for instance, quite easy to recognize that the school system and the in-migration phenomenon were important considerations with regard to system operation; but it was not possible to deal meaningfully with either one. No attempt was made to suggest and analyze *fundamental* changes in the schools as an alternative means of reducing subemployment, despite the schools' dominant role in supplying persons who are subemployment prone. The complexity of such an undertaking was simply too great. For the same reason, it was impossible to make any inroads into the problem of quantifying the relationship between the flow of in-migrants and the state and character of the rest of the subemployment system. For analysis purposes, therefore, in-migration was assumed to be constant (and inconsequential).

With regard to geographic limits on the system, coverage was restricted to the confines of the model city itself and this reflected, not so much the play of demographic, economic, or topographical factors, as the federal government's requirement that model city areas should contain no more than 10 percent of the city's total population.

From both a functional and geographic viewpoint, then, the subemployment analysis dealt with a system of very limited scope. But no analysis can deal with a "total system"; some restriction is always necessary. One need only assure that, when the boundaries have been set, the objectives developed for the resulting "subsystem" are neither unrelated to nor inconsistent with the higher level objectives of the broader system. Thus, to the degree that reducing subemployment in the model city and moving toward parity of occupational distribution between the model city and the remainder of the SMSA were compatible with the objective of improving the overall model city environment (or conditions in general throughout the city), the reduced system scope was acceptable. To the extent that they were incompatible, then the decision to focus on lower level objectives was poor and the results of analysis suspect. Such incompatibility is, of course, possible, particularly if efforts to cure subemployment in the model city are pursued to such extremes that other functions, either inside or outside that limited area, are badly neglected, or in-migration increases beyond the city's capability to absorb it. But, within reason, it seems inconceivable that successful accomplishment of the objectives set forth for the model city subemployment system would run counter to other, higher level objectives either for the model city or the entire Dayton area.

On the other hand, a systems view that was defined, geographically, by limits of the model city may have been a deceptive one. There was probably good reason to be concerned about the particular problems that are faced by subemployed Blacks. But, if that was to be the focus, then the entire West Dayton area (where the city's Blacks were concentrated and of which the model city population was only about half) would have been a more sensible area for analysis. This is especially so since the population of West Dayton, exclusive of the model city, was growing whereas the number of people in the model city had remained relatively constant since 1960. Similarly, there would be good reason for concern about subemployment — of Whites and Blacks — throughout the SMSA, a concern that would dictate analysis of the problem on an SMSA-wide basis. But to limit the subemployment system to the model city, to concentrate on part of a part of a problem, could not but jeopardize the project's credibility. It may well have meant that critical issues were never really uncovered and understood.

Summary

The sum of these comments regarding the technical problems that confronted the subemployment analysis does not and cannot lead to any final, objective conclusion as to whether or not the work was acceptable as a basis for program decisions. Quite clearly, there are serious questions about some aspects of the analysis and, consequently, about the confidence that it merits. On the other hand, it seems fair to say that the analysis did result in a more concise, rational conceptualization of the model city's subemployment problems, a better insight into the past effectiveness of various means of dealing with them, and the rudiments of a quantified model of the system. As to specific, reasonably supportable findings, the following seem to emerge as having potential importance for program planning and execution purposes.

1. The planned *total* capacity of the new subemployment system was reasonably well suited to the needs of the model city population. This conclusion, however, was highly sensitive to the actual status of undercount males and the ability of CEP and NAB to live up to their stated expectations.
2. The division of total capacity between male and female clients, however, was inversely related to the ratio of males and females in the subemployed population.
3. The mix of existing and predicted job openings was working against the achievement of occupational parity, especially since institutional skill training programs were required to be aligned with this mix.
4. Resources might be better spent to keep young people in school rather than to help already subemployed dropouts find work.

In the next section, we will examine how these findings (and the remainder of the analysis) were actually used by the city.

APPLICATION OF THE ANALYSIS AND LESSONS LEARNED

Research for the subemployment analysis was begun in April 1968 — although the model city population survey was begun earlier — and finished in mid-August. In late October, the final report was submitted to the PPB director whose task it was to prepare a digest for review by the city manager with subsequent presentation to the city council. The press of other commitments, however, prevented completion of this digest until May 1969. During the interim, no one except the PPB director read the final report, nor — with one exception that will be discussed shortly — did anyone ask to read it or express great concern that it had not been forthcoming. Following its completion, no action was taken on the digest.

The subemployment analysis, in other words, has had no influence whatsoever on the allocation of resources or formulation of policy — a fact that cannot be attributed to a lack of technical credibility, for no one (save the PPB director) was aware of how credible the analysis was. Nor can it be for want of concern about subemployment. Key administrators all agreed that this was one of the city's most critical problems and much high priority activity was under way to deal with it. Why, then, was the analysis ignored so completely?

Part of the answer lies in the fact that no decision maker in Dayton's management was faced with any *immediate* resource allocation or policy commitments for which the analysis could supply guidance. Most important decisions with regard to subemployment were outside the hands of city management. Funds and policy were, for the most part, under federal control. This would suggest the almost painfully obvious conclusion that useful analyses — in the sense that they can and will be used by city governments for decision-making purposes — must address issues on which city management can make the decision itself or, at the least, exert strong influence on the outside authority that does make the decisions. And this may well exclude some of the

city's most urgent problems from the list of appropriate sub-
jects for analysis. Concern about subemployment, no matter how
great, was unlikely to be translated into concern about an analysis of subemployment when city management was relatively
powerless to act.

This conclusion is underlined by the fact that the one person
who did show a keen interest in the analysis and a pressing need
for it did so because she believed there *was* room to act. In mid-
September, the project group received several urgent requests
for the results of its analysis from the woman responsible for
drafting the employment section of the model city planning proposal. In her view, the content of a total subemployment program for the model city had by no means been settled by the
commitments to CEP and NAB. Viewing these two activities as
one part only of a total program, she was anxious to explore
additional alternatives that might use general purpose model
city funds to augment CEP and NAB. If she were correct, there
had indeed been an opportuunity to allocate resources to other
subemployment programs or approaches on the basis of local
ideas and decisions; but this had not been clear when the analysis was in progress. Unhappily, the final report was not yet far
enough along to permit a response to these requests before the
October deadline for submission of the model city proposal.

These events suggest that in the future another prerequisite
must be met if useful analyses are to be done for city government: namely, that the analysts should neither be compelled nor
permitted to remain isolated and aloof from the administrators
who will use their work. An initial contact with these managers,
made (as it was in Dayton) at the beginning of a project is not
enough to assure that the completed analysis — perhaps four to
six months in preparation — will be compatible then with the
city's needs. Situations may change and alter the most suitable
direction for analysis. Information uncovered by the analysts
may indicate that objectives should be modified or criteria re-
stated. If adjustments to these developing situations are to be
made, there must be reasonably frequent interchanges between
managers and analysts as the work progresses — indeed, managers must take an active part in the analysis work. At the out-

set, when analysts are relatively unfamiliar with the urban environment, and city management unsure of the strengths and limitations of analysis, a close working relationship is a necessary basis for mutual education and accommodation. Management's involvement in the work will enhance the probability that a potentially useful analysis will be produced and actually used. Had better contact been established and maintained in Dayton, the analysis team might have had a far clearer idea of its mission — perhaps even a direct charge to tailor its work to the deadlines and textual requirements of the model city proposal.

This leads to a third and related failure of the Dayton project — the question of timing. It seems almost axiomatic to say that analysis should precede action, not follow it. Yet, through a coincidence of timetables, NAB, CEP, and systems analysis arrived in Dayton simultaneously. The analysts were faced with the horrendous task of examining a system that was in a state of almost violent upheaval. No one knew exactly how NAB and CEP would either operate or cooperate. The only sure thing was that both programs were being initiated as rapidly as possible and that, together, they would alter the shape and influence of every other subemployment program in the model city. The analysts had little choice but to try their best to keep up with the implementation phase of decisions they should have helped shape in the first place. Had the effort been started six months or so before its actual commencement in April 1968, the analysis (modest as its technical success may have been) might still have had some practical value for it would have supplied the background information needed by the CEP director and would have been available to assist the drafters of the model city proposal. Barring this, it could be useful only if it were viewed as the beginning of a continuing effort to improve the city's understanding of and response to its subemployment problems.

To summarize, three factors prevented the Dayton analysis from serving a truly useful purpose for city management: first, the project dealt with a problem area where no immediate significant resource allocations or policy commitments needed to be made or could be made; second, it was conducted in an atmosphere of infrequent contact between city management and the analysis team; and third, it was begun so late that it got caught up in the implementation stage of the very decisions it should have preceded. Any one of these would have been enough to diminish interest in the project. In combination they eliminated any immediate usefulness that the Dayton analysis might otherwise have had. Having drawn these conclusions, we turn for purposes of comparison to a very brief discussion of analytic work in East Lansing.

Fire House Location in East Lansing

In 1963, a study of East Lansing's existing two-station fire department recommended that it be enlarged by the addition of two new stations. Since that time, the city's fire chief had pressed repeatedly for implementation of an expansion program; the city manager, however, not thoroughly convinced by the 1963 report, had asked with equal persistence for more evidence that would prove why the fire department could not make do with what it had or revamp the two stations already in operation. Both officials saw the ICMA project as an opportunity to resolve these questions and establish a viable development plan for future fire station facilities. The analytic approach, taken with technical assistance from the National Bureau of Standards, was to adapt to the specific requirements of East Lansing's street network a general purpose computer model developed as part of the Northeast Corridor (NEC) Transportation Project. In the model, each street intersection in the city was identified as a numbered "node" and each street connection between nodes as a "link." The program calculated the optimum path between any two nodes using whatever criterion the user wished. Traditionally, fire houses have been located using either a distance and/or time criterion. With a network model, such as the NEC program, various locations for a station are proposed, and the program computes the time to reach all other nodes in the city from each node proposed for the station. Iso-time lines are drawn around the proposed locations and the resulting maps are used to select the most favorable site. In East Lansing, city management concluded that this traditional criterion was not entirely satisfactory. They agreed that travel time from a fire house to other nodes in the city was important, but believed that not all nodes were of equal concern to the fire protection system. Nodes, they felt, should be weighted in proportion to the fire hazard inherent in nearby structures.

To translate this concept into quantitative terms, considerable effort was expended by the city's project group developing a weighting factor based on the probability of fire occurring in various kinds of buildings. The final formula for this weighting factor used the actual history of fires in the city and correlated the probability of fire in a structure with the number of occupants, the height of the building, the construction type, the age of the building, its square footage, and the land use. Each node in the city was given a total weighting factor equal to the sum of the individual weightings for all structures in the vicinity of that node.

Using these total weighting factors for the nodes, a proposed firehouse site could be evaluated by finding the least-time path between that site and each other node in the city (or in the area to be served by the station), multiplying the time along these paths by the weighting factor assigned to the destination node, and then summing these products for all nodes served by the station. The site with the lowest total score — designated "penalty points" — was then considered to be the best.

Computer runs based on this procedure produced some unexpected results. First, the two existing fire stations seemed to be satisfactorily located given the city's current distribution of structures and population. Second, if future growth patterns evolved as forecast, it appeared that augmentation of these two stations by two new ones — as recommended in 1963 — was neither necessary nor advisable. Instead, the city should abandon the present main station and replace it with two new facilities in quite different locations. This meant the operating cost of a fourth station would be avoided.

There is no question that the East Lansing project was considered highly successful. Asked if the study had demonstrated the usefulness and applicability of systems analysis to urban problems, the city manager gave an unqualified "yes." [8] In his view, the project had solved the fire station location question and pointed the way to other promising areas for analysis. This success is of great interest, of course, because the East Lansing analysis contrasted sharply with the Dayton experience in several respects. Most obvious, and perhaps dominant, is the technical simplicity of the firehouse problem relative to subemployment. But even the East Lansing project is not beyond severe technical criticism and we must look beyond that issue to draw a complete comparison between the two.

One thing that stands out clearly, for example, as compared to Dayton, is that a decision on fire station facilities was needed and that East Lansing, itself, could make this decision and then commit its own resources to action.

Another sharp contrast with Dayton was the active involvement of city management in the project work. It seems reasonable to suggest that this involvement grew out of the aforementioned need to make decisions and commit resources; but, whatever its cause, both the city manager and the fire chief were strong advocates of the analysis and members of the city's analysis team, a team that met regularly and frequently throughout the project. The importance attached to this participation is borne out by comments taken from the project team's final report to ICMA:

> From the city's brief experience with the systems process we would argue that there are two distinct roles to be played. On the one hand you have the problem expert, the person or persons most familiar with the objectives of the study. In a city, this might be a mayor, city manager, planner, or any other department or combination. The second role must be filled by the program expert; the person who because of his technical ability will construct the system model.
>
> Roles must be clearly understood by participants. The problem expert should not interfere with the technical aspect nor should the program expert interfere with the problem and its requirements. . . . The two kinds of experts must work closely through all stages.[9]

Apparently, East Lansing's management concluded that analysis could not be left solely to analysts. Instead, they defined specific roles that should be played by line management and analysts, respectively, and became sensitive to instances in which the participants stepped outside these roles.

A final difference between the subemployment and fire facilities projects was that East Lansing, in return for the costs of analysis, received a product of lasting value. Dayton's analysis produced little of on-going usefulness; East Lansing's node/link model could be applied to a variety of problems that might require analysis in the future. Just as the model was suitable for locating fire stations, it could also be used, with some modifications, to locate schools, maintenance depots, police stations, and so forth. Provided it is kept up to date, in other words, the model can become a permanent tool for city management.

THE QUESTION OF COST

One last issue deserves attention before this case study ends — the question of the resources spent on the analysis projects. If only direct salary payments and computer charges are included, and if the writer is charged at a rate similar to that used for the Dayton staff, then the total direct cost of that project was between $10,000 and $12,000. The elapsed time for its completion was more than six months, including preparation of the final report but excluding the model city survey which began in November 1967. Costs incurred by East Lansing and NBS during the firehouse study were also between $10,000 and $12,000. Two questions need answering: Were these costs reasonable considering both the decisions that each analysis sought to influence and the city's capacity to support analytic effort? Even if reasonable, were the expenditures worth it?

The first question can, with some assurance, be answered affirmatively on both counts for both cities. New firehouses, exclusive of equipment, cost in excess of $150,000. Yearly operating costs including equipment maintenance, salaries, and so forth, are substantial. Clearly an analysis costing $10,000 was not un-reasonable viewed against program expenditures of that magnitude. In Dayton, too, the cost of analysis was small vis-à-vis the $5 million being spent on subemployment programs. As to the cities' capability to support analysis efforts of this kind, a $10,000 project seems more than reasonable when viewed against budgets of about $65 million and $2 million for Dayton and East Lansing, respectively. Just how many such analyses these cities could support is a moot question although it is likely that the perceived usefulness of early analytic efforts will have much to do with city management's opinion of how much it can "afford" for analysis in the future.

Turning now to the question of whether or not the expenditure was worth it, the answers in East Lansing and Dayton are at opposite poles. Clearly the East Lansing study was worth it. At reasonable cost, the city received effective assistance with a decision-making problem as well as a computer model with potential applicability to several other problem areas. Dayton received neither of these; the project was an adjunct to the management process, not a part of it. Analysis tried to deal too quickly and too broadly with an extremely complex, little understood problem — a problem where outside influences left city management with little room to maneuver. The lessons seem clear: Analysis of urban issues will be worthwhile only if city administrators and analysts assess carefully and in advance what is expected of analysis, whether or not analysis can, in fact, deliver in accordance with these expectations, and what the city can and will do with the results once the work is finished.

APPENDIX 2-A

Numerical Analysis of the Subemployment System

Of primary interest to the analytic work in Dayton was the way in which the three major system components interacted as a total operating system and how well this system was likely to progress, over time, toward accomplishment of its objectives. As a reference for examining these interactions, a simplified system diagram was used (Figure 2-A1). Very little was known about several of the important parameters in this diagram, but there did appear to be enough data to assess how the system might operate (i) under different assumptions regarding these uncertain parameters and (ii) under different policies regarding the operation of CEP and/or NAB. To do this, a simple equation was used.

FIGURE 2-A1.   SIMPLIFIED SUBEMPLOYMENT SYSTEM DIAGRAM

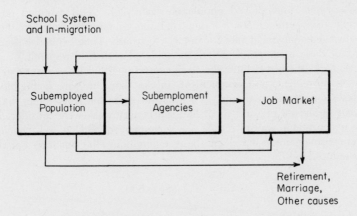

From the diagram, the following terms were identified:

B = Backlog of subemployment.
J = Job placements of subemployed.

P_r = Probability that a subemployed person will be retained on the job.

A = Additions to the subemployed backlog from the school system and in-migration.

L = Losses from the subemployed backlog due to marriage, retirement, and other causes.

Over any stated period of time, then, the reduction in the backlog of subemployed (ΔB) is simply:

$$\Delta B = (P_r) \ (J) - (A - L)$$

Data about A and L, unfortunately, were almost nonexistent. It was assumed, therefore, that contributions to A made by in-migration were relatively small and in the short run, at any rate, could be ignored. A, then, would be almost completely determined by the number of young people leaving school and entering the work force. The maximum number possible from this source was estimated at 1,600 per year of which 600 would not have completed high school. If it was assumed that 1,000 of this maximum number *do* enter the work force and that half of these entrants find employment by themselves, then about 500 of the 1,600 (250 of each sex) would become part of the subemployed population each year. (This assumed unemployment rate of 50% for new entrants is roughly equal to the known unemployment rate for model city youth. Time expired before any of these assumptions could be validated with field research.)

As to L, there was little choice but to assume that losses from marriage, retirement, and disablement, in the short run, are negligible. Losses due to out-migration, or withdrawal from the work force, that occur because a person cannot find satisfactory work were considered an unacceptable way to reduce the subemployed backlog and, hence, were also ignored. Based on these assumptions, the equation could be reduced to:

$$\Delta B = (P_r) \ (J) - 500$$

Even with these simplifications, the number of system operating conditions that could be examined were very large and only a few were considered. The purpose was to see how quickly the backlog of subemployed would be reduced to negligible size under each of the assumed conditions. The results served several purposes: First, they indicated that the new subemployment system (under almost any set of assumptions short of mass in-migration) was capable of substantially reducing Dayton's model city subemployment backlog — provided that current placement and retention expectations for NAB and CEP were fulfilled. Second, the results re-emphasized the importance, for Dayton policy makers, of making a careful, explicit decision regarding their own assumptions about male undercount. Without such a decision, rational program planning would be impossible. Finally, the calculations provided some insight into the implications of operating the new system under various policies regarding the ratio of male placements to female placements and showed that current federal policies on this ratio were not necessarily suitable.

CHAPTER 2

1. Details of the SLFP work have been described in a number of publications available through the George Washington University Bookstore. Of particular interest is: Selma J. Mushkin, Harry P. Hatry, et al., *Implementing PPB in State, City, and County: A Report on the 5-5-5-Project* (Washington, D.C., SLFP, 1969). The complete list of project jurisdictions included five states (California, Michigan, New York, Vermont, and Wisconsin), five counties (Dade, Florida; Davidson, Tennessee; Los Angeles, California; Nassau, New York; and Wayne, Michigan), and five cities (Dayton, Denver, Detroit, New Haven, and San Diego).

2. Letter from the City Manager of Dayton, Ohio, dated March 18, 1968.

3. See, for example, U.S. Department of Labor, *A Sharper Look at Unemployment in U.S. Cities and Slums* (Washington, D.C., Government Printing Office, 1966).

4. Descriptions of both these programs are oversimplifications, but they serve to clarify the differences between the two. In point of fact, NAB and CEP each planned to make substantial use of concepts and techniques of the other.

5. The reasons for this are not at all clear. It could be the result of increased intellectual capacity. It could just as easily be a feeling of self-confidence and self-esteem engendered by successfully coping with the school system; or it could stem from the imposition by employers of needlessly high academic achievement as a prerequisite to being hired.

6. Harry P. Hatry and John F. Cotton, *Program Budgeting for State, County, City,* State-Local Finances Project of the George Washington University (Washington, D.C., 1967), p. 52.

7. "AIM-JOBS, Cleveland's Attack on Unemployment," *Ohio-Bell*, October–November 1968.

8. Of interest is the fact that the manager's "yes" was given even though the analysis does *not* answer the question posed by the city initially. East Lansing wished to know whether it "needed" two, three, or four fire stations. The node/link model, however, accepts as one of its inputs the number of stations in the city and then assists in finding the best sites for these stations. It will, for instance, help locate one station optimally (based on the time/fire hazard criterion) and will determine how many penalty points, in total, are associated with the optimal location. It will do the same thing for two, three, or more locations. But the basic decision

as between actually building, say, two or three stations rests on trading off the added cost of the third station against the reduction in penalty points for the total system that the third station will buy. This trade-off, of course, must be based on human judgments regarding the value of a penalty point. Apparently, the city manager was satisfied that analysis would enable him to take a more convincing stance before the city council, despite the subjective aspects of his recommendations.

9. Undated report entitled *ICMA Systems Analysis Study* prepared by the East Lansing systems analysis project team, pp. 8, 9.

The Progress of Analysis and PPB in New York City Government

Carter F. Bales

Carter F. Bales

Carter Bales is a Principal in McKinsey & Company, Inc., and directs the public practice consulting group in McKinsey's New York office. Over the past four years, he has directed a dozen major projects for the City of New York, including program analysis and development projects in housing, education, hospitals, and environmental protection. He has also worked on a range of projects for other governments and for industry. He received a Bachelor of Arts degree in Economics from Princeton University and a Masters degree from the Graduate School of Business Administration, Harvard University.

CHAPTER 3

THE PROGRESS OF ANALYSIS AND PPB IN NEW YORK CITY GOVERNMENT
(Carter F. Bales)

THE SUBJECT OF THIS CASE is the introduction of analysis and the development of a Planning-Programming-Budgeting (PPB) system in the largest municipal government in the United States — the City of New York. The study has a single central proposition: Analysis and PPB have a major role to play in city government but — to be successful — they must be introduced into the bureaucracy through a carefully fashioned, phased strategy. Experience in other governments and in corporations has demonstrated clearly that several years are required to introduce change — in attitudes, approaches, and systems — into a complex institution. The strategy employed over the first three years in New York and the lessons learned are the story to be told.

To date, no other major city has applied analysis to its public problems on a scale equivalent to New York City's efforts. Some have tried to install a PPB system, hoping then to develop and use an analytic capability; but none of these endeavors has ever been fully implemented. Like its counterparts in these other cities, New York's administration saw potential value in both a PPB system and an increased analytic input to the city's decision-making process. In contrast to these other cities, however, the priorities assigned to PPB and analysis were reversed in New York. Primary emphasis was given to analysis. In retrospect, this reversal emerges as the most critical element in shaping the outcome of the city's efforts.

✻   ✻   ✻   ✻   ✻

The case begins with a brief introduction to the dimensions of the challenge to analysis and PPB that is present in the government of New York City. It then turns to a discussion of the strategy formulated to foster analysis and PPB in the city. A description of the progress achieved and the problems and frustrations encountered follows. Finally, conclusions are drawn on the success of the New York City effort, and some observations are made for the benefit of other urban governments facing similar challenges.

The effort to infuse analysis into the city government has been led by the Bureau of the Budget (BoB), particularly the program planning unit. Consultants from McKinsey & Company, Inc., worked closely with Bureau and agency personnel throughout the project.✻ The case covers the period from the beginning of the project in late 1966 through the midpoint of the third PPB cycle in the fall of 1969.

The Setting of the Story

New York City, like other municipalities, has come under increasing pressure during recent years. A tremendous clamor for improved city services has erupted — from white middle-class areas as well as the ghettoes. Concurrently, the real need for many programs has sky-rocketed. To cite a few examples: the city's welfare rolls have doubled in four years to over one million persons, yet nearly 50,000 jobs paying wages above the poverty level go unfilled each year for lack of skilled applicants. The city will need over 500,000 new housing units during the next decade, but construction costs have risen so rapidly that only 15,500 units in private and public housing were started in

---

✻ The writer served as head of the McKinsey team.

1969. Reported crime has grown at an astonishing rate — robberies, for example, rose 70 percent from 1967 to 1969, despite an 11 percent increase in police patrol. And fire alarms have increased 70 percent over three years, with false alarms and nuisance fires now constituting 65 percent of total alarms.

The strain placed on local government by these and many other unprecedented changes is aggravated by the bleak financial picture. With the federal and state governments preempting the high-leverage taxes tied to growth in national income and to inflation, cities are left with a very slowly growing revenue base. In recent years, New York City's revenues have grown about 5 percent annually. Mandatory costs, by contrast, have grown nearly 15 percent per year. (These are the costs of merely "staying even" — e.g., union wage settlements, civil service wage increases, welfare costs, and price increases in purchased items.) A new city tax program, increased state aid, and numerous ad hoc actions helped close the budget gap during the first few years of the Lindsay Administration, but major reductions had to be made in the fiscal 1969–70 budget.

City management has been ill-equipped to meet the dilemma posed by these conditions. Despite a "strong mayor" charter in New York, there is little tradition of strong central management. Historically, the Mayor has been seen as a resolver of crises and an adjudicator of agency disputes rather than an "executive" or "manager" like the president of a corporation. To be sure, the Bureau of the Budget has exercised close control over the agencies through central preparation and administration of a detailed line item budget. But although the Bureau has been one of the strongest in the country, its ability to exert a positive rather than merely a restraining influence on agency operations has been limited. So long as departments stayed within their budgets, the city's top executives seldom interfered.

Under these circumstances, a "conventional wisdom" or fixed view of agency mission and methods tends to emerge. Commissioners and other appointed personnel in the city's departments, who usually are not experienced executives, generally accede to the career managers who have come up from the ranks. And often the latter — particularly the professionals such as policemen, firemen, and teachers — are trapped in traditional ways of operating. Consequently, with no agreed-on substitute for profit as a measure of efficiency in government, productivity is likely to lag. Work practices remain fixed or deteriorate, and capital equipment is not substituted for labor quickly enough. Even more important, there is little impetus to search out fundamentally *new* ways of accomplishing (or defining) an agency's purposes. The system is per se antithetical to change.

Thus, most city departments come to view themselves primarily as "service providers," and attempt to meet growing needs for service with incremental increases in service levels. These marginal improvements to existing programs (usually adequate in the past) have not been sufficient to meet today's burgeoning demands on the city. The upheaval in urban demands requires a corresponding "upheaval" in urban management. New and vastly revised programs are called for, and even currently effective programs need major improvement to stretch the limited budget dollar further and further. City governments are being forced to leave behind their conventional role and become "problem solvers." And, in the Lindsay Administration's view, this new role could best be fulfilled through a major commitment to increase the use of analysis in its decision making and to recast its planning and budgeting process in a PPB format.

FORGING THE STRATEGY FOR ANALYSIS

In introducing analysis and PPB, city management wished to advance two objectives:

> *To attack the city's major problems and opportunities directly in order to make significant improvements in city services,* that is, to create new programs or make major improvements in present programs, not merely to budget in a more rational manner.

> *Gradually to build a capacity for self-analysis and innovation into the agencies of the city,* that is, to develop the agencies' ability to initiate program improvements by themselves.

In practice, these two objectives could be in conflict, and this potential had considerable influence on the way in which the analytic component of the total analysis/PPB project was defined. Pursuit of the first objective would imply a highly selective and sharply focused analytic effort and extensive use of centrally directed special analyses. Little agency involvement would be necessary, except in the implementation phase. Pursuit of the second, by contrast, would imply a broad-scale effort to involve and teach agency personnel. Moreover, the problems tackled in pursuing the two objectives might also differ. For the first objective, the studies undertaken might challenge agency purpose and cut across individual agency jurisdictions — sometimes leading to drastic program revisions. For the second objective, analysis would be focused more appropriately on insular issues that concern individual agency heads, such as justifying budget increases or improving the efficiency or effectiveness of present programs.

Thus, to strike a balance between the two objectives, it would be necessary to combine a series of special centrally initiated studies of major issues with a broader joint analysis effort within the agencies. That is why BoB elected to define what it meant by "analysis" in very broad terms. Usually, "analysis" refers to the kind of cost/effectiveness evaluation (developing and presenting relevant information on the full implications — cost and results — of alternative courses of action) that should take place in building a budget within the framework of a budget system. BoB went beyond this concept in order to mount a balanced, broad-based analytic effort. Many studies would be undertaken, in the traditional style, but other special task force studies would be linked to the budgetary process quite loosely. In addition, other analytic and managerial improvement projects (e.g., improvements in information systems) would also be included under the rubric of "analysis." In short, the evolving PPB system would be viewed as an "excuse" for almost any analytic effort that would contribute to the two overall objectives.

This expanded view was justified by the pervasive need for analysis in city operations. Many of the important decisions that face New York are not strictly budgetary, although all decisions ultimately involve the allocation of resources. Often decisions deal with ways to improve the effectiveness and productivity of specific programs, without changing the dollar figures shown in the line item budget. Thus, in practice, the budgetary aspects of these decisions are often less important than other considerations. For example, development of improved rules for deploying policemen, firemen, or sanitationmen by time and location increases program productivity but does not affect the budget.

Not that budgetary considerations are unimportant. On the contrary, the findings of all analyses should be explicitly translated into budgetary terms before final decisions are made. Stretching the limited budget is critical to improving city services. In addition, the budget can be a powerful tool for change in a resource-constrained bureaucracy — especially in New York City where close budgetary control can be exercised through the line item budget.

Besides being cast in broad terms, New York City's approach to the introduction of analysis and PPB went to great lengths to accommodate the obstacles to innovation that are traditionally present in the bureaucratic setting. Rapid, smooth, citywide implementation would be possible only if every agency possessed: (1) a strong administrator who recognized the value of PPB and would support its development in his agency; (2) a well-developed internal analytic staff capable of initiating high-quality analysis; (3) problems that are inherently "analyzable," i.e., with agreed-on measures of program results and known, quantifiable relationships between input and output; and (4) basic information on agency operations, e.g., how resources are currently deployed among agency activities, and what results are being achieved.

It seemed self-evident in New York that agency administrators differed markedly, both in their willingness to base decisions on analysis and in their ability to control their agencies. Indeed, although Mayor Lindsay strongly supported the effort, most administrators and key career bureaucrats did not seem to consider either analysis or PPB useful. Nor was there any staff in most agencies oriented toward and trained in analysis. Many areas (e.g., human resources programs) lacked clearly defined or agreed-on social objectives, adequate measures of results, and knowledge of how resources are actually related to results. Rudimentary operating data were often not routinely available.

To cope with these problems, a strategy was developed whose broad outlines were described as follows by Budget Director Frederick O'R. Hayes in testimony before the Joint Economic Committee of Congress in September 1967:

New York City in initiating a planning-programming-budgeting system has pursued a strategy sharply different from that of most other state and local governments. Our overall approach has, deliberately, been opportunistic, rather than systematic and comprehensive. We have concentrated our efforts on analysis, rather than on program structure and accounts, and we have focused on sectors of high apparent yield. . . . One reason for this approach was the conviction that the massive effort to classify expenditures by program categories, to articulate and quantify program objectives, and to establish the mechanism of the program plan, all on a government-wide basis, would literally suffocate the basic concept of PPB as a means of rational choice among alternatives. But more important, our strategy was based upon a recognition of realities — the strengths and weaknesses, the constraints and limitations inherent in the existing pattern of municipal government.[1]

In practice, these principles were translated into a fourfold working strategy for introducing analysis and PPB:

1. Concentrate on thorough analysis of a few priority issues.
2. Generally play down the development of PPB as a formal budgetary system.
3. Install important PPB features as justified to stimulate and support analysis and help assure analytical decision making.
4. Make the effort genuinely useful to the agencies by jointly analyzing issues of interest to the agencies and tailoring the PPB system to each agency's special management needs.

Carefully Selecting a Limited Slate of Issues

Since analytic manpower was expected to be in short supply, only a few issues could be tackled at a time. To quote Allen Schick: "To try to analyze everything is to end up analyzing nothing." [2] And, to produce usable results, the issues and problems for analysis would have to be selected with great care.

In its selection process, New York sought to strike a balance between importance and feasibility. Insofar as possible, issues chosen for analysis were those that were of critical importance both to the heads of major agencies and to the Mayor and the Budget Bureau. But, early in the effort, it was decided to sprinkle the slate liberally with issues of high opportunity so that relatively easy and quick results would be forthcoming. The absence of any analytic input whatsoever to most city programs offered rich opportunities for such a "skimming the cream" strategy. (The proportion of high-opportunity issues has declined as more and more analytic projects have been completed.)

A good deal of time was spent in developing an inventory of issues and clearly establishing their relative priorities. Tentative lists of problems needing analysis were drawn up for each agency, and then modified and refined in several rounds of discussions between knowledgeable personnel in the agency and the Budget Bureau. A separate list for citywide and interagency issues was developed in the same way.

From the beginning, issues were given informal priority rankings according to four criteria: (1) the importance of the program; (2) the urgency of the analysis (e.g., were options about to be lost? was there an opportunity to establish a useful precedent?); (3) the feasibility of performing the analysis, securing decisions, and actually implementing the decisions (e.g., were quantitative data readily available? did decision makers agree on the general approach to the problem?); and, finally (4) the speed with which results could be obtained (i.e., when would results be visible to the agency and the public?).

As issues were selected and defined, and the early analyses began to make headway, analysts' understanding of the issues deepened. The inventory of issues was continually revised as analysis uncovered new issues and eliminated some of the old ones. At present, with several years of experience in analysis, each agency has a well-defined reservoir of issues to probe.

Preferring Analysis over System

The short supply of analytic manpower did more than constrain the number of issues that could be analyzed. It also forced a choice between the expenditure of effort to develop PPB system features[3] and use of the same resources to pursue analytic projects. In New York, there was a firm belief that the real payoff from the total analysis/PPB effort would come from improved policy formulation and budget decisions, and that these improvements, in turn, rested more on analysis than on system. The competition for analytic resources, therefore, should almost always be decided in favor of analysis.

Other factors also entered into this preference. There was, for example, a strong conviction that system building at the expense of analysis could throttle future efforts to develop an analytic capability. System structure seeks to insure that budget decisions are based on analysis, primarily by tying analysis closely to the budgetary process. In many ways, however, analysis is inherently incompatible with the budgetary process. Allen Schick, in particular, has cogently described the antianalytic character of the budgetary process.[4] He points to the routine nature of most budgetary decisions, the insular viewpoint created by the bottom-up nature of budgeting, and the strength of well-established budgeting traditions. Existing budgetary processes in New York seemed to confirm the Schick paradigm and it was feared that the net effect of tying analysis tightly to budgeting would be precedence for the latter and relative impotence for the former.

The final reason for concentrating on analysis instead of system structure was to produce early results and gain early credibility for the overall effort. The development of a PPB system structure invariably takes years while individual analyses can be initiated, completed, and implemented much faster, often in a matter of weeks. Nothing, it was felt, would build momentum for the effort better than visible results produced early in the effort.

Phasing the Installation of Important System Features

Although primary emphasis was placed on analyzing issues, the Lindsay Administration was also committed to the gradual development of a complete PPB system. The structural features of PPB were recognized as valuable for several reasons. To begin with, they would provide improved information for analysis and decision making. They would also offer an improved basis for budgeting resources at the margin since agencies are forced to justify their budget requests more completely. In addition, they would help institutionalize analysis by orienting agency thinking more toward programs. Moreover, as progress was made toward developing system features, the Budget Bureau believed it could achieve an additional benefit, e.g., the capability to budget several years ahead.

Thus, the development of systems features was made part of the total effort from its beginning. But these features were to be installed only where they would help promote analytic efforts or an agency's understanding of its own operations. Furthermore, it was decided to develop the various systems features at different times in different agencies, depending on their apparent usefulness to each organizational unit. Thus, basic program structures would be adopted only after some analytic experience had been gained, and these structures would adhere to agency (not citywide) objectives and organization. As the analysts' understanding of programs improved through analysis and as agency thinking became more oriented toward programs, the basic structures could be refined and improved.

A similar view would be taken toward the measures of program effectiveness commonly associated with structure: they would be developed slowly as a by-product of analysis. Special efforts to develop indicators of effectiveness were thought to be of little value until analytic work had provided a clear understanding of the intricacies of individual programs. Indeed the choice of such indicators would require some knowledge of the relationship between program input and output and firm assurance that the indicator did approximate "real" program results. This would require that analysis come first.

Work on developing multiyear projections would be almost completely deferred. A multiyear perspective was felt to be superfluous for reaching decisions on many programs, for instance, those that were static or followed a simple growth pattern. For others, this long-term perspective was not feasible. Crime patterns five years in the future, for example, cannot be predicted or meaningfully related to expenditures on police. Hence, some prototype multiyear projections would be developed, but work would go forward at a measured pace. Understanding the present would take precedence over predicting the future.

Finally, information systems, too, would be developed as a companion effort to analysis. First priority would go to information only where lack of basic data proved utterly crippling to the analytic effort. But, in general, the refinement of information systems would await the completion of enough analysis to permit a clear definition of what information was really needed. (In retrospect, this proved wise, for in those few instances where information systems were developed before analysis, progress was slow and fitful.)

Insuring the Usefulness of Analysis and PPB to the Agencies

The Bureau of the Budget believed from the start that the agencies would have to see genuine value for themselves in the analysis/PPB project before they would give adequate time, thought, and cooperation to the effort. Making PPB solely a tool of the Budget director and the Mayor would inevitably lead to failure. To insure its usefulness, the analysis/PPB effort was to embody three characteristics.

First, top priority would be given to the development of an internal analytic staff in each agency. All of these agencies had recently been through the massive reorganization of the city's administrative structure in which a large number of smaller, often conflicting and overlapping units had been grouped together into ten "superagencies." It was hoped that an analytic staff within each of the ten could demonstrate the more general potential of analysis by helping the new administrators to understand and organize their larger responsibilities. Funds were promised for recruiting program planners, and candidates were channeled to agency heads by the Budget Bureau, which planned to provide on-the-job training to agency line and staff personnel. Administrators were also encouraged to use outside consultants if the agency could not otherwise meet its analytical needs.

Second, a "joint team" would be established in each agency to guide the analytic endeavor and the evolution of its PPB system. Members would be drawn from the Bureau of the Budget (program planners, examiners, engineers, and performance standards analysts), their counterparts in the agencies, and the City Planning Commission. The Deputy Budget director and the five assistant budget directors would each be responsible for directing between one and three teams. The teams were expected to provide a means of training agency personnel, to insure that agency needs and viewpoints were given adequate consideration, and to facilitate close cooperation between the Budget Bureau and the agencies during the start-up analyses and the systems definition work. During later stages of the effort, the Budget Bureau hoped that agency personnel would take the initiative so that a healthy competitive relationship could be established between the Bureau and the agencies. Agency participation was also expected to strengthen its commitment to using analysis. The teams were also supposed to facilitate communication both between the Bureau and the agencies and among divisions within the Bureau.

Finally, credibility for the effort was to be built through the visible support and participation of the Budget director and the Mayor. Wherever possible, budgetary and other decisions would be based openly on analysis — whether performed by the Budget Bureau or an agency's staff. Moreover, BoB resolved wherever possible not to use analysis performed by an agency to reduce that agency's total budget but, instead, to guide the agency in realigning its spending among programs. During the implementation phases of the program, support by the Mayor and Budget director often took the form of direct discussions with agency heads on the desirability of supporting the analytic and PPB efforts.

IMPLEMENTING THE STRATEGY FOR ANALYSIS

The strategic decision to concentrate initially on analysis and to manage the gradual development of the system features of PPB according to the needs and appetites of the individual agencies led to a straightforward plan for the analysis/PPB project. This basic plan stayed constant over the three-year period after 1966, although the relative emphasis assigned to its different parts changed.

The first year was devoted entirely to performing special analyses of selected major issues of Mayoral or BoB concern. In the second year, the effort was expanded: although special studies were still carried out, the major emphasis shifted to working with the agencies to analyze issues of particular interest to them and to develop selected PPB systems features. Now, at this writing, in its third year, with the effort well launched, work continues on developing and strengthening systems features but at a considerably reduced scale. The primary emphasis has shifted back toward analysis.

The following sections trace the city's experience since launching the effort and discuss specific examples of progress and problems.

The First Year

During late 1966 and throughout 1967, the Budget Bureau's new program planning unit concentrated on probing a few high-opportunity issues. Besides achieving the primary goal of bringing about substantial program changes quickly, these analyses helped establish the credibility of the effort. More important, they built the program planning staff's understanding of the inner workings of agencies and programs, thus providing the basis for fitting further development more closely to each agency's individual requirements.

The following analytic efforts were among those completed:

Expanding and Targeting Police Patrol

With rising street crime a major issue facing the Lindsay Administration, efforts were undertaken to expand and target police patrol. A program was developed to return patrolmen to the beat by substituting lower paid civilian employees for patrolmen in desk jobs. The police trainee program was expanded and trainees were assigned to traffic duty so that traffic patrolmen could be reassigned to regular patrol. And a budget decision was made to hire 3,000 new patrolmen.

Plans were developed for concentrating the expanded patrol in high-crime locations during high-crime periods — notably 6:00 P.M. to 2:00 A.M. A Tactical Patrol Force was created for special assignment to high-crime areas, and a legislative proposal for a "fourth platoon" to work from 6:00 P.M. to 2:00 A.M. was drafted. To further expand patrols, the concept of an "effective patrol unit" was developed. This was based on the hypothesis that deterrence is directly related to the visibility of patrol (the frequency that patrol passes a given point) and the speed of patrol response to a call. This concept led to the use of one-man cars and foot patrol in low-crime areas, thereby releasing more policemen for assignment to high-crime areas. Walkie-talkies and scooters, introduced to speed response, are two other changes that were initiated.

Stimulating Small-site Industrial Renewal

This analysis led to the inclusion in the capital budget of funds for an industrial renewal program. The concept was to use the city's urban renewal powers to assemble small industrial sites and then sell them (at "write-down" prices) to developers or companies that might otherwise migrate from the city for want of suitable space for expansion. The city would also assist in training the new workers hired by the companies moving to these sites. The analysis focused on the economics of the program, including the potential loss of jobs to the city without such a program, the additional jobs that could be created, and the value of employment for the presently unemployed or subemployed target group of workers. The city's projected net investment of $9 million in land write-down and training costs was compared to the potential payoff from 1,400 new jobs created, 1,200 families prevented from going on welfare, and 350 families actually removed from the welfare rolls. These benefits showed projected savings of $18 million in welfare payments and lost taxes.

Developing an Air Pollution Abatement Program

Attacking the problem of air pollution required investigation of a myriad of technical and administrative abatement alternatives, complicated by the developing technology of air pollution control, the large number of pollution sources in the city, and the lack of basic data on emissions. Emissions were analyzed by type (sulphur dioxide, particulates, carbon monoxide, hydrocarbons, and oxides of nitrogen) and by source (refuse incineration, space heating, power generation, industry, and transportation). After screening for feasibility, the program alternatives were evaluated in terms of projected reduction in emissions and capital and operating costs to the government and the private sector — both over the next 5 years. This analysis resulted in a balanced 5-year strategy and program for attacking each type of pollution. A number of changes were also made in the local air pollution control law.

Although little agency participation was expected or achieved during this first year, the Budget Director and the Mayor strongly encouraged agency heads to hire analytic staff. As a result, nearly half the major agencies hired some staff during the first year. Predictably, the new analysts were uneven in quality and experience. For this reason, and because of variations in the administrators' attitudes and the tractability of agency problems, their impact, too, was uneven. Nevertheless, a start had been made.

Besides carrying out a handful of major studies, the Budget Bureau's new program planning unit undertook to improve the analytic content of the fiscal 1968–69 expense budget. After the regular agency budget requests were received, the staff identified several budget issues in each major agency and carried out quick analytic probes to provide a basis for better budget decision making. In addition, Budget Bureau staff recast the budget for several agencies in rough program terms.

The Second Year

By May 1968, after one-and-a-half years of analyzing individual issues in most major agencies, the groundwork had been laid to approach PPB more formally. This year, each agency was asked to analyze a series of issues jointly with the Budget Bureau and then to prepare a program-oriented budget submission. Most agencies were also to begin developing selected PPB systems features, for example, program structure and effectiveness measures. The broad purpose was to teach personnel in major agencies throughout the city how to carry out PPB and to build organizational momentum for the effort.

The First Formal PPB Cycle

The first formal PPB cycle (for the fiscal 1969–70 budget) began in May 1968 with a brief program definition effort. Each joint team compiled a rough inventory of major issues to be analyzed, developed a rudimentary agency-oriented program structure, and identified the major data gaps. In addition, measures of program results and cost were tentatively selected for the more advanced agencies. All these items were reviewed with the agency head and the Budget director. The Budget Bureau then triggered the analytic phase of the cycle by issuing a program guidance letter to each agency around midsummer. These letters specified high-priority issues for analysis, spelled out the Mayor's broad priorities for the agency, and provided some general funding guidance.

Agency staff, assisted where necessary by Budget Bureau joint team members, then began analyzing the high-priority issues specified in the program guidance letters. Where severe difficulties were encountered, requirements were scaled down in an effort to obtain usable results. Each agency prepared a budget preview submission (a brief and tentative document) for review by the Budget Director and, in some cases, the Mayor. Due October 1, this submission summarized the results of the analytic efforts by program, including preliminary budget dollar estimates. Most agency heads were not as deeply involved in formulating these recommendations as it was hoped they would be.

After this first round of reviews and a meeting between the Budget Director and the agency head, a second budget guidance letter was sent out in early November to assist each agency in revising the budget preview submission and preparing the final budget submission, due in mid-December. This final document was not expected to differ fundamentally from the preview submission; the analysis was to be improved and data included on appropriation totals, expense budget line schedules, and performance.

This initial experience with formal PPB procedures proved enlightening in several respects. First, it confirmed BoB's earlier conclusion that efforts to develop a program structure could be very time-consuming and, even when completed, might be of marginal usefulness for analyzing issues or making budget decisions. Second, the reactions of some agencies to the joint efforts suggested that administrators and their staffs were convinced that cooperating too closely with BoB would work to their disadvantage when budget allocations were made. Nevertheless, as the budget cycle unfolded, the joint teams began to function more effectively and agency performance, in terms of developing well-supported budget requests, markedly improved.

Concurrently, the PPB system staff of the Budget Bureau was working to lock the PPB system into place. Computer programs were developed to facilitate the coding of crosswalks linking the program and appropriation budgets; and a process was developed for periodically updating the program budget on the computer to keep the program and line budgets in balance. For a few agencies, assistance was provided to integrate the program and appropriation structures into a single dual-purpose structure.

Variations in Agency Efforts

As expected, mixed results marked the effort during the second year. At the beginning, agencies varied widely in terms of the four basic characteristics that determine the ease of adopting analysis and PPB, namely, the attitudes and abilities of the administrator, the availability and caliber of analytic staff, the tractability of agency problems, and the state of agency information systems. After experience with the early issue analyses (the program probes undertaken in the first year), and the hiring of an analytic staff in some agencies, three stages of agency readiness for further development could be distinguished: the "pre-analysis stage" (Stage I), where the four preconditions for easy success were completely absent; the "joint-analysis stage" (Stage II), where help from the Budget Bureau still seemed necessary to advance agency performance; and the "self-analysis stage" (Stage III), where the agency appeared ready to move forward on its own. Thus, at the beginning of the second year, Budget Bureau and agency personnel worked to fashion a separate approach and system for agencies in each of the three stages of evolution.

Having entered the year at different stages, the agencies tended to widen their differences as the first PPB cycle unfolded: several spurted forward, many others moved forward moderately, and a few remained virtually at a standstill.

Agencies in Stage I (pre-analysis) possessed none of the preconditions for early acceptance and use of analysis and PPB. Their administrators were either uninterested or openly hostile — even in cases where successful analyses had been carried out in the first year. Usually these agencies managed programs that were difficult to analyze quantitatively, had an insufficient analytic staff, and lacked basic information on their operations. The Human Resources Administration and the Parks, Recreation, and Cultural Affairs Administration were the two clearest examples of Stage I agencies.

For these agencies, the accent in the second year continued to be on thoroughly analyzing a few important issues to prove the value of analysis, to familiarize agency personnel with the analytic process, and, hopefully, to gain the administrator's commitment; only minimal system requirements were imposed. Although a joint effort was proposed, the Budget Bureau expected to initiate the analyses and carry the analytic burden. If necessary, the decisions flowing from these analyses would be made by the Mayor or the Budget director and imposed on the agencies, sometimes with assistance from external project managers. This was recognized as a relatively high-risk tactic, but the ultimate payoff in improved decision making was felt to warrant the conflicts that might develop. Concurrent with these efforts, the Budget Bureau kept pressure on the administrators to hire analytic staff and to initiate selected information improvement projects.

Except for a few Budget Bureau studies, little progress was expected or achieved in the Stage I agencies. In large part this was because the problems facing them were so difficult to analyze and basic information was unavailable. Analysts were hired by most of these agencies, but they were unable to produce early results. Information improvement efforts were begun, but they were generally low priority. Overall, there was little reason for administrators or key career managers to change their original skepticism about the effort.

For example, the head of the Human Resources Administration (HRA) appeared to give PPB a low priority and the commissioners of the departments and the staff nominally charged with responsibility for analysis were indifferent or even antagonistic toward the effort. Some argued that program options did not really exist since their programs were controlled by state and federal statute. They also seemed to believe that the Budget Bureau, as a lay agency, was overstepping its bounds in inquiring into the substantive provisions of HRA programs.

The agency's PPB effort got under way slowly and fitfully. Its analytic group — too small, short of high-quality staff, and plagued by personnel changes — became enmeshed in discussions about the ideal program structure. The result was much time spent on constructing a very detailed program structure that was not used in the agency's budget submission or in the information systems improvement effort. In addition, agreement could not be reached on a slate of issues for analysis. The Budget Director's program guidance letter requesting joint analysis on several issues produced no positive results, and only a traditional budget submission, lacking analytical support, was prepared. Efforts by Budget Bureau staff to carry out several analyses on their own were unsuccessful.

It is impossible to single out any one cause for the lack of progress in HRA. BoB personnel found themselves hampered by what they believed was an absence of cooperation. On the other hand, analysis leading to actionable recommendations is extremely difficult in the human resources area and it is questionable whether quick analytic results would have been possible even with the enthusiastic backing of agency personnel. Prototype analysis of these problems has not been done elsewhere. There was and is little knowledge available on the real impact of human resources programs on the poor (e.g., the impact of welfare and job training programs on the incentive to work). In some areas, there is little agreement on the desirability of various objectives and, in others, an almost complete absence of important basic information.

The causes of slow progress, then, seemed to be many and too deeply rooted to be overcome in a year or two. It was concluded that several years of following essentially the same strategy would be necessary to move these agencies even to the joint analysis stage.

Most City agencies were in Stage II (joint analysis) at the beginning of the second year and appeared to offer great opportunity for improvement. In general, these agencies possessed some internal analytic staff (usually with weak quantitative skills), and their problems were relatively amenable to quantitative analysis. Basic data on operations were imperfect, but usable. In most cases, the administrator, the commissioners, and other key agency staff were neither enthusiastic about nor opposed to the PPB effort — they remained uncommitted. Among the agencies entering Stage II in the second year were the Environmental Protection Administration (EPA), the Housing and Development Administration (HDA), the Economic Development Administration (EDA), and the Transportation Administration (TA).

The approach used with Stage II agencies was to rely more heavily on cooperative effort through joint teams and to add some system features to the analysis. At the beginning of the annual PPB cycle, the joint team identified the issues to be analyzed and compiled them in a rough inventory for discussion with knowledgeable agency and BoB personnel. The priorities for analysis were then negotiated by the Budget Bureau and the agency. After selecting a limited slate of issues, joint analysis was begun and special steps taken to involve the agency head. To insure that the conclusions and recommendations emerging from analysis clearly belonged to the agency, agency personnel were encouraged to take the lead in analysis, with BoB program planners providing assistance as required. The Budget Bureau evaluated the analyses later as part of the annual PPB cycle.

Besides analyzing issues, the joint teams began work to design and install selected system features in Stage II agencies. Rudimentary agency-oriented program structures were built, and an effort was made to reach agreement on them with the agency head. Where the agency was ready, the team attempted to construct a computer-based crosswalk or, in a few cases, to develop an integrated program and appropriation structure. More information systems improvement work was also undertaken in Stage II agencies.

Progress in Stage II agencies varied widely. In several, the internal analytic efforts began to produce results and the agency head seemed to find real value in the project. The Environmental Protection Administration (EPA) is an example. Before the first PPB cycle began in May 1968, only a few significant analytic efforts had been completed for programs within EPA. The study of air pollution control, completed the preceding Fall, has already been discussed. Another, a Bureau of the Budget staff study, indicated that a shorter replacement period was warranted for sanitation trucks; this provided support for an agency request for replacement of the entire fleet over a two-year period with new and larger trucks.

Efforts to involve EPA in the first PPB cycle were initially unsuccessful although the EPA Administrator hired both the senior Budget Bureau examiner for EPA and the Mayor's assistant for EPA for his own analytic staff. Budget Bureau and EPA personnel worked together closely, but results were few. The agency's budget preview submission was late and the small amount of analytic work that was finished did not provide strong support for the incremental funds that were requested.

Progress was spurred by the Mayor's increasing concern for the cleanliness of the city's streets. He created, in January 1969, a special Clean City Task Force, chaired by an assistant director of the budget, and charged this group with reviewing all of the sanitation department's operations. He asked the task force to meet every two weeks with him and the Policy Planning Council.

The resulting crash analytic effort produced important program changes. For example:

- A new and accelerated procedure for removing abandoned automobiles from the streets succeeded in reducing their number at any one time from nearly 4,000 to about 1,000.
- A successful pilot project involving the use of plastic and paper bags instead of metal garbage containers promised to increase department productivity.
- A program to substitute large-volume detachable metal containers for regular garbage cans at high-volume stops resulted in significant increases in productivity.
- A successful special bulk-refuse drive was aimed at selected geographic areas suffering from a large backlog of bulk.
- Experimental efforts were made to reduce the waiting times of loaded trucks at the transfer stations.
- Saturday overtime was initiated in some of the vehicle maintenance and repair shops to maximize the number of trucks available for Monday's peak collection and reduce missed and night collections.

Relationships with agency personnel improved markedly during the task force effort. The administrator began to see some value in the effort. Personnel in the sanitation department also cooperated more as they became better acquainted with the Budget Bureau personnel and recognized the unusual opportunity to educate the Mayor to their problems. Throughout the project, the EPA director of program analysis continued to win over agency personnel by performing demonstrably good analysis and working closely with them.

By the time that budget decisions drew near, a much improved base of agreed-on information was available for negotiating the decisions. The task force had prepared a rough production function for the collection activities of the department, and agreement had been reached on the increased productivity expected of the new trucks and the increased volume of refuse to be generated by the enforcement of the apartment house incineration aspects of the city's air pollution control law. On the basis of these and other calculations, a decision was made to add 850 men to the 10,000-man force. In return, the department agreed, voluntarily, to realign some of its present resources toward more important programs. Sanitation men were transferred from manual sweeping to regular compactor collection and mechanized sweeping, the sanitation enforcement patrol was reduced in size and reorganized, and a "civilianization" program was instituted.

As the PPB cycle drew to a close, it was clear that analysis had become an accepted part of the agency, thanks largely to the efforts of the internal analytic staff. EPA had become one of the most advanced agencies in terms of analysis and PPB.

It is important, of course, to acknowledge the relative straightforwardness of the problems under study in EPA and the general availability of usable information for analysis. Ordinary operations analysis usually was sufficient. Program objectives were clear, as were measures of effectiveness. Simple conversion formulas were adequate in most cases to express the production function of a program. Usable measures of results (e.g., backlog as measured by number of truck shifts uncollected, efficiency as measured by tons of refuse collected per man-day) were available, indeed, were routinely used in operating the department. Work assignment schedules yielded the actual deployment patterns. And the line budget itself provided a reasonable basis for estimating costs. Thus, it was logical to expect significant and rapid progress in EPA.

Unfortunately, several other agencies seemed stalled in Stage II. Very little headway was made in the Transportation Administration, although its problems are subject to relatively straightforward analysis. No analytic staff was hired and little real analysis took place. Those in charge of each area in the administration wrote their own narrative portion of the budget submission. Not surprisingly, the managers accepted the existing organization and methods without question. In essence, these narratives justified current operations and asked for expansion funds. The managers viewed the undertaking as similar to budget preparation in past years, only with a different format. In addition, the staff preparing the submission seemed to feel that top management was not deeply interested or involved in the effort. The resulting submission, although complete as to form, was nonquantitative, and not useful for decision making.

Agency personnel carried out only two analyses leading to real decisions as part of the PPB effort. One dealt with converting operating bridges to fixed bridges, and led to the inclusion of funds in the budget to achieve the potential savings. The other dealt with measuring the volume of street reconstruction needed annually. A few other analyses, such as one on coordinating street and sewer construction, were useful although nonquantitative.

In several areas in the Transportation Administration, fledgling analytic efforts were stymied by the absence of the most rudimentary data. For example, the number of street miles by class of use was not known. Despite these gaps, agency personnel showed little interest in initiating a full-scale information improvement effort.

The absence of a full-time, qualified analytic staff was the greatest obstacle to developing substantive content in the effort. The central administrative personnel who performed the bulk of the work had neither the time nor inclination for analysis, and staff personnel had neither the time nor the ability.

The most critical factor in whether an agency stalled in Stage

II or made continued progress toward Stage III seemed to be the attitude of its top management. In those agencies where an analytic staff was hired and actively encouraged by the administrator, favorable results emerged. Where the administrator's actions were unenthusiastic, the effort lagged. For the latter cases, BoB continued its efforts to sell the value of analysis by analyzing agency issues itself and, sometimes, incorporating the results directly into agency budgets.

At the beginning of the second year, no agency had quite reached Stage III (self-analysis), but a few agencies were close, needing only stronger analytic skills and more time. These agencies had developed the conditions necessary for successful implementation of PPB: the administrator was interested in using analysis in his decisions; an internal unit capable of self-initiated, high-quality analysis had been started; the agency's issues and problems, although complex, were susceptible to quantitative analysis; and data that could be used to derive measures of program cost, output, and future levels of need were routinely generated as a by-product of managing operations. The agencies had gained some experience in defining program structure and were able to generate reasonable cost data by program. Through analysis and discussion, they had evolved generally accepted program effectiveness measures. Finally, the effort to build competent information systems had gathered some momentum and was beginning to produce real benefits.

For agencies near Stage III, the desired competitive relationship between the agency and the Budget Bureau could begin to exist. Issues for analysis were jointly agreed on or separately initiated, and analyses carried out by the agency were submitted to the Budget Bureau for evaluation and decision as part of the annual PPB cycle. The agencies nearest Stage III were the uniformed services or para-military agencies — the Police and Fire Departments.

The Fire Department, with a competent staff and assistance from outside consultants, moved strongly from the beginning to develop PPB. Early in the first year, the commissioner agreed to employ an assistant commissioner for operations analysis, an experienced analyst who had worked in the federal government and who provided the impetus for much of the department's subsequent analytic work.

In the second year, a major joint effort was undertaken by the internal staff, with the assistance of the RAND Corporation,[5] to model the department's extinguishment operations. Normal procedure was to send three pumpers and two ladder engines in response to each fire alarm, despite the high proportion of false alarms and nuisance fires (65 percent of alarms) and the wide variability in need for equipment at fires (e.g., structural fires and nonstructural fires require different equipment). The purpose of the model was to pave the way for developing a "flexible response policy," under which the fire apparatus dispatched would depend on the probable nature of the fire. The intent was to model the probability of various types and intensities of fires, considering factors such as location, season, day and time of week, weather, etc. By means of predictive modeling based on historical fire alarm and report data, the incidence of types of fires would be correlated with other social factors, such as number of housing code violations, incidence of reported crime, etc. Such a model would improve the department's ability to predict fires and to deploy its apparatus.

Although these massive modeling efforts required well over a year to complete, early findings were sufficient to suggest changing general department policy from a standard response of three pumpers and two ladders to two pumpers and one ladder.

While the modeling effort was under way, the internal analytic staff, working closely with Budget Bureau personnel and outside consultants, undertook a number of other program improvements, including:

- An analysis of the optimal fire apparatus replacement cycle, which resulted in reducing the cycle from 20 to 15 years.
- An analysis of the geographical incidence of fires to provide an improved basis for locating new fire stations and consolidating several present fire stations.
- An analysis of the department's fireboat fleet, which led to reducing the fleet's size and changing its deployment.
- A simulation of fire dispatching procedures to isolate bottlenecks and streamline the process.

A strong effort to develop an analytically based budget sub-mission was also undertaken by the same three-part team. Line personnel were deeply involved in preparing the submission, which was built up in terms of the new program structure, for which a computer-based crosswalk had been built. The depart-ment's own budget hearings were held in terms of this new struc-ture as were the ensuing budget decisions by the Budget Director and the Mayor. The department also decided to administer the budget in program terms.

Again, the success of the effort must be attributed partly to the straightforward nature of the problems and the availability of information. Most problems in the Fire Department, while com-plex, are subject to quantitative analysis. Objectives and meas-ures of effectiveness are clear-cut. As with EPA, the data used for managing operations were often adequate for analytical pur-poses. However, as with every agency, improvements in infor-mation were needed. For example, to begin to relate fire damage and duration to response level, the actual manning at fires had to be recorded. For this purpose, a new data collection system on the fire trucks was instituted.

The agencies near Stage III were still some distance from having fully installed, operating PPB systems. Although they were more advanced in their analysis than other agencies, they had only begun to deal with the host of high-leverage issues con-fronting them. They were still in the process of developing foundations of a full PPB system — namely, well-understood programs and adequate program information.

In the second year, besides the formal PPB effort, a number of special studies were undertaken for the Mayor or the Budget Director. As before, an ad hoc team was assembled to tackle each issue, usually on an accelerated time schedule. For example, a basic study was undertaken to discover the cause of the rapid growth in the welfare rolls and to develop an experimental train-ing incentives program to help offset it. The recent rapid rise in uncontrolled rents was also studied, and this analysis led to the new rent stabilization law.

The Third Year

In May 1969, on entering the fiscal 1970–71 budget cycle, the stage was set for a significant advance in most agencies. Analytic staff had been installed in nearly two-thirds of the agencies, and the Budget Bureau program planning staff had compiled a two-and-a-half year history of analysis. Working relationships had been established between the Budget Bureau and agency personnel, and both knew which issues should be studied and where the major data gaps lay.

By this time, the agencies were spread out even further in their analytic and PPB system accomplishments, making individual treatment even more important. Fire, environmental protection, and police had passed into the self-analysis stage. The Housing and Development Administration moved strongly into Stage III at the beginning of the cycle. The Economic Development Administration, the Transportation Administration, and the Parks, Recreation, and Cultural Affairs Administration remained in the joint analysis stage. Finally, a few agencies remained in the pre-analysis stage. The Human Resources Administration was the primary example; but equally limited progress had been made in the Corrections Administration and the Health Services Administration.

On the basis of the results of the prior cycle, a number of changes were made for the fiscal 1970–71 effort. Budget submission requirements were streamlined and simplified so agencies could increase their concentration on thorough analysis of a limited number of key issues and programs and reduce their analytic efforts on lower priority programs. Even greater emphasis was placed on joint analysis of major problems, and more time was allotted to the analytic effort. In addition, more attention was given to the development of adequate information and accounting systems.

Although it is too early at this writing to measure the results of the third year, progress seems to be satisfactory. Understanding of agency programs continues to grow and most agencies are still moving toward self-analysis.

CONCLUSIONS

Success or Failure?

Clearly, if the analysis/PPB project in New York City is judged in terms of its systems features or the completeness of each agency's annual PPB submission, then progress over three years has been small indeed. On the other hand, if "success" is related to the number of substantive and important decisions made and implemented and to changes in the attitudes and policies of agency management, then a more sanguine conclusion is justified. To be sure, most of the program decisions attributable to PPB have come from joint Budget Bureau/agency analytic efforts. But evidence, cited earlier, suggests that this is changing as more agencies approach the self-analysis stage. Moreover, our observations indicate that increasing success with analytic projects *is* beginning to change the agencies' views of their missions and the best approach for carrying them out. As experience with successful analysis accumulates, the effort gains in respectability and agency personnel begin to view it as a normal part of their operations. This has happened in the Police Department, the Fire Department, parts of the Environmental Protection Administration, and the Housing and Development Administration.

Of course, the degree of success has varied substantially from agency to agency. But this was expected — indeed, was made an integral part of the overall strategy — and the results confirmed our assessment of the four characteristics most critical to an agency's capacity for PPB and analysis: (1) the administrator's attitudes and management style; (2) the availability and strength of an internal analytic staff; (3) the analytic tractability of the agency's problems; and (4) general condition of the agency's information systems. Early and relatively easy success was achieved in the uniformed services — police, fire, and sanitation — where all four of these characteristics favored the PPB effort. Slower and less permanent success is evident in a large middle group of agencies where one or two of the characteristics raise

102 *Carter F. Bales*

obstacles. Finally, in a few agencies, these obstacles have been so great that the value of analysis has not been established at all.

Emphasis on People

Despite the substantial accomplishments of the past three years, the city still faces the problem of sustaining progress. It is difficult, if not impossible, to build a heritage of analysis into an agency unless that agency attracts and holds competent people. People, in fact, are the most critical element in a program improvement effort — fresh, questioning, bright people in substantial numbers. They should have no duties other than analyzing problems and otherwise helping to improve the quality of decisions. And they should represent a mix of skills and orientations. All they need to have in common is quantitative good sense, a belief in action, and a sense of urgency.

During the first year of the New York City effort, the Budget Bureau hired 15 program planners, most of them directly from graduate schools of economics, public administration, business, and law. The staff was more than doubled in the second year. Similar, though smaller, recruiting efforts were launched in many of the agencies. And a large summer intern program has been run each year, both to augment the permanent staff and as a recruiting device. Plans are now being laid to double the size of the staffs.

Outside consultants have also been used in many instances to tackle major problems. Besides extra hands, they have contributed scarce skills (e.g., expertise in computer modeling) and have coached city personnel in techniques of analysis. Occasionally they have led efforts jointly staffed with city and consultant personnel. McKinsey & Company, Inc., has served the Bureau of the Budget for nearly three years and recently began work for a number of agencies throughout the city. The New York City — RAND Institute has been under contract to the city for two years, and several other consultants, notably certified public accountant firms and computer software houses, have also been employed.

New York's heavy emphasis on separate analytic staffs — composed largely of new employees — does not argue against training permanent city employees in the new approaches. However, in our experience, this is the more difficult route. In some cases, permanent employees have become deeply involved in the analytic process. But there is a tendency for career employees to revert to their "proper" roles and for analysis to be forgotten.

At present, most of the analysts are young and were recruited directly out of graduate schools. Owing to salary limitations and the scarcity of experienced analysts in general, the city has had little success in attracting and retaining more experienced, career-oriented analysts. In addition, staff turnover has been fairly high. Only the charisma of Lindsay and Hayes has attracted and held the current staff, and without such human magnets, the supply of young analysts would probably be quickly depleted. With this degree of uncertainty about the adequacy of future staffing, a permanent role for analysis is by no means assured.

Beyond Analysis

By itself, good analysis, leading to wise decisions, followed by efficient implementation, is not sufficient to solve many problems facing the cities, today. Other, deeper changes must also take place in our basic urban institutions. Many aspects of city government should be decentralized to make them more responsive to the neighborhoods. Unions must become more agreeable to new work incentives and new methods. The Civil Service system must become more receptive to change. And new forms of organization outside government's control — such as public benefit corporations — must be tried.

There is also a critical need for more funds — a need that can be met only by reordering national priorities. The cities' revenue base is woefully mismatched with their program responsibilities. Without a massive infusion of new funds, significant improvements in municipal services will be impossible. Money remains the cities' first problem.

New York has shown that analysis can help improve the management of America's cities. But solving the problems of urban America will require far more than just better management.

CHAPTER 3

1. Frederick O'R. Hayes, "PPB in New York," *The Planning-Programming-Budgeting System: Progress and Potentials.* Hearings before the Subcommittee on Economy in Government of the Joint Economic Committee, Congress of the United States (Washington, D.C., Government Printing Office, 1967, p. 95).

2. Allen Schick, "Systems for Analysis: PPB and its Alternatives," in Joint Economic Committee, Subcommittee on Economy in Government, *The Analysis and Evaluation of Public Expenditures*, vol. III (Washington, D.C., Government Printing Office, 1969, p. 825).

3. In speaking of the "system features" of PPB, I am referring primarily to the development of detailed program structure, the recoding of line budgets to the program structure, and the preparation of so-called "multiyear programs and financial plans." The development of formal information systems to capture data on program results is also included.

4. Schick, *op. cit.*, pp. 817–834. See also Aaron Wildavsky, "Rescuing Policy Analysis from PPBS," *Public Administration Review*, March/April 1969, pp. 189–202, for a more extreme view.

5. Now the New York City—RAND Institute.

New Jersey Housing Finance Agency

Robert P. O'Block

Robert P. O'Block

Robert O'Block studied engineering at Purdue University and obtained his Masters degree from the Graduate School of Business Administration, Harvard University, where he is currently enrolled in the doctoral program studying Production and Operations Management. Recently, Mr. O'Block has been employed by McKinsey & Company, Inc., where he has worked on studies for the City of New York dealing with stimulating private new residential construction, improving the effectiveness of welfare rents, affecting the use of rehabilitation to upgrade the quality of the existing housing stock, and developing the City's new rent control program. Mr. O'Block has written several articles and has recently co-authored two books, published by the Division of Research, Harvard Business School: *An Economic Analysis of the Housing and Urban Development Act of 1968*, and *Urban Analysis*.

CHAPTER 4

NEW JERSEY HOUSING FINANCE AGENCY
(Robert P. O'Block)

NEW JERSEY, the most urbanized state in the Union, is sandwiched between the New York and Philadelphia metropolitan areas. The centers of growth in New Jersey are in the commuter suburbs, the ocean resort towns, and islands of industrial development, all outside the established cities. The state's largest city, Newark, with a resident population of over 400,000, exhibits in an acute form the afflictions of the old central cities of the northeast. Until recently, the state and its cities lacked any comprehensive policies for dealing with the contrasts of growth and decay in their urban areas. The absence of focused central city development has created one of the state's critical problems, the continuing deterioration and abandonment of its housing stock.

The New Jersey Housing Finance Agency (NJHFA), created in 1967, was assigned the difficult task of developing and implementing a statewide housing program. This case describes the introduction of an innovation in analysis into one part of NJHFA's work, the process of financial analysis of housing applications. Because financial analysis is crucial to achievement of the Agency's objectives, and because the Agency is an important factor in the entire state housing effort, innovations of this sort could have far-reaching consequences.

NOTE: This chapter describes conditions in New Jersey and in the New Jersey Housing Finance Agency as they existed in the Spring of 1970. Changes subsequent to that date may not be reflected here.

In order to measure the extent of these consequences, several major questions will be examined: How will innovation in a small but critical part of an Agency activity affect other aspects of its work? How do management attitudes and the nature of the organization influence the introduction and effective use of a new method in analysis? What will the human and organizational effects of this change in operations be? What effect will internal Agency changes have on other agencies and organizations in the housing field? What problems develop from the introduction of a new technique of analysis?

The case first describes the background and institutional complexities of the New Jersey housing situation and the history of NJHFA. A second section explains the analysis procedure, including the computer program used to implement it. The final section discusses the computer system's impact on Agency operations.

The Housing Situation

New Jersey's housing need has two components: one results from the inability of present new construction to fulfill current requirements arising from population and household increases, the other results from the large number of substandard or deteriorating units in the existing stock. The gap between newly constructed units and population and household needs is serious and averages approximately 5,000 units annually. Minimum needs to replace demolished units and rehabilitate substandard units are estimated at about 420,000 units, almost one-third of all housing in the state.[1] The latter need is categorized programmatically as follows:

Program Action	*Dwelling Units Affected*
Demolition, clearance and replacement	200,000
Major rehabilitation	220,000
Total	420,000

The present annual production rate of 40,000 to 45,000 new units is already falling 5,000 units short of meeting the needs arising from increasing population and new household formulation. If we add to this an additional 42,000 units per year over a ten-year period which would be necessary to replace demolished housing and perform major rehabilitation of substandard units, the total state production rate required would be 87,000 to 92,000 units, more than double the present rate. Furthermore, any serious state effort to produce low-rent housing, which is the most critical element of the housing need, would represent a dramatic increase over the 2,000–4,000 units produced annually by existing public assistance programs.

Many organizations at all government levels participate in the housing production process. The Federal Housing Administration (FHA), Veterans Administration, and other agencies administer fragmented and grossly underfunded federal programs; in New Jersey, the Division of State and Regional Planning, Department of Community Affairs, Relocation Department, and others work specifically to channel state housing resources; in the cities, Local Public Housing Authorities, Zoning Boards, Renewal Committees, and so forth, are conduits for federal and state programs and protect the rights of cities. Community groups emerge to sponsor housing or to impede the government bulldozer; builder/developers coordinate the efforts of many development team members: land surveyors, architects, contractors, lawyers, bankers, etc.; and finally private and public investment are needed to provide capital for construction. While not all of these groups work together on each project, a successful program requires numerous organizations working at various levels to implement any single housing project. Each group must develop a working relationship with the other housing actors, for without all the parts, the whole cannot succeed.

The New Jersey Housing Finance Agency

The New Jersey Housing Finance Agency is a state-authorized self-supporting institution in, but not of, the Department of Com-

munity Affairs. The Agency's primary job is to help implement
a new statewide housing development program by financing low-
income and moderate-income housing construction and rehabilitation.

By law, NJHFA must pursue the following goals:

• Stimulate housing construction through grants and long-term
  below-market interest rate loans to qualified nonprofit and
  limited-dividend sponsors.
• Promote construction and maintenance of viable communities
  by encouraging quality design and imaginative site planning,
  and seeking proposals with promise of advancing racial and
  economic integration.

The NJHFA was chartered to play a major role in housing
development, one which would coordinate, package, and finance
various housing programs. The executive director formulated the
Agency's specific goals as follows:[2]

> The initial goal is to provide a great deal more housing pri-
> marily for low-income and moderate-income groups, as quickly as
> possible, although it is very hard to provide for the low-income
> because of the high cost of land, construction, and financing.
>
> One of our other goals is to foster the growth of nonprofit hous-
> ing development corporations . . . we obtain not only a greater
> degree of local involvement, not only citizen participation and
> owner-occupancy through co-ops, but also more low-income
> building.
>
> In addition, I think we should be providing for middle-income,
> not as our first goal, but as a by-product in the attempt to provide
> economically integrated communities or developments. NJHFA
> is a better vehicle for this than FHA because we have more flexi-
> bility in setting acceptable income limits.

NJHFA programs are supplements, rather than substitutes, for
federal programs. The Agency subsidy mechanisms are legally
targeted to moderate-income and middle-income groups, those
with incomes of approximately $6,000–$15,000 per year. To serve
low-income families, i.e., those earning less than $6,000, NJHFA

programs are combined with federal subsidy programs, making possible a wide range of rents for each project. One Agency objective is to support projects tending to maximize the use of federal subsidy money, as well as private sector equity employed in the project's capitalization. Recognizing the limits of federal subsidy appropriations, the Agency must rely primarily on its legislated financing mechanisms.

The following financial tools are at the Agency's disposal for project financing:

- The Agency's tax-exempt bonds, issued at a rate of 2%–4% below going market rates, are usually purchased by high-income investors. The bond proceeds are used for both construction and permanent mortgage financing.
- A legislative appropriation of approximately $1.25 million per year is made for the revolving Housing and Demonstration Grant Fund which allows the Agency to make direct grants or interest-free "seed money" loans to nonprofit sponsors for development of housing proposals and plans.
- $12.5 million was appropriated by a November 1968 referendum for Agency use in one of the following ways:
  a. as an interest subsidy applied to decrease rental or carrying charges;
  b. assistance by subsidy or outright grant not to exceed $2,000 per unit for special assistance subordinated to the federal mortgage loan, with repayment of principal and interest, if any, deferred until the federal loan is paid or released.

Because of its character as an autonomous authority, the NJHFA has a special stake in the financial soundness of the projects it assists. Bankruptcy of one of its mortgages would jeopardize the NJHFA's credit rating and impair its ability to meet the principal and interest obligations on its bonds. But the Agency cannot afford to be excessively conservative in its lending either. Beyond the motive of its social goal of promoting housing developments not otherwise attractive to private investors, the NJHFA has a direct financial interest in financing projects in volume. Agency operating costs, by law, must be met from the proceeds of the Agency fees added to the monthly mortgage payments and are not covered by annual appropriations.

The financial analysis of applications is crucial to assessing the chances of success or failure of proposed projects and, ultimately, of the Agency itself. Each application must be analyzed in detail to determine whether sufficient revenues can be obtained to cover building support costs,[3] whether the sponsor can credibly manage the project, the mortgage amount the Agency should issue, and so forth.

The computer system described here was the result of a collaborative effort by the Agency and staff members from the Harvard Program on Technology and Society. While providing technical assistance to the state, the Harvard group sought to employ the Housing Finance Agency as a sounding board for ideas and to accumulate information, ideas, and experience which would advance their research efforts.[4] In return, NJHFA expected to benefit through implementation of techniques and transferal of ideas developed at Harvard. The computer applications described in this case were developed by the author, who was a research staff member at Harvard, and a member of the NJHFA staff.

In the spring of 1968, when the collaboration with Harvard began, NJHFA was completing its first nine months of operation and, like most young organizations, facing many problems. Only $50,000 was appropriated by the legislature for start-up expenses and salary; as a result, most staff members worked part-time for the first few months. Thomas V. Seessel, who was Executive Director, was the first person to hold this position in the Agency. Graduated from Dartmouth College and the Woodrow Wilson School at Princeton, Mr. Seessel's work experience was concentrated in Human Resources Development Planning, an area where he was directly responsible for numerous innovations. His only housing experience was as Director of the State Division of Housing and Urban Renewal in New Jersey, a position he held for six months prior to joining NJHFA. Ralph I. Brown, Director of Policy and Programs, is a graduate of Columbia Law School, where he was awarded the E. B. Convers Prize for the best original essay on a legal subject for his work, "Tenant Relocation in New York City." His experience in housing was gained during a five-year term with the progressive New Haven Redevelopment Authority.

In New Jersey little experience, either technical (financial, economic, etc.) or organizational, existed upon which the Agency could draw in establishing its programs and policies. A planning or research and development staff had not been developed. Most early planning and organizational designs were developed incrementally from either the traditional bureaucratic way of doing things, i.e., drawing experience from the FHA and the New York State Housing Finance Agency (the only other state housing finance agency in existence at that time), or incorporating the previous staff experience gained from work in progressive quasi-public organizations such as the New Haven Redevelopment Authority. These factors, plus the dynamic and dominant personalities of both the Executive Director and the Director of Policy and Programs, created an organization structured as a single functional unit with no distinct subunits or functions requiring full-time management and control. In addition, procedures had not yet been clearly established for internal transactions, allocation of resources, or rewards and punishments. Decisions on these matters were largely in the hands of the Executive Director and the Director of Policy and Programs. Figure 4-1 is a schematic approximating the organizational structure.

For the moment, this fluid organizational structure was adequate, for no one really expected NJHFA to do much in the early years; the politicians were not breathing down their necks, and clients were not banging on their door begging for financing. There was, in fact, not much to do in a functional, implementation sense but learn, organize, and plan. Because their task and functional areas of responsibility were only vaguely defined by the legislature, this short-term task-force-like organization recognized that many changes and revisions in the organizational structure and legislated policy and programs would occur during NJHFA's development.

The organization and its stage of development also influenced the goal formulation process. Although goals, objectives, and strategies of implementation were discussed with other influential

FIGURE 4-1. EARLY ORGANIZATIONAL STRUCTURE OF THE
NEW JERSEY HOUSING FINANCE AGENCY

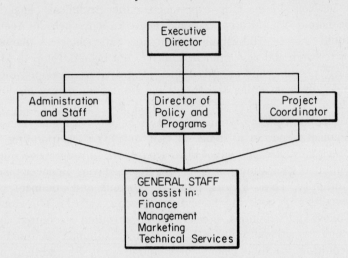

people in state government, the values and personal predisposi-
tions of the two top-level managers guided the Agency at this
time. One of them said:

> In the last year, we have concentrated our energies in all areas
> on becoming operational but we've still not fully developed what
> we ought to be doing. This is still a band-aid operation. . . .
> We've been inventing as we go along, and this is one of the rea-
> sons it takes so long to start up. Other similar experiences have
> shown that 6–8 years are necessary to become fully developed.
> . . . We have to be different here from other groups in the
> housing area and this is where conservatism pops in: we almost
> become bankers . . . we are not allowed to lose in any of our
> developments . . . if we lose, we are in trouble, and that means
> bankruptcy.[5]

Given the complexity and magnitude of New Jersey's housing
problem — the many factors to consider, lack of knowledge on
most, and the multi-dimensionality of the housing decision-making process, etc. — it is easy to see why a logical and thorough

hierarchy was not established. Some of the conflicts facing the Agency were described by the director:

> We sort of go in conflicting directions between moderate-income housing and low-income housing, between urban involvement and rural involvement. We're not quite sure whether we want to cover the state generally or whether we want to concentrate on a few geographic areas.
>
> I think we have to be prepared to do all kinds of things if they are good things and the right things. It seems that what we're really asking is what priorities do we have at this point? When an application comes in, how is it evaluated? Do we use a point system, do we use a narrative, what do we use? . . . Do we put the greatest weight on the possibilities that a program can succeed because it's a good program or do we put it on geography, or do we put it on local contributions? We've got a few basic criteria here but in the final analysis a negative rating on one category could kill a whole project. . . . It is pretty clear that there are at least 15 or maybe 20 very key indicators and there is no easy way to evaluate them.[6]

DEVELOPMENT OF THE COMPUTER PROGRAM

The collaboration began with a consideration of the many factors and their relationships necessary to formulate housing policies and programs. The decision maker developing policy or making decisions on specific project applications must consider many factors related to the supply and demand for housing, including social, psychological, political, demographic, and economic factors, as well as the condition of the existing stock. Figure 4-2 presents a schematic of the key policy variables identified in our initial 1968 analysis of the state housing system.

It is not possible in any study to pursue in depth all these variables. Policy and programs must be rationally targeted to certain variables to achieve a desired result. We sought first to identify the key, controllable variables and then to investigate their importance in the Agency's decision-making processes and requirements. We decided to study first the construction cost

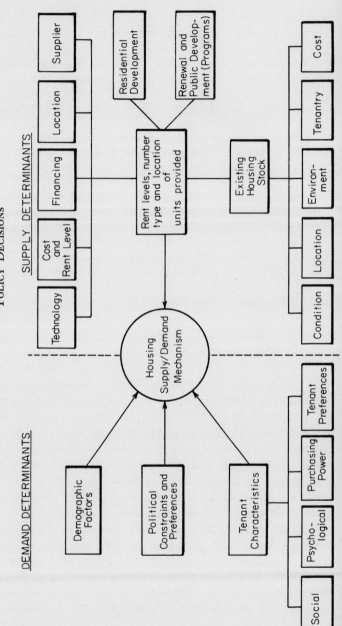

FIGURE 4-2. FACTORS INFLUENCING HOUSING POLICY DECISIONS

SUPPLY DETERMINANTS

Technology

Cost and Rent Level

Financing

Location

Supplier

Residential Development

Renewal and Public Development (Programs)

Rent levels, number type and location of units provided

Existing Housing Stock

Condition

Location

Environment

Tenantry

Cost

Housing Supply/Demand Mechanism

DEMAND DETERMINANTS

Demographic Factors

Political Constraints and Preferences

Tenant Characteristics

Social

Psychological

Purchasing Power

Tenant Preferences

and financing variables that top management thought were crucial to successful program development and implementation. Once this area had been defined adequately and understood, other, less quantifiable areas — e.g., social, political — could be similarly probed.

The key variables initially identified by the Agency related to the financial and economic consequences of specific project proposals. To determine whether a proposal should be financed, the Agency evaluated the implications of alternative cost assumptions, financing schemes, and so forth. To help define and assess the trade-offs involved in these project-specific decisions, a number of computer programs were developed to enable one to quickly and accurately make financial and economic "go" and "no-go" decisions and to pinpoint specific project characteristics which were out of line.[7] Rationalization of this process would ultimately give top management a firm grip on the key variables related to the financial success of the Housing Finance Agency.

Before introduction of the computer program, analysis procedures were relatively unstructured. Most analysis and evaluation was done by one of the two top-level managers, who was very good with a slide rule. However, pressure of time and numerous other responsibilities naturally limited the amount, accuracy, and comprehensiveness of his analyses. While the concepts of housing finance are quite simple, the mass of calculations and numerous repetitions required due to constantly changing assumptions was overwhelming. Lack of staff time and the problem's size and complexity led to numerous calculating errors, delays in getting the numbers "in shape" and a general feeling of frustration, and, consequently, avoidance of this task by the individual(s) involved. One staff member said:

> How many deals have never become deals just because of delays or because we have to redo the numbers . . . we'll meet again and think about what we've got to adjust, and somehow we never get down to business. The calculations are too long and involved and most of us don't have the time to perform the analysis.

Figure 4-3 shows an FHA mortgage application form for below-market interest rate financing under Section 236 of the 1968 Housing Act.[8] Over 100 items must be computed and filled in. Moreover, when one variable is changed, the remaining items must be recomputed, for most items are a function of previous values and calculations. Just outlining and explaining these forms required a 200-page Urban America handbook. These labyrinthine forms account for much of the bureaucratic red tape, long processing times, delays, bottlenecks, etc., characteristic of mortgage applications. Given the many housing variables (land, construction and operating costs, fees and financing schedules, subsidy programs, financing alternatives, etc.) and the need to perform many computations repeatedly, we investigated the feasibility of using computers to calculate quickly and accurately the information required for mortgage application evaluation.

Our analysis of Agency operations indicated that the relatively fixed set of computational procedures involved in housing finance was very amenable to computerization. Adequate data were also available. We did not need to define the process to be computerized, only to insure that the model included all relevant variables and parameters and presented the computer's output in a format useful to housing finance officials.

The developed computer programs employ simple mathematical equations to replicate the financial relationships in housing construction and operation, shown schematically in Figure 4-4. For a housing project to be financially feasible, the mortgage interest and amortization charges associated with construction plus yearly operating expenses (including profit and real estate taxes) must be less than or equal to total annual project income, which in turn must be less than or equal to the tenants' ability to pay rent. All planning and construction costs are summed to arrive at a total project replacement cost. The investor's equity position, mortgage term and interest rate, profit requirements and so forth, in turn determine the equivalent "rental" implied by a given total cost over the project life. By taking operating information, appropriate rents and income levels are determined. One advantage of the computer system is that each factor included in the program is treated as a variable. Any proposed change can be

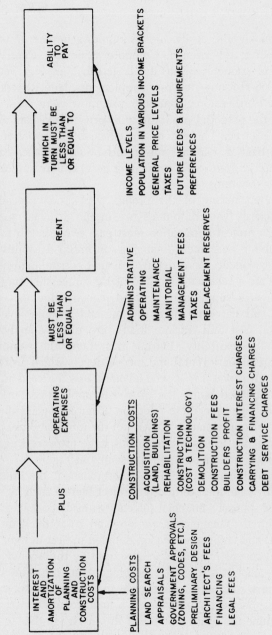

FIGURE 4-4. PRINCIPLE OF THE HOUSING ANALYZER MODEL

tested quickly and easily and its resulting impact on any or all of the factors determined. Computer programs were also constructed to examine various available subsidies, e.g., Section 236 of the 1968 Housing Act, rent supplements, land writedown, and so forth. Furthermore, computer programs were constructed to evaluate the potential profitability to private investors of Agency financed projects. This reflects the effects of depreciation, interest and amortization, capital gains, return on equity, and many other profit criteria. Figure 4-5 presents a general flow diagram of the computer programs.[9]

An understanding of the project application procedure will help to clarify the computer's use in the financial analysis. In practice, a project application must pass two administrative hurdles to obtain permanent financing: an initial feasibility analysis and a subsequent, more detailed, issue-by-issue analysis. Figure 4-6 presents a schematic outline of the processing stages. First, cost estimates subdivided by land, construction, operating, financing and carrying charges, rent and income levels, along with legal cost and income limits, are quickly analyzed as a package for feasibility. During this stage, the computer calculates preliminary rental and income levels which a project will theoretically serve; if rents and incomes served exceed administratively established limits, the proposal (application) must be reworked or face immediate rejection. Computer-generated output constitutes approximately 80%–90% of the information required for project-specific decisions during this stage of processing. Illustrative output from one project is presented in Figure 4-7.

Once preliminary feasibility is established, the Agency systematically examines additional project factors such as site, marketability, sponsor's financial solvency, subsidy packages available and required management, design, and so forth. Concurrently, architects and engineers develop detailed project design specifications and cost estimates, which are used by the Agency to determine the amount of the final mortgage. Here the computer plays a secondary role and is used only to update the sponsor's cost estimates. Before final closing,[10] a final computer run is made to determine the exact amount of the mortgage the Agency will issue. If costs exceed those previously agreed on, the Agency

FIGURE 4-5. FLOW DIAGRAM OF HOUSING ANALYSIS MODELS

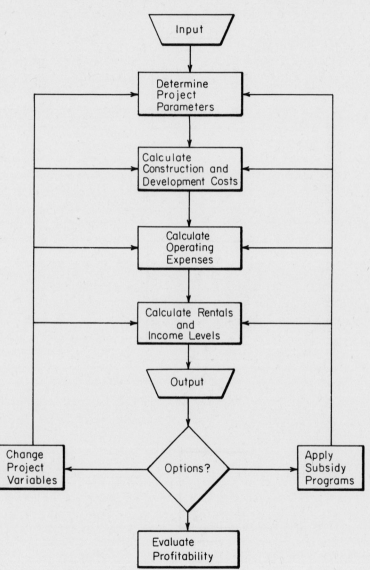

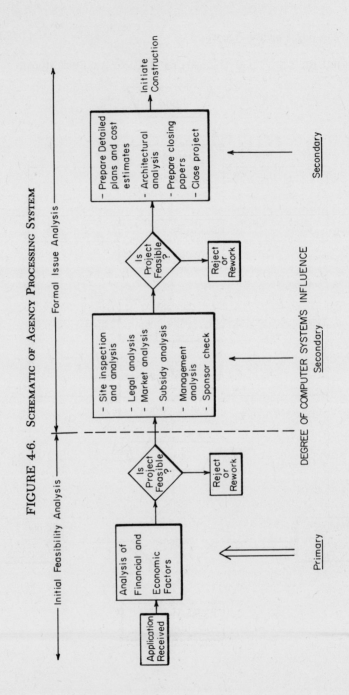

FIGURE 4-6. Schematic of Agency Processing System

FIGURE 4-7.
Illustrative Computer Output

SECTION 236 FEASIBILITY ANALYSIS
PART A: BASIC INFORMATION

(1) Mortgage Terms:
A. HFA Mortgage	$ 4915000
B. Interest Rate (per cent)	6.25
C. Length (years)	48

(2) S.236 Subsidy:
A. Yearly Amount per $ of Mortgage	0.039767
B. Total Yearly Subsidy	$ 195455

(3) Rents and Unit Breakdown:
A. Basic Rent Factor[1]	0.609383
B. Total Yearly Mkt. Res. Rents[2]	$ 500376

UNIT TYPE	NO. OF ROOMS	NO. OF UNITS	MARKET RENT	SECTION 236[3] BASIC RENT	MIN. RENT [4] SUPP. RENT
1 bdrm	4.0	46	168	102	31
2 bdrm	4.5	22	185	113	34
2 bdrm	5.0	92	205	125	37
3 bdrm	6.5	46	240	146	44

PART B: FEASIBILITY ANALYSIS WITH UNADJUSTED INPUT

(1) Feasibility at Regular Income Limits:

UNIT TYPE	NO. IN FAMILY	MIN. S.236[5] INCOME AT 25 PCT.	REGULAR INCOME LIMIT[6]	SEE NOTE	REGULAR INCOME SPREAD[7]	POSITIVE FEASIBILITY 1-YES, 0-NO
1 bdrm	1	$4896	$4860	1	−36	0
1 bdrm	2	4896	5670	1	774	1
2 bdrm	2	5424	5670	1	246	1
2 bdrm	3	5424	5915	1	491	1
2 bdrm	4	5424	6155	1	731	1
2 bdrm	2	6000	5670	1	−330	0
2 bdrm	3	6000	5915	1	−85	0
2 bdrm	4	6000	6155	1	155	1
3 bdrm	4	7008	6155	1	−853	0
3 bdrm	5	7008	6400	1	−608	0
3 bdrm	6	7008	6640	1	−368	0

(continued)

FIGURE 4-7. (continued)

(2) Feasibility at Exception Income Limits:

UNIT TYPE	NO. IN FAMILY	MIN. S.236 INCOME AT 25 PCT.	EXCEPTION INCOME LIMIT[8]	SEE NOTE	EXCEPTION INCOME SPREAD	POSITIVE FEASIBILITY 1-YES, 0-NO
1 bdrm	1	$4896	$5350	1	454	1
1 bdrm	2	4896	6550	1	1654	1
2 bdrm	2	5424	6550	1	1126	1
2 bdrm	3	5424	7650	1	2226	1
2 bdrm	4	5424	7650	1	2226	1
2 bdrm	2	6000	6550	1	550	1
2 bdrm	3	6000	7650	1	1650	1
2 bdrm	4	6000	7650	1	1650	1
3 bdrm	4	7008	7650	1	642	1
3 bdrm	5	7008	8800	1	1792	1
3 bdrm	6	7008	8800	1	1792	1

[1] Basic rent factor is the number used to derive the subsidized rents under Section 236. Subsidized rents equal market (unsubsidized) rents times the basic rent factor.

[2] Total yearly market residential rents — these are unsubsidized rents.

[3] Section 236 basic rent is the effective rent achieved through use of the 1%, 10-year below-market interest rate loan.

[4] Minimum rent supplement rent is the lowest rental attainable under the Section 101 Rent Supplement Program. Minimum rent supplement rental equals market rent times 70%.

[5] Minimum Section 236 income at 25% is the household income necessary, assuming 25% of income spent for rent, to support the subsidized rents (Section 236 basic rents).

[6] Regular income limit is the administratively established limit (a function of family size) above which families are not eligible to receive Section 236 subsidy. This limit is approximately 135% of Public Housing income limits.

[7] Regular income spread equals the regular income limit minus the minimum Section 236 income at 25%.

[8] Exception income limit is the administratively established limit above which families are not eligible for Section 236 subsidy. This limit is approximately 90% of Section 221 (D) 3 limits.

can reject the project or postpone its mortgage commitment until the figures are adjusted to satisfy both parties — the Agency and the sponsor/developer. In each instance, the computer is a controlling and monitoring device for the Agency and insures that any cost changes submitted are reflected accurately in the mortgage.

Before the computer system was installed, five part-time project managers, also responsible for other Agency functions, performed by hand the lengthy calculations to determine project feasibility whenever time permitted. Often applications sat on desks for weeks until the analysis could be performed and verified. In some cases, calculations for one project had to be repeated 10, 20, or 30 times. Once final cost figures are agreed upon and a mortgage commitment is made, the Agency legally must provide the sponsor with the contracted sum of money; staff errors or oversights must be borne by the Agency.

Our investigations showed that, even with the careful attention given it by the staff, many errors still crept into completed project forms. When informed of this, the general managers regretted the fact, but said given the numerous staff responsibilities, it was unlikely that more time could be devoted to the analysis task. Reasons stated above, i.e., lack of funds, part-time staff and no previous experience, all contributed. Further, much of the analysis work was being performed at night and obviously fatigue and long work days contributed to the errors. The author witnessed several of these work sessions, one lasting until 2:00 A.M. Also contributing to the possibility of errors was the fact that no individual or staff function was directly responsible or accountable for the analysis; the responsibility was divided among five part-time employees. Not only could financial failures bankrupt the Agency, but they could become political weapons to be used against the existing state administration. Thus, accurate calculations were crucial to Agency operations.

In summary, the computer system replicates the numerous hand calculations traditionally performed in housing analysis. More importantly, it determines costs and benefits accruing to government, tenant, and private investor and enables housing officials to evaluate quickly many more programs and policies.

How the Model Was Implemented

Initially, a series of weekly meetings and interviews was devoted primarily to discussing the computer system's requirements, capabilities, and potential uses; defining the appropriate parameters and variables to be included; and eliciting the general goals and specific objectives for housing in New Jersey. Simultaneously, work had begun at Harvard to construct the initial prototypes and to incorporate the financial characteristics peculiar to NJHFA processing procedures. For the system to satisfy NJHFA requirements, it would have to duplicate exactly the existing analytical procedures; then, if successful, the system could be expanded to perform additional tasks and provide further information. The prototype system constructed actually duplicated the slide rule calculations formerly performed by the staff. Interaction with and feedback from the Agency during this stage of development was essential.[11]

After the system was constructed and preliminarily debugged, and the time-sharing equipment — i.e., a teletype terminal connected to a computer via telephone lines — had been installed, the system was presented to the NJHFA for testing. Figure 4-8 presents a picture of the terminal being used by the NJHFA staff. Before this could begin, however, a short training program was conducted to familiarize the staff with the mechanics of using the time-sharing system. These sessions included two working classes run by the telephone company, several formal and informal lectures given by the researcher, and internal instructional sessions held by the staff, where they actually prepared the input data, ran the models, and interpreted its output. During this training and testing period, the system was changed slightly to satisfy the Agency's working requirements. Only if the inputs and outputs were presented in the form and quantity desired by the staff and if all relevant decision-making variables were included would the system have a chance of becoming an integral part of the Agency's day-to-day activities.[12]

Several problems developed in teaching the staff to use the system. The first was to overcome the staff's basic distrust of

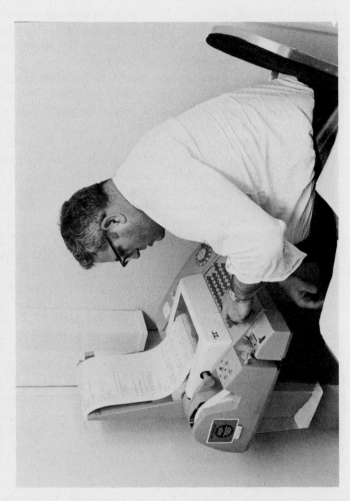

FIGURE 4-8. COMPUTER TELETYPE TERMINAL IN USE BY THE AGENCY

computers and their fear of actually operating the system independently of those who had designed and constructed it. There were those in the Agency who refused to use even a slide rule or a desk calculator, and to them the thought of using a computer was completely unacceptable. These fears and reservations, however, were dissipated gradually as the system was implemented and experience in operating it was accumulated.

To insure the installed system would be properly used and maintained, one staff member was assigned the responsibility for overseeing its activities. He was taught the mechanics of the system's programming language; the general characteristics of time-shared computer systems; how to operate the computer (via remote teletype console) to perform the tasks assigned to it by the Agency; how to explain and interpret the output to individuals outside the Agency (investors, community groups, builders, etc.); and how to transmit his knowledge to others in the Agency, so as the Agency grew, the staff expertise would also increase. The assigned staff member was brought to Cambridge and subjected to an intensive training program established for these purposes. He became the advocate and guardian of the system within the Agency. "I learned an awful lot when I was up there in Cambridge," he commented. "I'm now much more confident about what I can do. And I've got some ideas about what these variables mean." The teletype terminal was initially placed in his office.

The time-saving features of the proposed computer system and the general arguments presented in our management approach to Agency problems were accepted eagerly. The staff's youth and initiative, the Agency's evolutionary environment, the unique complexity of housing finance analysis, and the lack of historical precedent created a favorable atmosphere for innovation. One member said:

> Obviously, the computer is faster with arithmetic and more accurate . . . it's a short cut . . . a time-saver because to do all those calculations by hand, wow! . . . With the computer you can run through a whole deal in one hour and you know definitely whether you have a deal or you don't.

This effort demonstrated that financial innovation, an Agency policy variable, was more important in the short run than a breakthrough in construction technology, i.e., bricks and mortar, a variable over which the Agency has little control. This is illustrated in a statement by Paul N. Ylvisaker, Commissioner of the New Jersey Department of Community Affairs:

I think that at this point in the development of the new approach we should avoid committing ourselves to any single method of construction of housing, or even committing ourselves to assigning top priority to innovations in construction techniques per se. According to some recent studies, the most optimistic estimate of cost reductions through new building technologies is about 10%, and this in turn reduces rents by only 3% to 5%. It may be that the most significant "technological" breakthroughs that can be made . . . through the consortium approach or otherwise . . . are in improved and more efficient systems of planning, financing, and administering the total development process of housing. Such improvements in "software" systems could well lead to greater cost savings, greater production, shorter time periods, and more participation by private enterprise generally than many of the more esoteric "hardware" systems of putting the pieces and materials of housing together.[13]

FIRST AND SECOND ORDER CONSEQUENCES OF SYSTEMS IMPLEMENTATION

As a society, we strive to stimulate, achieve, and adapt to technological innovation. Our interest in technology is far broader than the simple technique or new machine. Secondary and tertiary consequences are equally important.

Technical developments almost invariably have the appearance of being "good things," because they invariably begin as a solution to some agreed-upon problem. The task of solving the problem is seen as "purely technical." The underlying assumption behind the phrase "purely technical" is that no "policy implications" are involved in the sense that one does not have to look

beyond the solution of the immediate task to consider further
ramification of one's action. . . . A seemingly unimportant "technical" change, however, produces a chain reaction — the implications of which were not seen in advance or sometimes not understood for a considerable period after the reaction had begun. . . .[14]

The use of the computer for financial analysis at NJHFA produced
both first and second order consequences.[15] Internally, the computer affected policy, organization, and individuals; externally,
it influenced the organizations the HFA encounters in day-to-
day business transactions.

First Order Consequences

As discussed previously, the analysis function is crucial to projecting the success or failure of individually financed projects
and, ultimately, of the Agency itself. The importance of financial
analysis, plus top management's concern over existing methods,
provided a neat technical issue that could be analyzed and improved upon. Initially, the computer system's success or failure
was measured by first order criteria, such as quality of analysis
produced, speed, accuracy, and output format.

First, the overall quality of analysis performed improved. Each
project application could be quickly processed through the computer to obtain an accurate and comprehensive analysis. The
relationships between all financial variables were now computed
for each run. This represented a significant departure from traditional methods where, once calculations were performed, perhaps
only half the numbers would be computed, or after one run-
through was completed, the impact of any proposed change, e.g.,
lower construction costs, would be merely approximated. The
automated slide rule with a memory could obviously out-perform
humans. In addition to quality increases due to the computer's
technical capability (a rationalization of the analysis procedures),
an input necessary to write accurate computer programs made

individuals more knowledgeable.[16] Two elements, more qualified staff plus computer software, have combined to produce improved financial analysis of projects.

Second, more alternatives could be examined for each project. Most of the staff could easily see the advantages of machine-aided analysis, once convinced the computer could perform the analysis task correctly. In many instances staff members suggested additional uses, tested more variations and generated enthusiasm beyond all expectations. Evaluation of combined subsidy programs, e.g., "piggybacking" a federal interest subsidy with a state loan and local tax abatement, was one of the successful "new uses." One member said:

> The main advantage of the computer is that we can look at options; we can look to change the land price before we even get an appraisal; we can have a best test and a worst test deal, and we can fool around with room rents and things like that before we reach a final decision.

Third, the amount of useful information, related primarily to specific projects, was increased and could easily be circulated to appropriate Agency members for examination and comment. Figure 4-9, for example, presents one circular that employed the computer output to derive specific conclusions. Data on all projects are now produced by the computer and recorded, along with information on other variables, e.g., site appraisal, sponsor's credit report, market analysis, etc., in a docket assigned to each entering application. This permits all relevant project information to be collected and reviewed systematically by the decision makers.

Finally, the staff time allocated to performing routine calculations decreased dramatically. The computer's speed and accuracy enabled it immediately to capture a large share of the computational work load. The five part-time project managers were relieved from "calculating the numbers" and were then able to pursue and accept other responsibilities. One project manager was quoted as saying:

Not only is this a major time-saving tool for us, but it's also a unique service to builders. . . . Within seconds, the computer comes up with the amount of rent a tenant would have to pay for the finished apartment. . . . It allows us to run instantaneous computations . . . to run through the whole thing with the developer in an hour and know whether or not we have a deal. It saves his time, our time, and makes for a better, more professional deal.

The time it frees up is valuable too. The hand calculations made us tired and frustrated and not as efficient in other activities . . . with the computer we're increasing productivity in the Agency quite a lot.

FIGURE 4-9. ILLUSTRATIVE INTERNAL REPORT USING COMPUTER OUTPUT S.236 & S.101-FEASIBILITY ANALYSIS

I. ADDITIONAL BASIC INFORMATION

A. Rehabilitation — Cooperative Development

B.
Unit Type	Number	Mo. Carrying Chgs.[1]	Down Payment
1 BR	4	$107.50	$200
2 BR	32	137.50	200
3 BR	27	168.50	200
4 BR	12	197.50	200

C. Initial closing to be held in February or March, 1969.

D. Anticipate market, unsubsidized, rentals on 15% of units.

E. New Jersey Housing Finance Agency direct mortgage of $1,055,209 — 35 year mortgage.

II. FEASIBILITY ANALYSIS

A. *S.101*[2]

1. Basic S.236 rents are below maximum allowable S.101 rents.

2. Paterson has a certified workable program.

3. All other project characteristics are compatible with rent supplement regulations.

B. *S.236*[3]

1. Actual

```
X = YEARLY SUBSIDY AT S1 MM (DECIMAL %)[4]
    X = .0408
MAXIMUM MORTGAGE = 1055209
TOTAL MARKET RENTS = 140994
BASIC RENT FACTOR = 0.6946
TYPE 1 TO CHANGE BASIC RENT FACTOR OTHERWISE TYPE 0
    K = 0
```

(continued)

FIGURE 4-9 (continued)

UNIT TYPE	NO. IN FAMILY	BASIC RENT	MIN. S.236 INCOME	MAXI-MUM REG. INCOME	SPREAD	$500 FEASI-BILITY SPREAD
1	1	75	2987	4995	2008	YES
1	2	75	2987	5535	2548	YES
2	2	96	3821	5535	1714	YES
2	3	96	3821	6075	2254	YES
2	4	96	3821	6615	2794	YES
3	4	117	4682	6615	1933	YES
3	5	117	4682	7155	2473	YES
3	6	117	4682	7695	3013	YES
4	6	137	5488	7695	2207	YES
4	7	137	5488	8235	2747	YES
4	8	137	5488	8235	2747	YES

2. Feasibility with an upward adjustment of 5.5% in the Basic Rent Factor for contingencies.

UNIT TYPE	NO. IN FAMILY	BASIC RENT	MIN. S.236 INCOME	MAXI-MUM REG. INCOME	SPREAD	$500 FEASI-BILITY SPREAD
1	1	81	3225	4995	1770	YES
1	2	81	3225	5535	2310	YES
2	2	103	4125	5535	1410	YES
2	3	103	4125	6075	1950	YES
2	4	103	4125	6615	2490	YES
3	4	126	5055	6615	1560	YES
3	5	126	5055	7155	2100	YES
3	6	126	5055	7695	2640	YES
4	6	143	5925	7695	1770	YES
4	7	143	5925	8235	2810	YES
4	8	143	5925	8235	2810	YES

III. CONCLUSIONS

Both the S.236 and S.101 programs are highly feasible in this development, even with a 5% contingency adjustment in the Basic Rent Factor.

[1] Monthly carrying charges.
[2] Section 101 rent supplements.
[3] Section 236 (the 1%, 40-year interest rate program).
[4] Yearly interest subsidy provided to the project by the federal government.

The computer, it should be recalled, simply replicated a standard procedure in existence since the beginning of housing finance. Many staff members were assigned traditionally to do nothing but calculate and check the accuracy of applications. In NJHFA, this task now is delegated to a computer system. Its implementation has increased the speed, accuracy, quality, and breadth of the analysis and has subsequently provided important information required to make project-specific decisions.

These direct consequences of the mechanization of financial analysis have created new possibilities whose importance to the HFA was highlighted by the views of a former high-ranking HUD official. After spending two days at the Agency in March 1969, he concluded that the computer system made it possible for the NJHFA to avoid the paralyzing red tape that seemed endemic to public agencies in the housing field.[17] His independent assessment also confirmed the expectation of the originators of the computerized methods that a different kind of processing system, and not just a speedier one, could ensue. In his words:

> That [different processing] system should identify the key decision points, and should make decisions early and use the decision process both to set parameters within which sponsors know they will be approved, and to educate sponsors to the realities of the development process.[18]

The second order consequences of this innovation in analysis stem in part from that "extra dimension" of the new processing system.

Second Order Consequences: Internal to the NJHFA

During this year of development and implementation, the policy framework, the organizational structure, and individual style and competence have all changed. It cannot be argued either that these *resulted* from the computer, or that they were entirely unrelated. We recognize the ultimate test of the computer's impact will be several years of use and observation. To what extent policy framework, organizational structure, and individual style and competence were accelerated or even shaped by the computer, we can't say with precision, but the author's views as an involved participant follow.

Policy Level

On the general policy level, the computer has indirectly led to redefinition of existing goals and objectives, investigation and definition of additional Agency powers and functions, and implementation of a more cogent and comprehensive housing development strategy. This has resulted, in part, from the freeing up of a tremendous amount of staff time, previously spent performing hand calculations, which can now be allocated to other problem areas.

The author feels that definition of financial analysis has given top management the confidence required to reexamine its legislated powers and responsibilities, in order ultimately to utilize more effectively Agency powers, capabilities, and resources. This has resulted in the initiation of several studies of policy issues such as potential sources and uses of funds, the power of eminent domain, creation of a centralized state financing mechanism for all community facilities, participation in Operation Breakthrough,[19] the use of federal interest subsidy with state financing, and many more. Although the computer's presence has in fact encouraged these activities, it will play a minor role, in most cases, in the development of solutions to these more difficult and complex policy issues.

Explicit consideration of many more variables has in turn expanded top management's decision space and enabled it to consider more policy alternatives. Management can now not only consider such factors as the demographic, sociological and technological state of the existing stock, etc., but also assess subjectively the impact of such variables on policy and program decisions. We have collectively studied not only the contents of these factors, but also the relationships among them. For example, the staff developed and implemented an analytic approach to market analysis. This included time series analysis of population and households, racial characteristics, vacancy rates, condition of housing, household income, and assessment of housing need for the designated market area. During the course of this development, the executive director asked the researcher to pursue ways to integrate the results of the market analysis with the computer outputs.

One area now being investigated is the Agency's role as an initiator, packager, and developer of deals. In many instances, the sponsor comes to the Agency with little or no idea of what the end product of his application will be. Often, he comes with only a plot of land asking general questions such as, "what kind of deal can be arranged? How much is it going to cost me? How long or what type of mortgage will I be able to receive from your organization?" Agency personnel are now better equipped to answer because the computer system has increased their understanding of the financial aspects of project development. Although Agency personnel lack the legal power to initiate projects, they are interested in adopting the role of project developer. These staff members must decide whether to be timid or inactive while waiting for a sponsor/developer to prepare a feasible package, or whether they should purchase options on land, prepare site and architectural plans, hire the contractor, prepare the financing agreements, and then find an adequate sponsor, developer, or community group to manage the completed project. Whichever approach is adopted, the Agency will, in any case, be more prepared to implement a comprehensive housing development strategy.

Organization

During the course of organizational evolution, the computer has been directly or indirectly responsible for definition of certain tasks and areas of responsibility, development of a new organizational structure, marked increases in productivity, competence, reputation, and organizational morale. In addition, decision making on individual projects now rests lower in the organization, freeing top management's time for other resource allocation decisions.

The computer's acceptance led initially to discussion of ways to improve the application processing procedures. With the computer performing the analysis work of five men, organizational reform and realignment of task definitions were obviously necessary. During the evolution of these reforms, several conversations revealed the Agency members' current thinking, as the following excerpt suggests:

> Soon the two project managers and I will be in adjoining offices. The computer will be in mine . . . it's a much more logical way of handling it. They can just say, run this project through the computer when you get a chance and see what it looks like. And, this will help just in terms of in-house communications.

One specific change implemented was the reassignment of the five part-time project managers. One was assigned the area of subsidy analysis, two became full-time project managers, one became a full-time executive, and the last was placed in charge of market analysis. The project manager's task also had to be redefined, for now more time could be spent organizing and managing members of the development team and less time "pushing the numbers," a task now delegated to the computer. Creating positions of subsidy analysis and full-time project management in turn led to examination of the old and eventually to development of a new organizational structure.

The new application processing structure employed the computer as an integrating mechanism to coordinate activities of all parties involved in project development. Project managers delegated analysis to a staff man in charge of operating the computer system. When a proposal was submitted to the Agency for analysis, the project manager, sponsor, an Agency executive, and the system's staff operator employed the computer to analyze the numbers, i.e., cost, rentals, and incomes served, to determine preliminary project feasibility. The following example illustrates this integrated working relationship:

> The director of technical services is the one who basically determines, based on the type of construction and his knowledge, how long a mortgage the Agency should grant, and whether this meets our standards of room design and everything else. So, he and the

builder were in there with the project manager figuring it out
and they called me in to give them some of the figures . . . with
the builder right there, we could show him the figures and within
pennies they agreed with what the builder had figured out. . . .
Then the director mentioned that this could only be a 40-year
mortgage because of the wood-frame construction but if it had a
masonry wall and brick veneer, he could give it a 50-year mortgage. They figured out by giving it to Mike (a staff engineer)
how much it would cost, roughly, to do this type of construction
. . . so all I did was increase the amount of the mortgage by that
much, the construction loan by 1/2 that much, and the length of
the mortgage from 40 to 50 years. Actually, we came out with a
lower carrying charge.

The location of the project management and analysis functions,
relative to other Agency functions, is presented in Figure 4-10
which shows the organizational structure adopted recently by
NJHFA. In contrast with Figure 4-1, the updated structure shows
the increased subdivision of managerial tasks by technical or
functional specialty. The technical services director manages engineers, architects, and project representatives; legal functions
are now performed internally by staff attorneys; the director of
operations (formerly Director of Policy and Programs) directs
the team of project managers and the subsidy and market analysis function. In addition, the management function has expanded,
e.g., administrative assistants now report directly to the executive
director. In the future, day-to-day operations are to be run by a
deputy director, thus freeing the executive director's time for
work on long-range planning, proposals for legislative change, and
general promotion and goodwill.

The computer system is controlled, allocated, and utilized by
the director of operations. The physical location is in the subsidy
and market analysis function (see Figure 4-10). Here, computations required to perform cost, subsidy, and market analyses are
carried out. The day-to-day use of the computer is initiated by
project managers who first work with sponsors to determine
whether the project's economic characteristics make sense. The
staff running the computer responds directly to the project
managers' requests. However, it should be noted that the subsidy

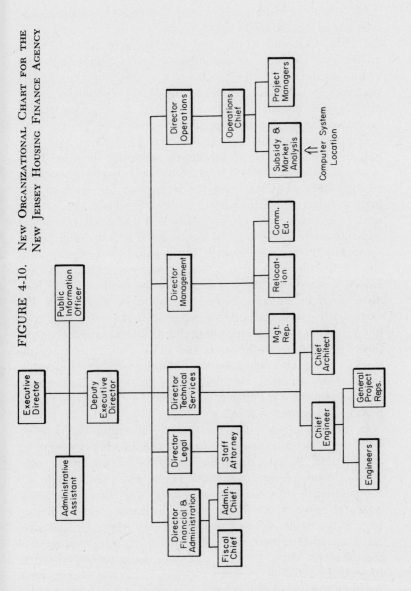

FIGURE 4-10. New Organizational Chart for the New Jersey Housing Finance Agency

analysis staff worked closely with the project managers and directors of operations to develop and structure the flow of information. Computer output and other relevant information on project feasibility are then submitted to the operations chief, who in turn consults with the director of operations and the project managers to determine project feasibility. If all analysis proves positive, the project is approved, and then submitted to the executive director for final approval.

During the analysis, the project managers call on the other four functions directed by the deputy executive director. Technical questions are handled by the technical services department; changes initiated by this group are incorporated by the computer to update and modify the project analysis. Similarly, management services changes, primarily operating and maintenance expenses and real estate taxes, are also incorporated and updated by the computer. Interestingly enough, the demand for computer services by the technical services, legal, and management functions has been surprising. Many new uses for the computer have been discovered (or intentionally created) by these departments. For example, the technical services department requested that computer programs be developed to perform moment-bearing calculations (i.e., determine the stress and strain characteristics of the steel structure and determine the optimum number of elevators to locate per structure). In addition, the financial and administrative department has initiated development of a management reporting and control system.

In the new organization, the resource allocation decisions related to project financing are made by the director of operations and his staff. In most cases, the executive director merely signs off after careful review of submitted data. Thus, the analysis and computational expertise and familiarity with the project data now rest lower in the organizational hierarchy. This is in contrast to the earlier decision-making process where the executive director and the director of policy and programs made most of the decisions. Other resource allocation decisions not related to projects, i.e., staffing, capital budgeting, marketing and so forth, continue to be made by top management, i.e., the executive and deputy directors.

In summary, few project decisions are made without using computer-generated information. To employ the computer system efficiently, a new organizational structure was necessary. In many ways, the computer acts, for part of the organization, like the hub of a large and complex wheel. As the organization evolves, the computer will continue to pay an important role in task structuring and designation of new areas of responsibility.

Individuals

The computer's sphere of influence encompasses approximately one-third of the staff, but many more have looked to it for assistance. During the course of constructing computer programs to replicate the financial analysis process, many unknown factors surfaced and were commented on by the staff. Each financial detail had to be closely examined, a fruitful educative experience for all those involved. In some cases, the staff's qualitative and intuitive understanding of the financing process was proved incorrect. One such observation is presented below:

> We've just finished about two or three hours of having Tom and Ralph run the programs, and we've been sitting here commenting on that experience. . . .
> The shame of this experience is that the tape recorder was not on. Strange numbers came out, and Tom was heard to exclaim, "Oh my————!" or something like that. I mean that should have been recorded for posterity. We got a little shook up when certain things came out and you saw how shocked we were that the coop project was running more expensive than the rental one. And, when we think about it, it doesn't surprise us because there were some extra fee allowances. But, the computer system forces us to focus more on our fee structure because it's got some problems that need to be adjusted.

This lack of complete understanding probably resulted from a combination of factors. In the state, housing finance was new and little experience or expertise existed. The many burdens and demands on the staff probably inhibited their spending a lot of time investigating and understanding small, nitty-gritty details.

And, in addition, sometimes human nature leads man to avoid the self-discipline required to investigate and understand completely any specific task, especially when he can get away with doing the minimum required to satisfy a requirement. The computer programming requirements tended to counter this tendency.

Increased knowledge and more available time have increased the self-esteem and self-confidence of individuals directly interacting with the computer system. During the early stages of organizational development, the staff was tackling unknown, complex and difficult-to-solve problems. The computer system provided a stable knowledge resource. The story goes, that if all other arguments fail, you can always fall back to the soundness of the numbers generated by the computer system and use these as strong and powerful bargaining tools. In addition, increased self-esteem and confidence led to an overall increase in organizational morale. This point was articulated by the executive director:

> It's a morale booster also. The staff feels much more confident about their own work, much better about it, because they are better able to handle it.

For certain staff members, the computer created an area of expertise which no one else possessed and increased their relative prestige in the organization. The analysis expertise and to some extent, the decision making, is now located lower in the organizational hierarchy. In the long run, the Agency's impact on the state's housing problem will depend on the competence and expertise manifested by lower-level staff. System implementation by top management has planted a seed low in the organizational hierarchy which is now prospering. Responsibility has been delegated, staff developed, and project decisions initiated by lower-level and middle-level staff. This situation develops completely the manager's role as a decision maker/coordinator and, in addition, encourages him to treat the lower-level staff with more respect. To succeed, the manager must have confidence in the staff product, for it contains valuable information concerning the potential success or failure of the project-specific decision-making process.

Coincident with the increase in relative status for certain staff members, one would expect to find others delegated to lower-status positions. Hopefully, the overall status increases will net out the decreases. Some, in fact, resisted the computer. For example:

> The computer is just something new. Just like ———— won't use the adding machine. She adds on her fingers and doesn't trust the machine . . . when you have someone like that and you throw the computer at them, whew!

But in the NJHFA, there was little evidence that certain people lost status in the organization, and during interviews even former opponents spoke very positively about the system. One explanation for their change in attitude was that they recognized the numerous benefits accruing to the Agency and probably related their status positions to the increased status achieved in day-to-day encounters with other members and groups of the housing finance community. In the long run, these people would accumulate more respect. They were members of a highly respected organization, one of the whiz kids.

Technology can produce negative as well as positive influences on individuals. First, the staff members operating the system may begin to ask only questions they know the computer is capable of answering. This could influence problem formulation, and stifle creativity, making the staff more dependent on the general capabilities established by the "system." This phenomenon is a general weakness of most technological systems and reinforces the position that the uniqueness, usefulness, and capability of a particular system is primarily a function of the ingenuity and thought expended developing it. Second, an individual's identity can be connected directly to the machine. In this case, the staff could become too dependent on the machine and less dependent on their own insights and initiatives. Similar to an army general stripped of his uniform, a staff member stripped of his computer may be incapable of acting. People tend to become too impressed with the machine's usefulness. This similarly influences problem formulation and forces us to differentiate between what the machine actually delivers and what it should deliver. Finally, as the machine becomes more and more expensive, both in staff time and dollar cost, the Agency may feel compelled to utilize the machine fully to get "its money's worth."

In the NJHFA, there has been some evidence to substantiate the above negative influence on individuals. However, these trends have been quickly countered by the hard-nosed approach of top management, objectivity of the staff, and the perspective of the researcher. This group has worked collectively to maintain a proper balance on the computer system's usefulness to the organization and individuals.

Finally, as staff members leave the Agency, they can proceed to their next job with a knowledge of how computers operate, what they can do and how they can be utilized to increase an existing organization's productivity and efficiency. This could affect the future career development of involved individuals.

Second Order Consequences: External to the NJHFA

The overall improvement of organizational efficiency has increased the respect for, confidence in, and influence of the Agency vis-à-vis other agencies and organizations in this field. In many ways, the Agency's second order impacts on other organizations are the most important aspects of the computer system's development. To achieve realistic solutions to the housing problem, concerned organizations need to work together toward the same objectives. The diverse, and often inconsistent objectives within existing organizations have often resulted in duplication of effort and reversal of favorable trends. A coordinated approach to the problem would obviously generate more impact. In the same way that the computer acts as an integrating agent within the Agency, the Housing Finance Agency can act as an integrating agent between the parties tackling housing problems in New Jersey.

First, the computer outputs are attached to the applications for funding to the federal government. The Agency methods of subsidy analysis have affected the FHA, increased the respect for the Agency and, in turn, given NJHFA applications much greater credence on FHA's list of customers. This could result in shorter processing time and eventually more funds. The Agency's increased self-confidence and influence is illustrated by the following comment:

> Just on the 236 thing, Hank uses the computer when he sends in his applications to the federal government. . . . The way Hank does it, the speed with which he does it, the precision and the way it comes out is far more sophisticated than the federal way and they don't do it in as much detail . . . we do much more careful homework and analysis than they do. So when we apply to them, they give it much greater credence, because it's done much more carefully than they do it themselves.

Another member said:

> It (the computer) definitely helps. We had our analysis on 236 before the FHA had one out. This was at a time when they had no guidelines for filling out the 236 application. They have a procedure now and it's approximately the same as ours. They accept our analysis without redoing the numbers. On other applications, they usually redo the numbers.

A federal official concurred on this latter point.

> On NJHFA's applications we only check to make sure the total construction cost is correct . . . we do not have to go back and check and recompute the numbers.

Second, similar respect is held by the builders, sponsors, and community groups who are immediately exposed to the Agency's computational facilities. As explained previously, one of the first steps in application processing is to determine preliminary feasibility. Often the builder actually comes in, sits in front of the computer terminal, and watches the results printed on the teletype. In many ways, this forces him to be more precise and thorough in developing applications for processing. The discussion between the builder and technical services director concerning masonry versus wood-frame construction is one of many examples where the computer has affected this group. The computer enables the Agency to provide better service to these customers.

Third, in dealing with local housing authorities and municipal governments, the Agency has influenced many decisions and in some cases attempted to influence local policy. For example, the Agency's view regarding negotiations with the City of Newark on a tax abatement issue is presented below.

When facing the tax abatement issue, the director instructed one member to use the computer to generate the cost and benefits accruing to the parties involved. Costs were measured in terms of the amount of tax abatement which could be issued or agreed upon by Newark and divided into the tax revenue received or the revenue not received, if some abatement was granted. Benefits were measured in terms of absolute and percentage reduction in rents charged to the tenant. His comment before his meeting with Newark officials was that when he arrived in the city, he was going to toss his computer output on the table and say, "this is the tax abatement we want, this is how much it's going to cost you, and these are the rent savings that are going to result." He would then ask the city to formulate an alternative position, the economic implications of which had already been calculated. In this example, a compromise position was achieved and the Agency was able to impose its view on a local municipality. No doubt the computer helped develop a stronger bargaining position.

Finally, the Agency has developed a major role in state government with regard to housing policy analysis and formulation. The Agency personnel direct and coordinate the efforts of the governor's office, Department of Community Affairs, State Planning and so forth. They are chosen to lead special studies, write and present federal testimony, and prepare white papers for gubernatorial candidates. In part, some of this increased responsibility has resulted from increased efficiency and expertise manifested by Agency members. This increased efficiency has, in turn, partially resulted from the computer's influence. Thus, in addition to the effects the computer has had on the Agency, it has no doubt influenced relations with other organizations, who now have greater respect for and confidence in the NJHFA.

SUMMARY

If the nation's housing problems are to be effectively attacked, new approaches and strategies must be designed. One such new approach was initiated by the New Jersey Legislature when in 1967 it created the New Jersey Housing Finance Agency and assigned to it the difficult task of developing and implementing a statewide housing program. The successful selection and financing of viable projects throughout the state is an integral part of the Agency's function, and crucial to the performance of this function is the financial analysis of housing applications. This analysis is critical in projecting the success or failure of projects and ultimately of the Agency itself. Mortgage defaults could damage the Agency's credit rating, impair its ability to make interest and principal payments to bond holders, reduce cash available for staff and operating expenses, and force ultimate bankruptcy.

To help define and assess the trade-offs involved in project selection, several computer programs were developed. With the help of the computer, financial and economic projections were made quickly and accurately. Rationalization of the application process gave top management a firm grip on the key variables related to the financial success of the Agency. Because of the importance of financial analysis to the total Agency function, this innovation has led to several significant consequences which have influenced Agency policy, organization, individuals, and even the organizations encountered in day-to-day activities.

Related to the immediate task of computerizing the financial calculations and improving the project-specific decision-making process, the following first order consequences have resulted:

- The overall quality of analysis performed has improved.
- The number of alternatives examined for each project has increased.
- The amount of useful information has increased and can easily be circulated for examination and comment.

- Staff time allocated to performing routine calculations has decreased dramatically.

Several second order effects, both internal and external, have resulted directly from systems development and implementation. On the general *policy level*, the computer's presence has indirectly led to redefinition of goals and objectives, investigation and definition of additional powers and functions, and implementation of a more comprehensive housing strategy. *Organizationally*, the computer has been indirectly responsible for definition of tasks and areas of responsibility, development of a new organizational structure, and increases in productivity, competence, reputation, and morale. *Individuals* have prospered, for the increased knowledge and available time have increased the self-esteem and self-confidence of individuals involved with the computer. Finally, the improvement of organizational efficiency has increased the respect for, confidence in, and influence of the Agency in the eyes of other agencies and organizations in its field.

As a result, the NJHFA is much better equipped to achieve its stated goals and objectives. Introduction of analysis was a small but, nevertheless, very important ingredient in building the competence and delivery capability required for the Agency to achieve its mission successfully.

CHAPTER 4

1. Alan Mallach, *Housing in New Jersey: Needs and Programs 1968,* New Jersey Division of State and Regional Planning, Trenton, New Jersey.

2. Quotations throughout this case from Agency staff members were obtained by the case writer through tape recorded conversations during the duration of the project.

3. Support costs include mortgage interest and principal payments, real estate taxes, profit, and operating and maintenance expenses.

4. This effort was one of several supported by Harvard's Program on Technology and Society. The Research Group on Technology, Business, and the City collaborated with groups in New Jersey and Boston to test and develop some of its hypotheses and designs in the laboratory of modern urban areas.

5. Statement recorded during interview with Ralph Brown, Director of Policy and Programs.

6. These statements represent the summary of an internal staff meeting held to discuss the goals and objectives of the Agency. Top management and key staff were present.

7. The author was also a member of the Urban Analysis Project, directed by Professor Maurice D. Kilbridge of the Harvard Business School. Professor Kilbridge is also Dean of Harvard University's Graduate School of Design.

A more complete description of the computer programs, their underlying theory and areas of application are presented in:

a) Robert P. O'Block, "Low-Income Housing: Goals, Actors, and Economics," in *Social Innovation in the City: New Enterprises for Community Development,* Richard S. Rosenbloom and Robin Marris, editors (Cambridge, Harvard University Press, 1968).

b) Maurice D. Kilbridge, Robert P. O'Block, Paul V. Teplitz, *Urban Analysis* (Boston, Harvard Business School, Division of Research, 1970), Chapters 8–11.

8. The Housing and Urban Development Act of 1968 established Section 236 of the National Housing Act to provide assistance to rental and cooperative housing for lower-income families. The assistance is in the form of periodic payments equivalent to the difference between the amount required for principal interest and mortgage insurance premium on a

mortgage at the market interest rate and the amount required for principal and interest on a mortgage at a 1% interest rate.

9. We chose to develop several small computer programs rather than one large program due to the scope and complexity of the financial analysis, many varied requests of the staff, and the space limitations of the computer. As computer programs were constructed and debugged, they were integrated into larger, more comprehensive models.

10. Final closing is the time when all mortgage agreements are officially signed by both parties.

11. Experience had taught the members of the Technology, Business, and City Group that such extensive preparation was essential to successful development and implementation of this technique. The author gratefully acknowledges the guidance provided by this group.

12. Unlike most modeling efforts, where only one or two technical specialists understand the computer programs, the NJHFA staff quickly grasped the internal workings of the programs since they merely replicated routine calculations. The staff's understandings of the program's internal structure would allow them to change and update the programs as required.

13. Paul N. Ylvisaker, Commissioner, New Jersey Department of Community Affairs, in a letter to Herbert Franklin, Executive Director, the National Urban Coalition, Washington, D.C., April 11, 1969.

14. Raymond A. Bauer, *Second Order Consequences: A Methodological Essay on the Impact of Technology* (Cambridge, M.I.T. Press, 1969).

15. First order effects are defined as those relating to the immediate task of computerizing the Agency's financial calculations and upgrading the project-specific decision-making processes. Second order effects are defined as the internal and external Agency changes that *indirectly* occurred as a result of systems development and implementation.

16. This aspect will be discussed in detail in a later section.

17. Memo to the Executive Director, NJHFA, from H. Ralph Taylor, former Assistant Secretary, U.S. Department of Housing and Urban Development, March 14, 1969. Mr. Taylor put it as follows:

> You are processing on a retail basis. As work load and staff expand, this will get you into the same kind of box that FHA has been in, and both the City and State Mitchell-Lama programs in New York. You will have to have more employees to process the greater work load. As this happens, each "processor" will focus on areas of greatest concern to him. The result can be a system wherein the "guy in the back room" who earns $15,000 a year gets overprotective; and the dynamics of a governmental review process work against his superior sticking his neck out to overrule.
>
> I am told that the New York City Mitchell-Lama program is shunned by developers because of this, and that processing through the State program takes a couple of years. HFA, New Jersey, will fail in its larger objectives if this pattern recurs.
>
> As an alternative, I recommend you use the capability inherent in

the computer program and the availability of computer time and people interested and skilled in the use of the computer as a management tool to develop a quite different processing system.

18. *Ibid.* He went on to say:

HFA now has the information for the computer. It can prepare run-outs showing the cost structure and rentals at different combinations of the key variables. The analysis can show the picture at a set of target rents, and the impact on rents of changes in the key cost factors, such as construction cost and taxes.

The objective is to set parameters within which the HFA and sponsor objectives can be accomplished. The sponsor can then be advised, in writing, that if the final project falls within the cost-rental parameters, including appropriate operating cost ratio, it will be approved.

The availability of the computer allows a testing-out of various combinations, and a presentation of these alternatives in specific terms. The discussion with the sponsor group at this point has two functions: (1) inform the sponsors about the hard issues, (2) the educational function is absolutely key when an agency is dealing with citizen group-type sponsors.

19. The federal government's program to encourage development and use of new technology in housing construction.

Systems Management in the New City: Columbia, Maryland

Mahlon Apgar, IV

Mahlon Apgar, IV

Mahlon Apgar is an Associate of McKinsey & Company, Inc. He specializes in the problems of strategy, organization, and management processes in the real estate development field. Mr. Apgar is a graduate in urban studies from Dartmouth College, Oxford University, and the Harvard Business School. He is currently a Visiting Lecturer at the Harvard Graduate School of Design. After Mr. Apgar received his Masters degree from the Graduate School of Business Administration, Harvard University, he was a Research Associate at the Harvard Program on Technology and Society and at the Harvard Business School. He has contributed articles to journals in the planning and development fields, and to the *Harvard Business Review*.

CHAPTER 5

SYSTEMS MANAGEMENT IN THE NEW CITY: COLUMBIA, MARYLAND
(Mahlon Apgar, IV)

COLUMBIA, in the words of entrepreneur James Rouse, "is a new city emerging from concept to reality." Fostered by his vision, it is the product of many generalists and specialists, representing a variety of disciplines. Their work has been marked by a wholistic view of the city as a "system" of interdependent parts, innovation in organization and methods, and a sensitive regard for the future residents. Consequently, they are demonstrating a significant alternative to the traditional patterns of urban growth, with the result that Columbia already has become the cynosure of corporate planners seeking new markets in urban development, and the favorite model for advocates of a national new cities policy.[1]

Because of the attempt to plan and build the new city in a comprehensive, integrated manner, Columbia is also an example against which to test the popular belief that the "systems approach," including the analytic and managerial techniques developed in our aerospace/defense establishment, will be effective in the complex process of urban change. This study will examine that belief, with the assumption that there will be continuing attempts by corporations and government agencies, which have

NOTE: Research for this study was completed in the Spring of 1969 and, therefore, subsequent changes in organization structure and management processes may not be reflected.

developed such techniques, to apply their knowledge to the long-range problems of urbanization.

Rouse felt that both cities and suburbs had lost their human scale, and that with increasing growth the needs would be even more acute. He saw an opportunity to create more "humane and responsive" environments, and was convinced that market conditions were ripe for such a product. The U.S. population was expected to increase from 180 million in 1960 to 262 million in 1985 and 360 million by the year 2000. Although the largest portion (22 percent) of population growth before 1930 had been in cities of over one million, between 1930 and 1960, towns and cities of 10,000 to 100,000 in major metropolitan regions captured half of the incremental increase. For every person added to the central city, two or three would be added to the suburbs. Rouse was certain that the bulk of urban growth would continue in these fringe areas around large cities. The pressure of population, and dissatisfaction with cities and suburbs alike, presented an excellent market potential for a different pattern of development.

Rouse believed that a "new city" was the best vehicle to take advantage of this potential. If large and comprehensive enough, a planned city could be a *prescriptive* rather than *reactive* form of development, creating new opportunities for economies of scale. Its most distinguishing features would be the integration of superior site planning with community facilities, shopping and employment centers, and new patterns of institutional development for community services that would meet human needs in a more sensitive and creative way. From his initial analysis, Rouse concluded that a population of about 100,000 was the minimum required to support the variety of specialized activities and institutions of a city. But if it were larger, its institutions would be likely to lose the sense of participation and personal control that give human scale to a community.

The master plan for Columbia (see Figure 5-1) is notable for its definition of interrelationships among the physical parts of an environment. The city is composed of 7 *villages*, each of which has several *neighborhoods*. These neighborhoods, which are Columbia's basic structural elements, are planned for 300 to 500 families. Each neighborhood has a center, including a modern-day general store, community facilities and playgrounds, a swimming pool, and an elementary school. The village center includes more specialized community and commercial facilities which can be supported by some 15,000 village residents. The town center, in turn, is intended to support all of Columbia's 110,000 residents, as well as serve consumer needs in the surrounding region of 250,000 to 400,000 with its department stores, boutiques, and specialized commercial facilities. Several industrial areas are located throughout the city to provide an economic and employment base. This structure is bound by a transportation network that includes a minibus system on its own right-ofway, and separate networks for pedestrians and cars. Approximately one-quarter of Columbia's 14,000 acres is devoted to open and recreational space, with parks, lakes, woods, riding trails, and sporting facilities.[2] In accord with an overall objective of offering a wide range of opportunities for individual choice, the villages and neighborhoods are planned to be diverse in character, housing type, and income range. Approximately 10 percent of the city's housing will be developed for low-income families by a nonprofit housing corporation formed jointly by the three major religious faiths.

Thus, the Columbia plan reflects an attempt to balance the vitality and variety of a city with the natural serenity of the countryside. Maintaining that balance will be a network of social institutions. Among the planning innovations, these institutions (religious facilities, health services, schools, libraries, community colleges) have required the most delicate and painstaking efforts, but may be the most enduring results of the development process. For it is through Columbians and their institutions that the vision and plans of the developers will be translated into the ongoing processes which mold a city and make it live.

SYSTEMS AND CITIES

A widely noted argument for the systems approach to new cities is espoused by John Rubel, who believes that a "new city

FIGURE 5-1. SCHEMATIC DRAWINGS OF

NEW TOWN

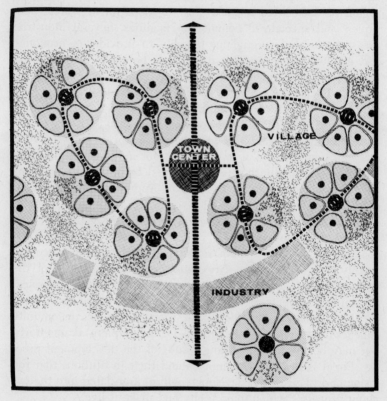

THE COLUMBIA PLAN

TOWN CENTER

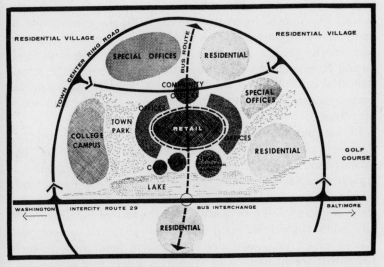

NEIGHBORHOOD CENTER

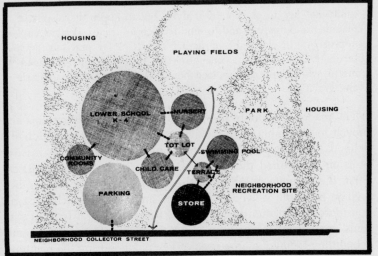

technology"[3] can be evoked by the creation of a market for the services of private industry and its cadre of managers, engineers, and scientists. The best way to do this, argues Rubel, is for the federal government to create a demand for the construction of many new cities, organized on a project-management basis, and executed by private firms. The competitive strivings and intellectual ferment that would ensue from such a challenge to our industrial capabilities would, he suggests, produce innovative accomplishments on a par with those of our missile and space programs.

Rubel, unlike some enthusiasts, does not argue that aerospace/ defense techniques should be "applied" to city building. The limits to such applications are evident. A human environment is a more complex organism than any space system; its structure is more diffuse; and its goals are subjective and evolving. But there is appeal in the suggestion that the task of building a new city, while beyond the grasp of our most advanced present techniques, might yet evoke and benefit from innovations in technique that would be of wide relevance. Rubel concludes:

> The "new city projects" would provide a truly unique opportunity not just to plan or to analyze, but to apply the results of planning and analysis and to modify theories, plans, designs, and approaches in the light of actual results. It is precisely such feedback that makes the concept of the "systems approach" meaningful, when applied to socioeconomic matters of such magnitude and gravity.

The reader may doubt the validity of referring to a systems approach in Columbia, because systems analysis, as conventionally defined (see Chapter 1), is not employed. The use of this expression is justified, however, by two principal characteristics. First, the ultimate objective of the development process — a city — is in principle viewed as a system, any part of which must be considered in relation to the whole. Second, several tools of systems management, such as formal quantitative models and scheduling techniques, are used at key points during the planning and development stages to analyze and control major project elements, including land use, cost, profitability, and development pace. These characteristics differentiate the project from conventional residential and commercial developments, which generally are the province of small investors and entrepreneurs using traditional management methods in single-purpose projects that are not systematically related to needs in their environment or evaluated according to noneconomic criteria.

We should thus ask three questions of Columbia as a pioneering American venture in using a systems approach to city building.

First, to what extent are the elements of a systems approach relevant to city building? Which parts of the development process are enhanced by, or require, the application of new methods of analysis and control? On the other hand, are there tasks essential to the process of creating a "responsive and encouraging" environment which are not susceptible to objective analysis?

Second, what are the human and organizational consequences of an effort to develop and implement new approaches to guiding the development of a city? What stresses are introduced into the implementing organization? Does a systems approach enhance the effectiveness of people and organizations in such a complex undertaking?

Finally, does the Columbia experience suggest that the unique challenge of building a new city would encourage experimentation and innovation in technique if fostered on a large scale? To what extent did needs inspire innovation in technique or in general approach?

To answer these questions, we shall examine both the approach to creating an environment in Columbia and several techniques for implementation. We begin with an overview of James Rouse and his company, their goals and prior accomplishments. These were the seeds both of the spirit and the structure of the Columbia process. We then examine two techniques which were devised early in the project cycle and were of major importance in refining the Columbia concept. The first was a work group of creative people whose ideas broadened the scope of what might otherwise have been a physical planning effort. The second was the Columbia Economic Model, an initial attempt to quantify the entire scope of the project and a prime discipline in keeping plans within the bounds of economic feasibility. As the plans were implemented, other techniques were introduced. A critical path analysis was the first comprehensive approach to scheduling numerous project elements, and resulted in a complete realignment of expectations and priorities. Finally, a land control system established a method of integrating actual and projected data about one of the project's key resources. Each of these techniques is evaluated in the ensuing discussion, which then concludes with an appraisal of their effects on the concept and the reality of Columbia.

THE ROUSE COMPANY

"Our business," according to Rouse, "is city-building. By this, we mean that we are either financing for others, through our mortgage banking division, or developing for our own account, in our development division, the buildings and the places that make up the American city."

He thus characterizes the work of an unusual American enterprise. By defining its business as the city, and by adhering to a unique mixture of private profits and public purpose, The Rouse Company (TRC) has placed itself squarely in the midst of a market created by the contemporary concern for urban life.

From an inauspicious beginning two decades ago, TRC is today nationally known as a community developer, and its president is regarded as a leading urbanist.[4] Rouse founded the company in 1939 as a two-man partnership. Until 1954 TRC served as mortgage loan correspondent for commercial banks and life insurance companies. The close relationships which were established with these fiduciaries, combined with an intimate knowledge of local real estate conditions, led almost naturally into real estate development. In 1954, the company began its first shopping center, and by the time that Columbia was announced in October 1963, the company had developed seven regional centers, and gained a national reputation for its innovation in the design of enclosed shopping malls and the quality of its product. Columbia launched TRC into the business of full-scale land development as an integrated producer of a whole environment. In 1964, a subsidiary called Howard Research and Development Corporation (HRD) was established to develop Columbia on a joint-venture basis with the Connecticut General Life Insurance Company.

The company has shown a five-year annual compound growth rate of 28 percent overall and a 40 percent annual growth rate in earnings. Net cash from operations (after mortgage amortization) has grown at the rate of 56 percent compounded annually. After initial hesitation during its first three years as a public company, the investing market responded both to TRC's past performance and to its prospects: its common shares in mid-1969 carried a price/earnings ratio of 40:1.

Today, TRC employs over 800 people in eight cities. It has completed and is operating 15 enclosed-mall regional shopping centers, an in-town residential and commercial development in Baltimore, and Columbia. In addition, another subsidiary, the American City Corporation, was formed in 1968 to apply the Columbia process to the inner city. The firm which began by financing the bits and pieces of the American city now intends to produce "more humane, more livable" environments in both new cities and old.

The president of this unusual company is a man of idealism, vision, and extraordinary business acumen. In a speech at Berkeley in 1963, Rouse spoke of the challenge of urban growth and defined his own view of the philosophy of community:

> American civilization depends on the kinds of cities we develop over the next 20 years. I believe that the ultimate test of civilization is whether or not it contributes to the growth and improvement of mankind. Does it uplift, inspire, stimulate, and develop the best in man? There really can be no other right purpose of a community except to provide an environment and an opportunity to develop better people. The most successful community would be that which contributed the most by its physical form, its institutions, and its operations to the growth of the people.

Rouse envisioned an "ideal community for people" as an inter-connecting series of small communities, separated by highways and open space, and unified by a center with cultural, educational, and recreational facilities. In the Rouse ideology, the urban structure would be a composite of the life of small towns — without the antiurban romantic traditions of 19th century Fabian Socialism or early 20th century communism — bound by the ideals of religious conviction and human concern.

If the words seemed utopian, the activities of the man belied them. For although none of his listeners at the 1963 conference realized it, Rouse had already begun his masterwork by acquiring secretively, in the manner demanded by our speculative land market, the site for a community in which he would attempt to realize that vision.

GOALS FOR THE COMPANY AND COLUMBIA

The mission of TRC, in Rouse's words, is:

> To conceive, design, and bring into being better places for people to live, to work, to shop . . . a better environment for the growth of man and his family . . a product for which the world hungers and for which it will richly reward the successful producer.

> We seek to build a corporate institution which is capable of undertaking and successfully completing real estate development built and managed to high standards of taste, beauty, human fulfillment, and profitability.

As corporate objectives, these are at once broad and vague, but they serve to infuse the organization with a sense of ideals and purpose which Rouse hopes will transcend the crises of day-to-day decision making and the pressures for profit. The rewards sought for the company's activity are vastly different from common managerial goals such as return on investment, earnings per share, or sales. According to Rouse:

Service, not profit, is the legitimate purpose of business, and profit is the reward for rendering imaginative and effective service. Furthermore, our profits will be most effectively increased by focusing on the quality of the environment that we are able to produce. It is better that we fail building that which is beautiful and humane than earn profit out of ventures that are tasteless, dull, and repressive to the human spirit. But it is lazy and irresponsible to give up on either purpose — to fail to work out the tough, demanding negotiations and compromises that are often involved in fusing taste, beauty, and public service with the realities of the marketplace.

Since its first shopping center, TRC's primary operating objective has been real estate development rather than investment. By minimizing its cash requirements in any project and retaining ownership and control, the company's aim is to benefit from the long-term values created by direct input of its knowledge and skills rather than to maximize short-term profits through rapid depreciation and turnover of its product. TRC has maintained an active, continuing interest in its projects by expanding, refining, and managing each beyond the initial development plans.

The goals derived for Columbia fit closely this conception of the corporation and the human community. As the project was beginning to take form, Rouse described these goals as:

- Providing a real city — not just a suburb, but a comprehensive balanced community.
- Respecting the land — we invited the land to impose itself as a discipline on the form of the community.
- Providing the best possible environment for the growth of people — here is the heart of the planning process.
- Planning from the needs and yearnings of people to the kind of community that will best serve and nourish their growth — by creating a dialogue between the people engaged in urban design and development and the behavioral sciences.
- Making a profit — we use the marketplace for people to cast votes for what they really want and care about enough to pay for. We recognize the dynamics of the market system as being fundamental to the democratic process, for it is through the marketplace that a free people can best make the complex

judgment of how, where, and when they wish to spend their earnings. Columbia, by producing an outstanding profit, will warn against the unmarketability of sprawl and lift attention to genuine respect for nature and family.

Conflict between the goals themselves and the people who implement them has been built into the company's strategy. The ability to manage this tension, which to Rouse is a creative and dynamic force, may make TRC not merely a company with a good product in a new and expanding industry, but an entirely new kind of institution with criteria for social as well as economic performance, using financial measures primarily as motivators for public benefit rather than solely for economic enrichment.

THE DEVELOPMENT PROCESS

Columbia reflects both an understanding of the requirements of the land development business and several management principles which have evolved throughout the company's history in community development. These have been instrumental in the Columbia process.

Characteristics of Land Development

The most important characteristics of large-scale land development are the magnitude of front-end investment and the length of lead time required.[5] In Columbia, both were unusually great: $23.5 million for land acquisition, and $1.7 million in predevelopment overhead were required, with annual carrying charges of 10 to 12 percent,[6] and three years of planning before the first cash inflow. Since payout is long-term and depends on future individual purchase decisions, the risks are high and so are the expected returns.

The developer also must draw on an outside financial source for the required investment. The Connecticut General Life Insurance Company provided debt financing for land acquisition and gained half ownership in the development organization for Columbia's income-producing properties. Through this arrangement, TRC was able to participate equally in long-term returns from land sales and income from HRD-owned property, with an initial investment of only $750,000.[7]

The third characteristic is the unusual variety and complexity of management tasks due to the nature of the product. In Columbia, both physical improvements and a social dimension are being created; 13,460 acres were originally acquired from 146 owners in a necessarily clandestine operation, which lasted 10 months and involved the creation of six "dummy" corporations. Twenty-three professional and academic disciplines have confronted an array of social, political, economic, and technical problems over a three-year planning period and a projected development cycle of 15 years.

The property must be managed until it is developed. Each type of land use must be planned in detail and coordinated with all other uses to produce an integrated scheme. Legal and political approval must be obtained for each land parcel prior to implementing those plans. Financial negotiations must be secured with an eye to constantly shifting credit conditions. Amenities as well as utilities are needed to attract house builders, jobs, institutions — and people. The physical elements and services of a city must be provided while the community is still countryside. The administrative machinery to operate and maintain an urban environment must be established from inception. Perhaps most critical, management systems and organizational depth must be built in an industry with little prior experience in sophisticated management.

In response to these requirements of community development, several principles that mark TRC's management style have evolved throughout the company's history. First, Rouse and his associates take a deep and continuing personal interest in their product. Second, they maintain close and complete control over both the production cycle and the inventory of finished products in order to maximize benefits from their "value added" to the land. Third, they have emphasized as their key factor for success in Columbia the creative, entrepreneurial talent which can transform raw rural land into an urban community within the constraints of an uncertain market.

The Columbia Process

The Columbia process (see Figure 5-2) is characterized by several distinct, though overlapping, stages: planning, predevelopment, in-tract development, and city management. Within these stages, the product flow moves Columbia from initial conception to implementation through land assembly, financial planning and resource acquisition, physical planning, engineering and land development, and industrial and residential marketing to managing the mature community. Because this process is viewed in TRC as a unified one rather than a series of discrete elements that could be explicitly programmed and evaluated, any attempt to describe the steps in the process must be simplified and somewhat arbitrary. However, the following listing should serve to identify the variety of interrelated tasks and skills which had to be integrated within the Columbia process:

STAGE I: Planning

- *Concept definition* was an intuitive, philosophical process which established long-range goals for an urban community and a particular style of life.
- *Area research* generated hard data on potential mixes of land use and socioeconomic composition which could affect the initial concept definition.
- *Detailed site analysis* was required to test the economic and the organizational feasibility of Columbia's goals before the decision to seek project financing for the specific site.
- *Initial staff* expansion and skills development in project management established an organizational capability for later phases which would require greater breadth and depth of skills than the company possessed.
- *Land use and financial planning* were especially critical in the

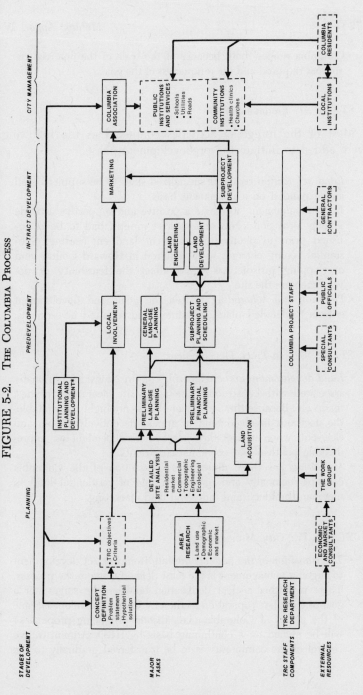

FIGURE 5-2. THE COLUMBIA PROCESS

*INSTITUTIONAL DEVELOPMENT IS A CONTINUING PROCESS BEYOND THE DEVELOPMENT CYCLE.

Columbia process both because of the scale of the financial resources required and the uniqueness of the goals.

STAGE II: Predevelopment

Most of the foregoing activities continued as the following
were added to initiate the predevelopment phase.

- *Land acquisition* required specialized skills to be supplemented
  and expanded on a permanent basis.
- *Local involvement,* to create a positive and supportive attitude
  among local politicians and interest groups, had to be established prior to detailed planning or land engineering. Substantial zoning changes were required in Howard County and
  overlapping jurisdictions could affect the feasibility of development on the site.
- *Planning and scheduling* related the goals and development
  criteria to detailed plans, schedules, and required investments.

STAGE III: In-Tract Development

- *Land development and engineering* comprised tasks traditionally
  associated with construction, including site clearance, utilities,
  roads, etc. Because these engineered tasks are highly predictable,
  the decisions involved tend to appear deceptively simple and
  clear-cut, when in fact they are heavily dependent on unpredictable political and economic constraints.
- *Marketing* has three dimensions: promotion of the Columbia
  concept regionally and nationally; sale of residential land to
  merchant builders; and industrial land marketing.

STAGE IV: City Management

- *The transition of the new community* from in-tract development
  to ongoing management is the least defined stage in the process.
  There is neither a clear delineation between the stages nor a
  goal of complete separation of the city from its developer. Some
  of the pieces of Columbia (i.e., income-producing properties)
  will be owned on a continuing basis by HRD. Administrative
  control of the community is to be transferred gradually to the

residents through the Columbia Association.[8] The Association's board of directors, which was initially dominated by HRD, has increasing resident participation. In time, residents will have full control of the Association. Planning and design control are effectively relinquished as portions of the development are sold to the eventual consumer, while complete control is retained for areas as yet uncompleted.

Pervading this entire process is the attempt to catalyze the development of social institutions. Several — including far-reaching innovations in the educational and health systems — were suggested by the work group. Others — such as the early establishment of the Washington National Symphony's summer pavilion — were the result of fortuitous circumstances. These institutions, and the city's new residents, are the infrastructure from which new institutions are expected to emerge to meet the changing needs of Columbians and link the concept to daily reality. In the transitional stage, it is important to the developers that the Columbia concept be diffused through the institutional fabric of the city, so that the course charted by future decision makers representing the Columbia polity will have a similar spirit and integrity. Consequently, local relationships again assume importance in order to maintain the continuity of goals and provide effective guidance during transition.

PROJECT MANAGEMENT

The project [9] form of organization is an important element in the Columbia systems approach. Its implicit objectives are: (1) to balance the individualized, highly specialized skills of traditional real estate development with those of planning, design, and the social sciences; (2) to maximize the effective utilization of the TRC support departments; (3) to relieve the president of day-to-day management problems; and (4) to insure top management control over major policy decisions.

From the project's inception, the principal operating functions were master planning, development, and sales. These were supported by a general administrative staff. Specialized services, such as legal, construction, and subproject staff work, were to be drawn from TRC departments. Overall control was the responsibility of a triumvirate including Rouse, the senior development division executive, and the Columbia project director. Neither functional responsibilities nor interdepartmental relationships were clearly specified. As the project moved into the detailed planning and development stages, this initial conception was modified considerably.

In late 1969, the Columbia organization, shown in Figure 5-3, included the three original functions supplemented by financial management, program control, land management, and engineering. Figure 5-4 shows the various TRC departments supporting the project at that time.

As an organizational system, the project has two significant structural characteristics. First, it recognizes the essential interdependence of many specialized skills and operating functions which are required at varying levels of management during every step in the process. Each unit in the development organization has to relate its day-to-day decisions both to the ongoing operations of many other units and to the overall objectives of the Columbia concept. However, the immense number and diversity of tasks to be performed, combined with the uncertainties of large-scale development, preclude any structural designs or management systems that would inhibit the flexibility or creativity of nonexecutive personnel to make decisions quickly. Any attempt to correlate levels of responsibility and authority, for example, would have to allow for the frequent assumption of authority for major expenditures by personnel in the field. Thus, while the project is ultimately controlled by the company's executives, they recognize a need for many integrators at different levels throughout the project organization.

Second, the structural design reflects the morphogenetic characteristic of organizations. As Columbia moved through the stages of development, the project organization was modified both in structure and in management processes. Several members of the initial project group emphasized the necessity for beginning with a flexible free-form organization which included the functions needed for the planning and predevelopment phases, but could readily absorb rapid increases both in personnel and in specialized functions. They also predicted some of the problems that were likely to result from growth and specialization. But their prophecy, while agreed to by Rouse and others, was balanced by the notion that the potential strength of the organization as a device for masterminding the creation of an environment lay in its ability to adapt to modifications in plans and to unexpected problems.

Other characteristics of complex projects are reflected in the organization. First, it represents a high degree of differentiation, harboring within the project group numerous professionals performing specialized tasks. Second, it operates in a rapidly changing and highly uncertain environment in which the complexity of subtasks being performed can become an impediment to successful management and successful accomplishment. Third, the techniques for coordinating and controlling critical functions have acquired substantial influence on the integration of specialized parts of the organization, beyond the direct influence of the managers themselves. Even as simple a tool as an economic model or a periodic cash flow statement can serve as a principal discipline on individual decision making. A more complex technique such as the critical path method or a project evaluation system can substantially alter opinions of middle management, who can more readily identify problems in implementing top management's decisions. In Columbia, these techniques have in effect shifted the types of influence exercised by one specialized organizational unit over another by highlighting problems which otherwise would have been overlooked.

The company's experience in regional shopping center development greatly influenced its application of project management in Columbia. Each shopping center project was submitted to a "projects committee" in the form of a tentative economic model. The project was then submitted by the individual project director (not the committee) to Rouse and thence to the board of directors for final approval. Working together on the committee, the project directors felt a mutual responsibility to Rouse, and assumed personal concern for all of the projects. Since each con-

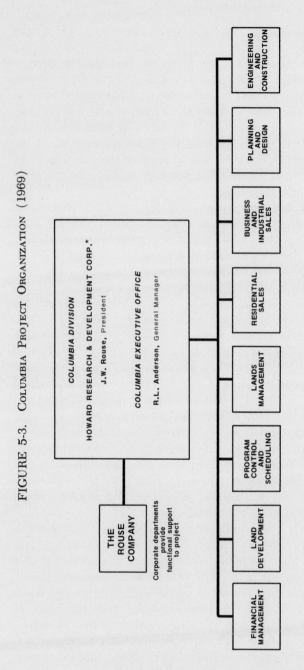

FIGURE 5-3. COLUMBIA PROJECT ORGANIZATION (1969)

* Howard Research & Development Corp. (HRD) is owned jointly by The Rouse Company (TRC) and the Connecticut General Life Insurance Company. TRC has a management contract with HRD to plan and develop Columbia.

THE ROUSE COMPANY

Corporate departments provide functional support to project

COLUMBIA DIVISION

HOWARD RESEARCH & DEVELOPMENT CORP.*

J.W. Rouse, President

COLUMBIA EXECUTIVE OFFICE

R.L. Anderson, General Manager

FINANCIAL MANAGEMENT

LAND DEVELOPMENT

PROGRAM CONTROL AND SCHEDULING

LANDS MANAGEMENT

RESIDENTIAL SALES

BUSINESS AND INDUSTRIAL SALES

PLANNING AND DESIGN

ENGINEERING AND CONSTRUCTION

FIGURE 5-4. ORGANIZATION OF
THE ROUSE COMPANY (1969)

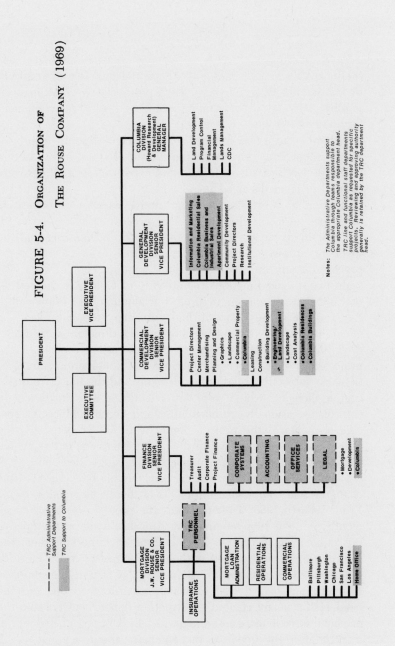

--- TRC Administrative
    Support Departments

▓ TRC Support to Columbia

Notes: The Administrative Departments support
Columbia through teams responsible to
the appropriate Columbia department head.

TRC line and functional staff departments
support Columbia as requested for specific
projects. Reviewing and approving authority
generally is retained by the TRC department
head.

sidered different goals to be paramount (e.g., profitability, aesthetic quality, tenant caliber), they felt that it was desirable to be continually aware of each other's perspective so that financial performance and project quality would be kept in a complementary state of tension.

Columbia appeared initially to be susceptible both to project management and to a committee system of control. In addition to the project staff, management and marketing committees were created to meet the need for a more systematic approach to coordination and decision making. Rouse wished to include as many people in the decision-making process as were relevant to the individual pieces of the overall project, recognizing that the diversity of tasks made complete control of the development process by any one individual or discipline seem unwise. The scale, scope, and functional complexity of Columbia created an entirely new dimension in project evaluation and implementation for which the company had not been prepared. Even the generalists who were outstanding project directors were inevitably limited in their ability to control certain aspects of the project over time, especially because of the numerous interfaces between subjective, qualitative elements and the objective quantitative elements which were easier to define and thus easier to control. Occasionally, responsibility and accountability for specific elements of the project simply were not accepted by any individual but were shifted to the management committee, which could absorb or diffuse the impact of any single decision.

Clear shifts in the management of Columbia have reflected the changing and complex requirements of the development process. From 1963 to 1966, a planner was the project director. For six months in 1965–1966, engineering decisions made at the operating rather than executive level became so important that "the project almost ran by itself without any direct controls," according to one executive. In 1967, as opening day neared, the emphasis in operations had shifted to major construction work and the head of the newly created construction department became the principal force in managing the project. In February of 1968, seven months after the opening, the company and the project were reorganized, and Columbia acquired a more definitive structure as an operating division of TRC (see Figures 5-3 and 5-4). In September 1969, the principal author of the economic model became general manager of the project, assisted by an executive experienced in managerial analysis and systems.

This history has made Columbia susceptible to diffuse lines of authority and decision making in its project management and committee systems. During the planning and initial development stages, the project director was a referee for conflicts between the planning and implementing groups and between old-line TRC executives and the Columbia "newcomers." Corporate executives became deeply involved in the details of the Columbia project because of its impact on overall company operations. The first project director recalls:

> It was a wild, helter-skelter period. No one was experienced in operating on this scale, and we were under enormous exposure and pressure. We really reacted to a crisis in decisions.

Initially, the close relationships of corporate executives provided an effective system of "personal controls." Rouse made strategic and operating decisions and had direct responsibility for control and resource allocation. However, with the project's rapid expansion, it became apparent that greater control would be required to maintain the integrity of the concept. One staff analyst foresaw some problems while the project was still in the planning stage:

> We will not have the time to document every system and procedure needed before opening day. The most urgent need is to develop operating procedures for our relationships with various governmental agencies. We must have an agreed-to operating basis, and development of the necessary systems will indicate whether agencies have the personnel capability to deal with us as fast as we want them to. We must develop systems and procedures for the land-development program; cost, tax, capital, cash accounting and budgeting; management reporting; and project programming and scheduling. These should be worked on as soon as possible just to get us to opening day. There is a considerable amount of work necessary to insure that we will be able to process the first land purchaser, the initial commercial tenant, the first

garbage collection, the first apartment house. All the systems and procedures must be developed to be compatible with the CPM (Critical Path Method) program, as well as our eventual IBM 360 system.

There was no institutionalized method in Columbia equivalent to the shopping center projects committee which could perform the control function. Moreover, there was no formal system for setting individual or subproject goals or priorities for resource allocation. A company-wide budget system was introduced in 1967, but was designed as a cost-accounting rather than control device.

The problem of control over the increasingly complex organization was compounded by an inadequate flow of management information. There was no formal flow or detailed reporting system; information generally originated at individual discretion from a variety of sources within and without the project. Management committee meetings were the principal method for exchanging and integrating information, but initially no specific agenda were set, and minutes were recorded only on an individual basis. In addition, the cast at these meetings shifted constantly (although Rouse and the project director were usually present), so that an integrated data base did not develop, even as a function of the committee device. With the start of land engineering and construction, formal agenda were set and minutes were recorded.

A Corporate Systems Department was established in 1966 to provide a focus for building management systems throughout the company. However, its function was understood by most managers to be an accounting one rather than an analytic one. Existing demands for data processing also forced it to concentrate on building its hardware capability. Although its capability for analysis has been steadily increased in both numbers and quality of personnel, there is little consideration of the systems group as problem solvers.

A system of project reporting also was instituted in 1966, in the form of project management files, maintained by the project director and department heads who had primary responsibility for each subproject (already there were over 100 defined sub-projects, each of a different magnitude and complexity). Each file contained: a budget analysis and current reports, CPM chart, monthly status report to support the project's schedule, design approvals, and a written summary of management decisions af-fecting the project. These files tended to function as a central repository of information prior to a mechanized system of man-agement information. The status reports often were submitted late, apparently because updating and review did require a sub-stantial amount of time; but by August 1966, over 20 Columbia managers were submitting status reports. Had the input data been quantitative rather than descriptive, they would have been more useful. Nonetheless, the reports reflected a fundamental change in management style and in the nature of the organiza-tion. They were evidence that the city was a hard product and that its production had finally begun.

THE WORK GROUP

The Columbia process, outlined previously, recognized the interdependency of physical and institutional factors in the en-vironment. From the beginning, the concept was oriented to spatial design, which required a knowledge and understanding of soils and streams. Rouse cautioned against preconceptions of shape or form, wishing instead "to let the design emerge from the natural environment and existing conditions."

He was also convinced that the environment could either foster or impede relationships between individuals, families, and the social institutions designed to serve them. "Communities," said Rouse, "should not be 'works of art,' but gardens in which we are a growing people and civilization." It was clear that the project team of physical planners and real estate developers would have to be supplemented by social scientists to provide the input to a "plan for people."

A work group was suggested for this integrating function, not as a coherent organizational unit, but as a "cluster of individuals," each with expertise in generally defined areas (e.g., education, health, recreation). Their commitment was not to find "a right way of doing things," but rather to explore uncharted terrain.

The selection of the group was critical, since this effort to coordinate social with physical planning would be the major guideline for the Columbia process. Rouse wanted people who were well known and whose ideas in their field were already legend. The project director, on the other hand, felt that a visionary project needed "young Turks whose ideas were on the cutting edge of society." The result was a compromise more toward the latter view. Members of the work group and their affiliations at that time included:

- Henry Bain, Jr. — Consultant in Public Administration
- Antonia Handler Chayes — Technical Secretary to the Committee on Education, President's Commission on Women
- Robert Crawford — Commissioner of Recreation for Philadelphia
- Leonard Duhl — Psychiatrist, National Institute of Mental Health
- Nelson Foote — Sociologist, Manager of Consumer and Public Relations, General Electric Company
- Herbert Gans — Professor of Sociology, Columbia University
- Robert M. Gladstone — Consultant, Economic Research and Market Analysis
- Christopher Jencks — Education Editor of *New Republic*
- Paul Lemkau — Professor of Public Health and Psychiatry, Johns Hopkins University
- Donald Michael — Resident Fellow, Institute for Policy Studies, Washington, D.C.
- Chester Rapkin — Professor of City Planning, University of Pennsylvania
- Wayne Thompson — City Manager of Oakland, California
- Alan Voorhees — Transportation Consultant
- Stephen B. Withey — Professor of Psychology, University of Michigan.

For six months during the summer and fall of 1963, the group met twice monthly for two days and a night — about 200 hours in all. It was important to have enough time for these "brain-storming" sessions to sustain a thought pattern in depth. Their problem was to take Rouse's general objectives and translate them into services and physical facilities. In addition, they were to analyze the areas of interaction of each service with other aspects of the community.

The process of the group was itself unique. Rouse was not seeking a systematic, "tight" cost-benefit analysis, but an inter-mingling of ideas and a general exploration of the possibilities. Said one member, "It was a mind-blowing exercise. Often we forgot feasibility altogether, even though every issue discussed was related to economics, either for the developer or for the residents." Nonetheless, their consideration of issues was detailed and comprehensive. As one memorandum described it:

> Each function was addressed, in turn, from individual and community health through libraries, active recreation, and the needs of homebound young members, or children, and the aged. The individuals with expertise in a given area prepared papers to articulate "optimum" conditions. These papers served as a grist for the interdisciplinary mill — and traditional boundaries crumbled. For instance, the church could serve a need in counseling and become part of the health system; nurses and doctors, in turn, would be part of the education system. Perhaps the library should sell paperbacks, private restaurants cater meals to the school system.

Consensus was not sought during the work group process. The responsibility to make the physical plan accommodate the insights generated from these "confrontations" lay with the planning team.

Indeed, the work group was not primarily concerned with specific outputs. Because of the parameters and level of abstraction in which they were dealing, the group decided not to codify or publish their results.[10] Many felt that it was impossible to capture the essence of the group's interactions. One participant called it "an intensely personal experience in thinking through and living with ideas subjected to the rigors of a systems concept where all parts are interrelated, and dogmas and traditional

standards are under constant scrutiny." Group members believe
that the work they did has affected the whole decision-making
process.

The work group's recommendations, which are embodied in
the physical and institutional plans, reflect neither the excite-
ment nor the unconventional composition of ideas and life-styles
which evolved in discussion. Indeed, to critics, the large investment by the company in the work group — estimated at $240,000
— seems to have resulted in making Columbia only a slightly
better suburb. Since their discipline was economic and social
"do-ability," utopian (or even democratic) flights of fancy were
tightly reined. The group suggested that American families want
the sense of belonging which comes from living with people who
make them comfortable, and thus social homogeneity at the
neighborhood level was recommended. A sense of security was
to be carried into the architectural design which Rouse strongly
felt should not be too "avant garde." The housing standard was
detached single-family units rather than high-density apartment
dwellings, since the single-home market was felt to be safer.
Their attempt was to build upon and improve existing suburban
life rather than to replace it.

Now, however, the issues which they raised predictively are
the problems which society faces: control of education, the generation gap, racial strife, and the need for pluralism in a technological age. In real terms, the group provided Columbia with
the background for institutional development, which is being
executed not by the developer but by those who ultimately will
assume responsibility for the city's institutions. For example, although a report on educational systems started an intensely political hassle at first, it has since provided guidance for the entire
county school system in curriculum, teacher-pupil relationships,
and physical layout. The Johns Hopkins University medical
faculty commited itself to develop a privately operated, com-
mercially financed community health system, oriented to preven-
tive medicine and positive health conditions rather than diagnosis
and cure. This is already resulting in a higher overall standard of
health care at lower per capita cost. The churches created a

"cooperative ministry" and agreed to build common facilities to be used by all the major denominations; they also increased the range of social services offered, while reducing overall capital costs. Some ideas, such as a community-wide communications system, with data banks and individual computer consoles in each home, remained in the conceptual stage because the hardware was not yet available at commercial prices. But even this concept did result in a decision to preservice lots with cable space, which would achieve future economies when the system could be made operational.

The work group had a substantial effect on The Rouse Company's organization, as well as the plans for Columbia. Its process of debate and discussion — sometimes pleasant, often tense — set the tone for an overall management style which Rouse calls "creative tension." The group (as well as the plan) was continually fluid in its process and responsive to feedback. Centers of influence and relationships changed often, not only because each member had respect for the other members, but because they were outside the norms and structure of the organization. The group reflected TRC's sensitivity to the use of corporate power in influencing institutional formation during Columbia's early stages. That role imposed a discipline on the developer by emphasizing the importance of pluralism and individual control within the unified concept which pervaded Columbia's planning. It suggested that the institutions most important in implementing the Columbia process were also those which the company would have to restrain itself from structuring and guiding.

THE COLUMBIA ECONOMIC MODEL

Most of the literature on new communities has emphasized the master land use plan as the key element. Superior site arrangements and the integration of community facilities and employment centers seem to distinguish new towns in both the professional and public eyes. Robert Simon, the developer of Reston,

Virginia, even regarded his plan of seven villages, a downtown, and an industrial park as "the blueprint for the future."

Similarly, Columbia's physical plan and its planning process have been widely reviewed as fundamental contributions to the state of this embryonic art. From the viewpoint of management, however, Columbia's most important blueprint was the Columbia Economic Model (CEM), for this simple and straightforward financial projection of cash flow over the entire project cycle gave the new community legitimacy as a business enterprise. While Reston had attracted widespread attention for its conceptual scheme and architectural design, it was underfinanced, and its cost-control system and cash projections were inadequate. Rouse intended to avoid the problems as well as the stigma of financial stagnation which had plagued other new towns. Therefore, even in the project's earliest stages, the CEM assumed great significance.

In a management era of simulation techniques and probabilistic models, the CEM may seem primitive, but its impact has been far-reaching. The importance of the assumptions and the use of the model as a tool in overall project management have extended its influence into most Columbia operations. Since the scale and complexity of the project preclude any individual executive from examining fully the implications of changes in development pace or costs, the CEM has in effect become an integrating device for the entire organization, with a role in every major decision — and most minor ones — that transcends the decisions of managers themselves. In the paragraphs below, we shall first outline the structure of the CEM and then describe its use and its impact on the organization.

Contents of the CEM

The economic model is a series of accounting routines based on general and specific assumptions, which are detailed at the beginning of each quarterly CEM report. Assumptions are made about specific development programs, development pace and scheduling, cash flow, the cost of financing, and current marketing strategy. There are seven categories of cost assumptions, as shown in Table 5-I. Once defined, each assumption is assigned to responsible executives by functional specialty or project element. Revisions are made continuously for both favorable and unfavorable reasons, including scheduling changes, cost changes, market reaction, and revisions in project specifications. The model is on a 15-year development cycle, with each CEM year corresponding to the company's fiscal and budget year, making model output consistent with financial statements and internal budget reports. The model includes the elements shown in Table 5-II, details of which are recomputed as necessary to include revisions in assumptions.

Four sets of input data are required for the model: (1) general financial data; (2) land development and sales data; (3) Columbia Association capital and operating data; and (4) HRD town-wide and in-tract costs. At present, these data are developed in two ways. For past years, actual accounting data on each phase are recorded. For future development years, project managers make assumptions based on development pace and expected land prices. These assumptions replace accounting data in input sets 2, 3, and 4 above. Five of the nineteen CEM sections are summary reports for the other fourteen elements. Figure 5-5 shows the interrelationships from stage to stage, each of which simply represents an aggregation of data.

Building the CEM

The original CEM (the Red Book), begun in 1964, was intended to identify the elements of profitability and define total financing needs. Through this process, the economic implications of development plans then emerging were evaluated, and an economic rationale was provided for plans and commitments that had already been made. Several attempts had been made to refine the data base and estimate total payout, but the Red Book was the first attempt to pin down commitments for specific land uses

TABLE 5-I: CATEGORIES OF BASIC COST ASSUMPTIONS

Land Development and Engineering

Estimates per lot for 15-year cycle.

Operating Functions

Costs for 15 functions such as construction and engineering, land development, etc., were determined for the current year. Projections for the 15-year cycle were then made based on the assumptions for pace and need*.

General Promotion

Expenses were projected for 15 years, assuming that costs would be highest in year 1, both in advertising and public relations, decline gradually in years 2 and 3 and sharply for the remainder (except for community relations) when merchant builders would be doing their own advertising.

Administrative and Corporate Overhead

Project administration and corporate expenses. County real estate taxes were significant because they would be computed only during the time land was held in inventory (between recordation and sale). This was finally estimated at 18 months.

Land Management (*Agricultural*)

Projected cash flow without interest or amortization over 15 years at a constant rate of $60,000. The CEM assumption is break-even because the amount is so small relative to the total.

Columbia Association

Initially costs were projected for general items such as "recreation in villages"; now they are identified as specific programs.

Columbia Development Corporation

Assumptions included only capital requirements of $1.5 million from HRD, but because of peculiar financing problems, these have taken about $4 million.

* An example may help clarify this process. In 1965, the planning department was preparing 50 per cent of the single-family lots needed in development years 2 to 4. A budget of $200,000 for year 1 would be increased gradually to $400,000 and remain at that level through year 10, when it was assumed to decrease because the planning process would have been routinized at 1,000 lots per year. The land-development function was assumed to decline by year 6 and be eliminated by year 12. Construction and engineering were directly related to annual pace. Institutional development would be high in years 1 to 10 and then decrease.

TABLE 5-II: ELEMENTS OF THE CEM

Net Proceeds From Development

Pretax revenues from gross land sales and miscellaneous income from land under development *less* town-wide and in-tract development costs

Land and Predevelopment Costs

Actual expenditures to date and projected costs for remaining development period

Composite Financing Position

Net debt, including land acquisition, predevelopment costs of planning and administration, and development costs *less* land sales proceeds and invested capital. Must be within limitations of peak debt set under the terms of financing arrangements with lenders

Columbia Association Cash Accounting

Summarizes revenues from assessments and capital, operating and financing costs

Columbia Association Operating Revenues

Recreation programs, day care centers, public works, cultural activities and administration

Columbia Association Costs

Neighborhood and village public facilities, day care centers, plazas, squares, parks, equestrian tracks, lakes, transit system, tennis clubs, equipment for public works, and safety

HRD Cash Accounting

Summary of cash flow from land sales and development costs during each development year

Consolidated Land Sales Proceeds

Proceeds from residential, commercial, industrial, public and other, calculated by multiplying projected unit space by projected unit price

Residential Sales Proceeds

Detached houses, townhouses, garden apartments, mid-rise apartments and high-rise apartments

Pace of Residential Development and Land Usage

Units sold and prices in 5-year increments of dwelling units and acres. Pace and proceeds of commercial and industrial land are divided geographically and by type of use

Pace and Proceeds from Public Land Sales

Schools, hospitals, churches, community college, highway programs

Town-Wide Development and Administrative Costs

Sewers, water, salaries and overhead, advertising and promotion, legal expenses

In-Tract Development Costs

Utilities, streets, etc., costs allocated to number of units assumed to be "finished" and sold in each development year

Lot Development Costs

Streets, sidewalks, landscaping, storm drainage, engineering, utilities, and overhead

FIGURE 5-5.   COLUMBIA ECONOMIC MODEL (SYSTEM FLOW)

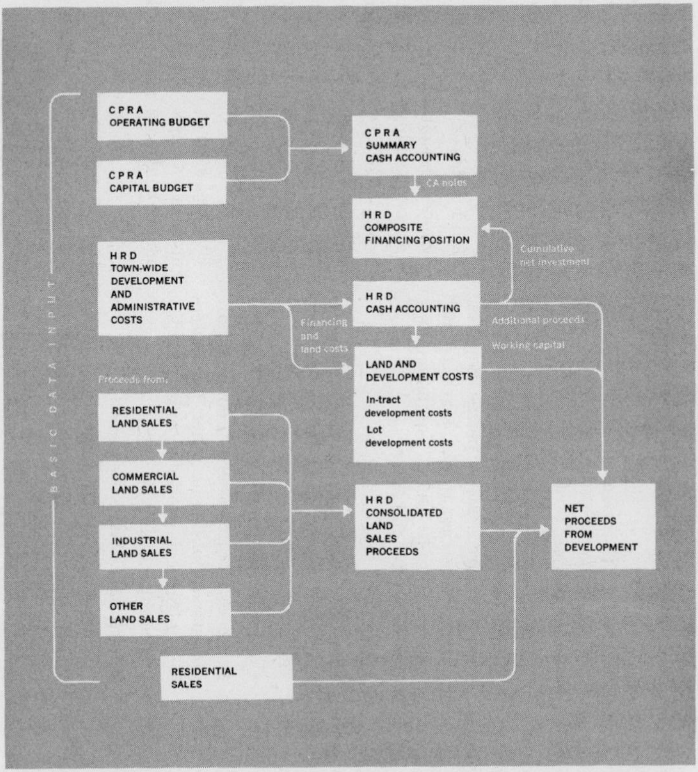

and refine infrastructure cost data. That first attempt consumed the full time of a financial analyst, as well as much of Rouse's time, for more than a year. It had several immediate effects:

- The original assumption of a very low-density residential development produced too low a payout, so that both residential density and the commercial/industrial base were increased. The conceptual definition stage, which had been highly aesthetic and subjective, was tempered by analysis of the optimum economic use of land.

- Areas of total uncertainty were highlighted and researched further. (For example, the initial plan allocated 300 contiguous acres of industrial acreage to be sold at one time, an unusually difficult undertaking.)
- The problem of reconciling the General Land Use Plan (GLUP) with the CEM was highlighted when it became clear that GLUP was using residential location as the primary development criterion, whereas CEM used commercial and industrial land location.
- The project group, composed principally of planners, was made forcefully aware of the need for a definitive rather than suggestive General Land Use Plan.
- As the elements of the first model were put together, total financing requirements shifted from $44 million to $47 million (plus a $6 million contingency figure). Program elements were reworked until the total was brought within $50 million.

Current Uses of the CEM

The model performs several distinct functions on a continuing basis. It gives TRC management and the HRD board an overall picture of profitability from land development for the entire project cycle. It also projects on an annual basis the total debt requirements of all project elements — a function critical to management because of the financing agreements with Connecticut General and other lenders.

The details required to make up this composite picture generate additional uses as a management device to:

- Identify and classify projected revenues and costs on a systematic basis.
- Establish development pace, which is the basic control factor.
- Establish priorities among development requirements.
- Establish guidelines for annual development budgets.

Information developed in the preparation of the CEM is also used for land use planning, tax planning, project scheduling, estimating staff requirements, marketing strategy, and many other elements of the project.

However, the model is limited in several respects at present. First, no projections are included for property to be developed by subsidiaries (and held for HRD's account), although Rouse expects these operations to produce a larger cash flow within a decade than all of TRC does today.[11] Second, no provision is made for inflation, so that price increases are assumed to result from added value rather than inflation. Third, profitability is not calculated by land use or geographic area. Consequently, quantitative comparisons of neighborhoods or villages can be made only on a cost basis, rather than by comparing profitability. In addition, the potential for organizing or evaluating the project through cost-benefit analysis of area elements or functional elements is limited, since there is no systematic attempt to relate results to expenditures.

Thus, the use of the model as a management control tool is only effective in cases where the cost projections required for updating are identified as irregular by the HRD treasurer and the general manager. For example, if the projected budget for landscaping a neighborhood is 20 percent higher than previous budgets or comparable projections, the HRD treasurer may require the responsible project director "to use fewer trees, cheaper trees, or alter his design" in order to meet the CEM objectives. Similarly, it is not a device for resource allocation, since it cannot evaluate alternative approaches to development areas within the total project.

Impact on the Organization

The CEM introduced an economic discipline into the intuitive, value-laden process of development. For the first nine to twelve months (June 1964 to early 1965), the land plan had been considered almost inviolable — an extension of the founder's vision. As a result, economic elements of the concept, such as industrial development, were by-products of a physical planning process, and the executives who became responsible for those functions in the organization had not been involved in shaping them. From mid-1965 on, a shift in discipline from planning to analysis began to take place. At the same time, Rouse began to relinquish his personal control of the project without having any ongoing system take his place in the decision-making process.

The CEM's impact on the development organization was felt in three major ways. First, it was a tool which required department heads and board members to continually examine assumptions, needs, and prospects for their own activities. The periodic updating for the HRD board of directors required specialized organizational units to evaluate their activity, expenditures, and staffing levels at least quarterly. For some (e.g., planning and design, industrial marketing), data preparation is still intuitive, but objectives and plans must be thought through nonetheless. The information generated is used in almost every phase of the project, including project scheduling, tax planning, personnel planning, and marketing. Thus, the *institutionalization* of data preparation and analysis has created specific channels for information and review in an open and continually shifting decision-making framework.

Second, while some key Rouse Company executives prefer to consider the CEM as a guideline, others feel that its greatest discipline is the pressure it puts on people to do their job. Connecticut General accepted it as a definitive control tool from the beginning. Rouse ties the achievements of the Columbia process to the disciplines of the CEM, and his executives have begun to use it as a negotiating tool. "Look," said a sales vice president, "the economic model says I've got to have this settlement this fiscal year. It can't wait 'til June. I've got to have it in May." Although the pressure induced by the CEM is substantial, it is welcomed by project executives as more rational than the less predictable pressures of several years ago, which were induced by a response to continuing crises. The general manager explained the effect on him:

> Most developers assume that fluctuations in sales are totally out of their control, and therefore that internal management can only respond to environmental factors. They don't push. But the

CEM tells me that my sales should be $18,907,000 this fiscal year. So far, we have $7.6 million with two months to go. What we are doing is making sure that someone is on each pending sale to make sure it's settled to meet each model category. If we have a production bottleneck, we can shift emphasis to another line. There is nothing I want to do more than meet that goal.

Third, the model insured that decisions made in Columbia's open and flexible task environment would be economically viable. For *planning,* the CEM was a device to limit functional specialists who assumed that they would need more equipment, time, staff, and money than the model would allow and who otherwise were not constrained by an authority structure. For *goal-setting,* the model was used as a motivating discipline to raise sales objectives to meet the required pace, rather than slackening the pace to insure achievement of objectives. Major long-term decisions, which characteristically were made intuitively in response to an "obvious" need or a crisis situation, were changed. At 2:00 A.M., while preparing the CEM for a board meeting in December 1966, two executives were trying to slice $1.5 million from the land development budget. According to one of them:

> If we hadn't had the discipline of the model, those programs would have gone ahead. The construction manager had orders to get those things done. He had his engineering plans for the whole thing. He was really shook. But we used the model to show him that it was all within the framework to keep Columbia a financial success.
>
> The development pace was increased by 5 percent on several successive models.
>
> We didn't make our sales pace the first year, so we had to spread that over the next three years' development pace to catch up. By May 31, 1969, we had sold land for as many dwelling units as we projected we would in 1965, so we are back on schedule.

The problem of where to extend major elements of infrastructures is now being resolved in line with long-term implications for the CEM, whereas previously the decision would have rested on personal judgment. Planning and design specialists may want a village opened in a certain location because of their primary concern for maintaining the integrity of the Columbia plan and ensuring its aesthetic quality. Marketing may want an industrial site prepared in a new area to meet the demands of a major customer who has been carefully cultivated. Both cases may require $1 million to $2 million in trunk sewer lines and roads. But once the investment is made, a much wider area will be opened up, so that the market potential for other uses over the *entire* area served by that investment must be sufficient to carry it, relative to investments in areas already being prepared for sale.

Although the CEM had significant impact on the organization, its even greater potential was not realized because of certain limitations. Since the board relies on the CEM as the only systematic reporting device, any changes that are reflected receive careful scrutiny, both from the board and from management. Consequently, those who monitor the input data and must answer to the board are reluctant to accept changes in assumptions unless they are "significant." The level of significance appears to be an intuitive measure, based on the degree of historical experience with a particular item. If there is too little experience with an item, or if substantial experience shows that it changes frequently or in some constant pattern, no change will be made. Officers feel safer not suggesting revisions in an assumption until experience makes them sure that it will not change again or be disproven, necessitating an embarrassing request for further revision.

One executive feels that there are two other factors which contribute to this reluctance. First, the sheer mechanical problem of testing changes in assumptions by hand throughout the project cycle, and including the implications for each section of the model, would be too great for any but the most "significant" ones. Second, the scale and scope of the project are so great that even minor changes produce enormous fluctuations in total profitability — and a projected million-dollar gain or loss in profits every quarter, even if spread through 15 years, is bound to raise questions among the most seasoned financiers.

The potential problem which some people in the project have observed, however, is that the lack of a mechanical capability to constantly analyze and reevaluate minor changes and detailed figures may prevent the early detection of nonoptimal decisions on sales objectives, prices, or lot costs. At present only gross effects, such as the use of increases in commercial land values to finance the increased costs of residential preservicing while maintaining marketable price levels, can be determined.

An Attempt at Computerization

In late 1966, a TRC senior systems analyst began an attempt to adapt the CEM to the company's 1401 G (16K) computer which was then used primarily for corporate accounting and mortgage servicing operations. The purposes of computerizing the CEM were: to make it easier to account for changes in model assumptions or actual results; and to increase management's ability to recalculate alternative mixes of housing types and development strategies. Previously, the burdensome nature of computing the model by hand had made it impossible to test the impact of all but the most major changes or events on either current or overall profitability. In addition, it was expected that other executives would begin to use the model as a planning and control tool.

Overcoming the organizational bias against the impersonality of "systems" and achieving acceptance for the machine's output were serious challenges for the analyst. "Systems men and their machines aren't really part of the Columbia process," said one junior executive who had recently joined the project.

The CEM analysis took approximately nine months with the analyst supervising the work of a service bureau programming team. The program was first run in preparation for the October 1967 board meeting. Because neither management nor the board were familiar with printout formats, it was retyped to appear identical to previous reports. Following that initial use, it was not used again and the analyst returned to work on other TRC projects.

The reasons for its failure to gain acceptance appear to be found in the fundamental problem of making systems analysis an integral process of day-to-day project management. By inference, however, there are several conclusions to draw. First, the attempt at a computer application for the most important management tool in Columbia was premature. Most managers viewed the computer as a calculating device and few knew of its potential for decision making. The Corporate Systems Department was new and heavily involved in other projects. No specific attempts were made to educate managers about the benefits they might receive from computerization so that many saw the attempt as irrelevant to solving their problems.

The second factor was that in 1968 there was a change in the administrator of the CEM. The new man felt that most important alternatives could be analyzed without the computer and that the actual report presentation, like the basic assumptions, was more a matter of intuitive judgment than calculation or analysis. He also lacked confidence in the quality of the program structure because many of the basic characteristics of land development were unknown by the program builders.

A final factor was the lack of confidence among executives that CEM analysis by computer was: (1) possible, or (2) worth the time and expense. As the computer model lies untested, however, so does the potential for further enhancing this sophisticated approach to the process of community development.

Cost Control and the CEM

An unanticipated effect of the CEM on the Columbia organization was its eventual use as a tool for controlling costs — not by original design, but as a function of the preparation and ordering of input data. In mid-1965, as the model was being refined, Rouse hired an accountant to develop a cost-control system for the project that would be completely integrated with the CEM and perform that management task for which the model was not designed.

Any new system would have to be developed within the context of Rouse's management philosophy. Rouse wanted to insure that the company's rapid expansion would not be hampered by controls that would limit the flexibility of project managers and staff to act quickly. In Columbia, however, the company was responsible both for managing the project and for Connecticut General's funds which were financing it. As a joint-venture partner, therefore, the company had at least an equal responsibility — if not a greater one — for controlling funds more tightly than in shopping center development.

Because of the project orientation, the company had not required departmental budgets on a periodic basis. Consequently, a large overhead factor was accepted as an operational characteristic for essential functions that were not specifically project-related or that were underbudgeted for a particular project such as research, leasing, and design.

The accountant believed that the company system would have to be revised for Columbia because the essence of management control for such a complex project would lie in "responsibility accounting." He wanted to design one system that would be consistent with all of the project needs, including overall financing requirements, the investors' interests, and the daily operational needs of project managers. He aimed to produce a framework in which corporate and project management could directly control costs rather than produce a series of accounting statements. Consistency also would be required to integrate the system with the CEM.

These problems were significant in day-to-day operations in that hectic year prior to opening. Internal pressures were intense. There had been a 15-month delay in the scheduled opening date. Decision-making responsibilities ebbed and flowed constantly because of continuing changes in details or unforeseen delays. Major commitments were made or revised in the field by middle managers or specialists closest to the point of decision in order to avoid the unnecessary delays of the management committee. Several executives warned that the project could be seriously out of control at that point.

Two major difficulties arose in implementing the cost control system. First, it did not interface directly with the existing corporate system or the perspectives of the accounting department. Second, the accountant had assumed responsibility for managing the CEM as treasurer of HRD and was unable to manage the cost control implementation phase. The system therefore lay fallow through the height of the planning and initial land development phases of the project, although problems raised by the lack of information flowing up to management about project flows and commitments continued to highlight the need.

THE CRITICAL PATH METHOD

Analysis and control of project scheduling were introduced during the planning phase, when Columbia was still conceived as an "environmental development," rather than a "land development" project. The elements of creating an environment were subjective and unpredictable. However, project scheduling requires knowledge of the relationships between project elements and a degree of predictability. Therefore, scheduling was difficult during the planning phase, but was feasible during implementation, because the tasks of engineering and building infrastructure were more ordered and straightforward production processes. Control over the latter was not only possible with the critical path method (CPM), but was recognized as necessary early in the implementation phase in order to coordinate, or even provide information about, the thousands of discrete activities then under way. Its impact as an information device was substantial. Its effectiveness for control was limited, however, because the subjective, unpredictable environmental considerations continued to be important in otherwise objective engineering and construction decisions.

Preopening Applications of the CPM

Early in 1965, the company had gained some first-hand experience with a CPM network designed in-house for a shopping center project. By that time, the commercial development process had been sufficiently routinized to make the application fairly simple and its schedule acceptable. In June 1965, a CPM evaluation report on Columbia stated that the scheduled opening date of September 1, 1966, could not be met.[12] Three suggestions were made: (1) shorten working time by extra shift work or overtime; (2) revise the logic to shorten the work sequence; and (3) revise the target date. Revising the logic on model homes and sewerage, for example, would have reduced the average number of overrun dates to 4 percent. The report recommended that the opening be delayed so that it would coordinate for control purposes with the first delivery of houses, scheduled for April 1, 1967.

Since the opening was a moment of strategic and psychological importance, no one in management was pleased or even willing to accept the consultant's dictum that delay was likely. Nonetheless, the CPM was a graphic portrayal of what was happening. Pressure was generated by several middle managers for a detailed application of CPM to be phased in throughout the project, where each phase would be keyed to specific objectives as they were defined for units such as a village or town center. They hoped also that the attempt to institutionalize this method would force a greater tie between information and control by requiring reports against goals that had been established, rather than written activity statements. The consultant's proposal identified four objectives for a CPM program:

- *In-depth planning* to meet the CPM requirement for detailed planning logic. Expected results were: (1) identification of problem areas; (2) definition of work packages; and (3) coordination between work areas.
- *Schedules* based on detailed CPM plans, continually available and revised to account for new information.
- *Monitoring* to compare the schedules with actual progress on a regular basis to determine project status.
- *Control* to evaluate the time impact of alternatives selected when problems are identified by project status reports.

The director of land development suggested that the CPM should serve three other functions:

- Defining and assigning responsibilities by department.
- Individual accountability for performance of each project element.
- Continuing feedback for evaluating progress against goals.

Management accepted the proposal for a full system designed by an outside contractor for three reasons. One analyst estimated that a 50 percent larger staff would be needed for the CPM operation if it were done in-house. In addition, the staff might remain idle four months of the year because of slack in the work load. Third, variances in computer requirements made it more economical and timely to use outside consultants and a service bureau. There was a final caveat: Since the initial program's results were discomforting to project executives, an internal analysis staff might find itself in an awkward interpersonal situation, which could in time restrict its information sources as well.

Between the June report and the following February, the director of land development and the director of program control were assisted by the consultant in preparing a detailed 2,000-activity network in the form of Gantt charts.[13] Data for the program were collected through the project status report, which included descriptive summaries of negotiations and activities by time period, but did not measure them against individual goals set for each project. The results then indicated that Columbia would not be ready for opening until June 1967.

Several events occurred in rapid succession, which marked a shift from *planning the environment* to actually *developing the land*. A senior project engineer with wide experience in large-scale construction was hired to expedite detailed land engineering and initial construction.[14] On-site construction began in May 1966. A TRC construction department was formed late that summer, and an experienced construction executive was brought in as a corporate vice president to coordinate the implementation phases.[15] One of his first acts was to establish a full CPM and scheduling team made up of two Columbia specialists and four analysts from the consulting firm. The networks were prepared by hand, and line managers met weekly with the team to update the schedule.

As Columbia neared the June 1967 opening, the entire project group was forced to accept a far more elaborate discipline from the schedule than at any time in the previous four years. A 30-man schedule review committee was established at management level, and included the legal, planning and design, finance, engineering, and construction department heads. This committee, which also met weekly, in effect replaced the management and marketing committees as the principal forum for decisions. It emphasized the shift in focus from overall Columbia marketing objectives toward meeting specific land development goals. "Opening may have been a 'marketing moment,'" said one member of that group, "but the schedule made us realize that we had to produce something in order to sell it."

CPM After Opening

"Pressure was so intense before opening day that we had forgotten to schedule the second year," remarked Columbia's project director. "So at the time we opened, we were already six months behind and didn't realize it." It was apparent that subsequent recycling would be necessary, and that delays would result as the group attempted to catch up. There was an abortive three-month attempt to use the scheduling system as a mechanism for objectively setting both individual and project goals. Target dates were estimated by the subproject manager concerned and modified according to engineering and construction estimates. The program control director managed this process, and in so doing he acquired a directive function. This in turn produced dissension that was considered dysfunctional by top management.

When the crisis of opening was past, the increased discipline and attempts at systematizing the control process, which had been imposed by the program on the entire project group, were eased in the implementation stages. In part, this was because the land development process had become more routinized, and because the project management team had become used to using CPM as a basic tool.

Even the management committee gradually began to reflect lessened tension. For the first two years, it met every week; then, biweekly. Now it meets every third week. However, there is still no conscious systematic grouping of issues requiring attention at these meetings. Thus, confrontations about "lost" or delayed projects still occur when the responsible manager does not know the current status.

To date, overall objectives for Columbia remain a function of the Columbia Economic Model, but they are not translated into specific daily or weekly goals for individual managers within the project. The reporting system is not formalized enough to pinpoint problems in scheduling subprojects or in the detailed negotiations with public agencies.

Two of the CPM's original proponents are now in a position to institutionalize its use. The director of land development uses schedules for planning, monitoring, and controlling each infrastructure project. The director of program control is responsible for coordinating individual schedules, monitoring and evaluating all Columbia land histories and projects, and administering related contracts. When it becomes operational, the Land Inventory and Control System will also be administered by him. Thus, while the CPM is being more broadly and systematically applied, its direct influence over individuals and the management process is concentrated in managers who favor its use and accept its discipline.

Implications for Management Control

The application of CPM in Columbia highlights several factors needed for a workable development control system:

- Thorough understanding of the development process, including relationships between activity components.
- Experience in estimating delays in both controllable and noncontrollable activities.
- Agreement of key decision makers on the methods and their willingness to act on the results.

Since community development represented a new dimension of tasks and relationships for the company, even the considerable collective experience of the project group did not provide a thorough enough understanding of the development process to apply CPM most effectively during the first two years. Planning factors in design and field construction could be quantified from experience. But neither the group nor the consultants could identify all of the activity components in the process, or put meaningful activity times on the entire procedure. Of greater importance, the lack of direct accountability for each activity, even when defined, meant that it was not always clear "who took over from whom or how the activities on the network would fit with each other."

Information collected through the project status reports was primarily descriptive and did not measure actual progress against plans; thus, it was not useful for monitoring and controlling the project. As a result, the system was initially built on inadequate information which necessitated continual schedule revisions and recycling. Smooth implementation of the system was disrupted by these changes and made its acceptance more difficult.

The least definable processes were the delicate negotiations and frequent reviews with a variety of public agencies. The company often proposed innovative service contracts to finance or operate public services where local authorities were severely underfunded and understaffed. Obviously, the qualitative, often political factors were extremely important. It was difficult to estimate the time of these negotiations in quarters, much less in days. It also was difficult to estimate the review and approval process, since the magnitude of Columbia represented a quantum shift in the amount of governmental control activities which would be required. Only after several years' experience with county agencies and with the whole development process is it now possible to quantify accurately the processing time for a subdivision application or title clearance. It is still difficult to estimate the negotiating periods with major institutions. Experience with these delays has indicated that the CPM is useful only after decisions have been made by the external institutions. It can take projects through the land-development process once specific targets have been set; it cannot be expected to monitor or evaluate projects under negotiation.

Both managers and analysts who were closest to the system forewarned of the potential problems in implementation which would result. They also pointed to the need for specific goal definitions if the CPM were going to be a successful control device. But the very fact of programming the CPM had either raised the expectations of its proponents or roused the ire of its critics to a point where the inadequacies and limitations of the method were somewhat clouded. As we have seen, pressure immediately before opening was extreme, and this led to greater reliance on the program, even with its inadequacies. In retrospect, however, its use may have been premature. It was implemented with neither complete acceptance by top management nor their willingness to impose its constraints on the organization. Yet it did effectively discipline the organization during the months of crisis before opening, and thus became a point of tension.

The CPM required information collection but could not tie the information to project goals for measurement and evaluation. It highlighted the day-to-day urgency of operations without a system for controlling them. And, as we have seen, it was applied while the political aspects of the community development process remained unsettled, although its objectives were designed to meet the controllable, engineered functions of land development. It required new knowledge to be created and led to a deeper understanding of the development process. Today, its place in the process is established and its use routine. But its potential effectiveness for overall project control has yet to be realized.

Land Inventory and Control System (LICS)

We referred to the Columbia Economic Model as the principal management-control technique used in the development process. Its function is to express the economic implications of development plans so that they can be evaluated and modified when necessary. It is particularly valuable in setting yearly goals for the development pace that must be met and in costing the elements (e.g., townwide roads) projected for a development year.

The General Land Use Plan geographically depicts these elements and general land uses (e.g., residential, industrial). However, neither the CEM nor the GLUP translates these elements into specific geographic land plots and uses. As a result, there is no rational method for evaluating alternative areas or plots for development which would meet the required development pace with minimum cash exposure for TRC, maximum utilization of expended capital, and maximum use of existing infrastructure. Additionally, there is no means of testing the impact of possible land use changes directly on the CEM. Within the overall management framework of Columbia, these problems are magnified by the complexity and range of land uses, and hazy zoning requirements for many plots on which uses have changed or have not been clearly specified.

The Existing System for Land Planning and Control

Determination of land use is presently made by evaluating each parcel in terms of "land characteristics," such as topography, physical features, adjacent land uses, the existing and proposed road systems, and its aesthetic character. General uses are also analyzed and "optimum" areas outlined throughout the site, based on marketability criteria of the target users. For example, one of the primary sales objectives in the first development phase was to sell as much industrial land as possible. Therefore, industrial areas had to be located in order to meet the marketing criteria of likely industrial tenants, who generally desire visibility and access to and from the transportation network and flat topography to minimize construction costs. Four primary industrial areas were located to optimize these criteria. The areas had to be preserviced with trunk sewers, water and electricity, and roads. Preservicing of industrial land also opened up approximately one quarter of Columbia's total land area designated for multifamily apartment and townhouse uses in the first development year — well ahead of CEM targets, and representing the equivalent of five years of residential sales.

Until recently, there has been no method for translating the marketing goals set by the CEM to the development alternatives made possible by preservicing. Thus, it has been difficult to plan any improvements strategically so that industrial, commercial, residential, and recreational development could be scheduled and located in area patterns which would minimize the acreage requiring substantial front-end investments for preservicing.

Land is considered to be "finished" upon completion of preservicing, regardless of its eventual use. It then becomes part of the finished land inventory. A ledger system for inventory accounting was evolved as demand for data on each finished parcel increased from a variety of company departments and county agencies. The ledger consists of formats for residential lots, apartment property, and commercial and industrial property. But variations in sources and demand for data over time have resulted in variations in format, so that neither the form nor the type of data entered is entirely consistent. The ledger is becoming voluminous as the pace of development increases. In March 1969, it consisted of 300 pages with seven lot listings per page.

The present system uses four major data sources which also change with the operational process. First, the county keeps maps and descriptive texts on each parcel. Second, data on land disposition to builders come from a variety of legal and financial documents, including option agreements, leases, sales contracts, purchase and construction mortgages. Third, data on sales by builders to individual owners or lessees are provided to the company in varying formats. Fourth, data on land development, construction, and final finishing progress are obtained by weekly site inspections conducted by the company. Only some of these data are posted on the ledgers, with the remainder going directly to the staff. As a result, progress data are neither complete nor consistent.

A variety of reports are drawn from the inventory ledgers, including weekly sales reports, project status reports, and CPM project schedules. These provide useful management information, but are limited in that they do not include budget and cost data to support the schedules or predictive data such as expected population growth by type and area for community facilities planning.

The existing system presents three major administrative problems. First, there are too many reports to be useful to the line or field project manager, with the result that they often are overlooked or underutilized. Second, maintaining the existing ledger is expected to generate a large increase in clerical manpower as the development pace increases; one estimate predicted a 200 percent increase in clerks. Moreover, continuing changes in data sources, ledgers, and outputs are expected to increase as the intensity and variety of development increase. Modifications or "add-ons" to the existing system will become more difficult to manage.

A New Land Use Model

In response to the need for a dynamic system for phasing the rest of Columbia's growth and better information for inventory control, a staff group began working early in 1968 to create a land development model (see Figure 5-6) which would translate the annual land use plans and goals of the CEM into actual geographic land plots.

The land use requirements outlined by the CEM in conjunction with the marketing demand for land and financial constraints imposed on the company are applied to Columbia's land inventory. The total inventory is divided into both preserviced and undeveloped land. Selecting from this inventory those combinations of land plots which will meet the required annual development program with minimum cash exposure for preservicing, the model then proceeds to calculate a set of CPM flow charts, indicating the time of development, target dates for the development process, and critical functions in the process. Using the time factors generated by the CPM and the existing debt position of the project, cost estimates for yearly advertising and overhead can be calculated. The model is then in a position to compute the annual cash position for the annual development program. Required expenditures are added to the past cumulative debt position and then tested against the debt ceiling to indicate the economic feasibility of the annual program. Reiterating this loop for every

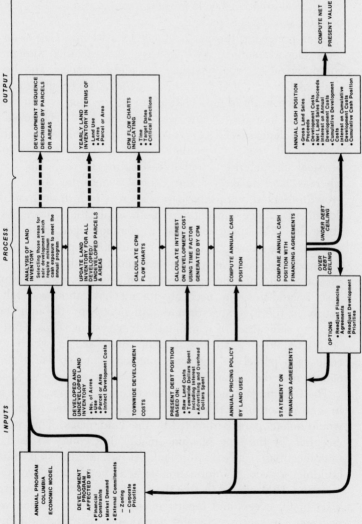

FIGURE 5-6. COLUMBIA LAND DEVELOPMENT MODEL

remaining year in the development cycle, a detailed development program and economic model for all of the land can be set up. Thus, by testing alternative development programs, the model can generate alternative development sequences and cash flow projections for specific land parcels.

After reviewing the proposed model with the Corporate Systems Department, it was apparent that detailed design and computerization would require outside assistance. The Federal Systems Division of IBM was approached. The resulting proposal was framed in terms of a total urban information system to serve as the data base for the land use model and as a mechanized land inventory ledger. The two uses were quite different: planning data would require a stable, use-oriented file related to the physical characteristics and infrastructure of each land parcel, whereas land inventory and control would be dynamic and growth-oriented, with information sources in historical and legal documents. Since the data for both applications were similar, however, IBM suggested that a common data base be developed. The entire proposal was not accepted, primarily because it would have been very costly to computerize both files. Project executives did not foresee benefits sufficient to justify the initial cost. In addition, the necessity for mechanization was felt primarily in the inventory data requirements and through the increasing difficulties of a manual ledger system. Thus, IBM was contracted to simulate the land inventory ledger which would code each parcel by legal and financial characteristics and by county recordation number.

The IBM project manager believed that it was possible to build in an XY coordinate referencing system in digitized form, which would relate parcels directly to the land maps. This was not essential for the land planning model, but could be used as a reference base, once established. As an interim step prior to building a second information system keyed to development planning, IBM agreed to give the Corporate Systems Department a set of file-access and report-generating routines, which would be general in nature and which would allow easy and rapid use of the files for geographic and demographic data being established for the land inventory. There was general agreement that the final step of a total information and control system would become necessary as development pace and complexity increased, and that it would become economically feasible as well. The remaining issue appeared to be whether the existing system costs would be recognized as excessive or at least as greater than the costs of building the land use model.

THE COLUMBIA PARADOX: HUMANISTIC MANAGEMENT AND SYSTEMS ANALYSIS

The systems approach in Columbia is a rigorous and logical thought process for planning and developing an environment. The objective of city building is defined in terms of basic human values (freedom, beauty, dignity), while managerial and economic goals are treated instrumentally as means to that end. In a project which demands the talents of myriad specialties, a continuing effort is made to infuse a philosophy and a sense of common purpose that encourage each specialist to transcend the limits and unique perspective of his profession. Within this framework, specific analytic techniques are used for explicit purposes to further the overall goals of the project.

However, the sophisticated quantitative and modeling techniques generally associated with systems analysis have not been applied for a variety of reasons. First, their advocates, within and without the company, have not been effective in justifying the required resources to support systems research, analysis, and implementation. Second, the current state of modeling art could not provide a useful tool which could comprehend either the dynamics of the city as a whole or the more subjective components of the development process. Third, many members of the Columbia project group continued to question the desirability of even attempting to build a set of mathematical relationships to replicate the human community. Finally, the organization's values, structure, and management processes have limited its capacity for gaining agreement on the ways in which systems analysis could or should be used. But powerful, though partial, techniques did produce a balanced set of disciplining forces which has kept an organic and evolving process moving toward previously established goals.

We have examined several analytic approaches which are employed in the project and provide substantive evidence that the unusual challenges of city building have evoked innovations in planning, organization, and managerial techniques. The CEM and CPM are tools for operational analysis which identify the problems and implications of past decisions on current courses of action and assist project executives in exercising routine control over many components in the development process. Two models also assist in functional analysis. The CEM quantifies the assumptions of an implicit development strategy and translates these into cash flows over the entire project cycle. The LICS (Land Inventory and Control System) is designed to have the capability of generating alternative development strategies and evaluating them according to stated economic criteria. Both models thereby provide a better basis for making resource commitments, although they are not used explicitly for that purpose as yet.

It is significant, however, that these techniques are *disciplines* on the development process, but not *determinants*. Neither the CEM nor the two control tools are actually used for allocating resources, determining land uses, or initiating subproject development. The CEM still is used primarily for planning, although it has the capacity for resource allocation. The CPM draws implications in terms of project schedules, but is not invested with the authority to change the logic or the sequence of the process in order to meet previously established goals. The LICS is being developed primarily as a control tool, although it also is intended to be a dynamic simulation model for planning and programming. Both systems guide the application of strategic project objectives, but do not evaluate alternative development strategies. They have, in effect, been modified to the subjective nature of the Columbia concept. Without such rigorous disciplines, however, the project would probably have failed to maintain its economic viability during the most critical development year, and thus would have been stillborn — another housing subdivision.

The work group was Rouse's pioneering attempt at the third

analytic approach — community analysis. It was formed in response to the need for melding social theory and research with economic reality. It enhanced the project staff's understanding of the "total system" by taking an integrative view in which principles were defined for each of the fundamental elements in the city, after which interfunctional relationships were examined for potential synergistic effects. The group's process was synthetic rather than analytic. The members of the work group made an extraordinarily inspired but inductive leap from a consideration of the city's component parts to the whole, which became the Columbia concept. As a result of that inspiration, new institutional arrangements are being attempted to apply knowledge and resources more effectively to the needs of the community.

Columbia thus reflects an interesting and prophetic paradox. The classic principles of the systems approach were espoused in the first definition of the Columbia concept. The rhetoric and allusions were precise; as one executive put it, "We stated our objectives, examined alternatives in land use and space, calculated the results in qualitative standards and cash flow, and then evaluated them in light of our objectives." "Indeed," he shuddered, "we sounded like RAND developing a missile." There was a strong and deeply infused commitment to a wholistic approach to analyzing human needs and providing for them, which was reflected in the work group's effort to integrate its deliberations across academic or functional boundaries.

Yet, the Columbia "system" is vague and unspecified. As a result, explicit trade-offs between functional elements are not analyzed, but are induced judgmentally. The work group's recommendations were oriented to single functions, with the exception of an integrated communications system to be used by homes, schools, and libraries. This systems approach remained at such a high level of abstraction that it was sufficient for general land planning, but not for day-to-day decision making. Operational pressures have caused decisions that were not optimal in terms of the total system because there were no generally accepted analytic processes to insure control.

The factors underlying this paradox are in part found in the unorthodox organizational environment of TRC. A flexible, free-form organization has evolved which has partially resolved the conflict between the constraints of time and money and the need for creative and continuing managerial response. An open communications pattern, an emphasis on individual relationships, and the traditional atmosphere of cohesiveness and "humaneness" in the company have resulted in a widely held skepticism of techniques or systems that are "impersonal" — especially those that would be used as controls or disciplines over individual action.

This style of management has been called "creative tension." "Management," Rouse once wrote, "is the art of organizing an environment which is comfortable, challenging, and fulfilling for the creative and diverse people within it." In other words, rather than organizing people, he has organized the environment in which they work. Rather than having to respond along rigid communications channels to commands established by higher authority, the individual acts freely to reach goals that he has established himself within an overall framework of concepts and objectives. The manager's long-accepted role as an integrator in resolving conflict has been transformed into one of maintaining a delicate equilibrium between organizational subsystems which are in a perpetual state of conflict. This is in effect an attempt to replicate within a task-oriented organization the necessary paradox of our social order which has been defined by John Gardner:

> The critical lines of tension in our society are between *emphasis on individual performance and restraints on individual performance*. This tension will never be resolved and *never should be resolved*.[16]

Creative tension has three predicates, however. First, those involved in the organizational processes must like and respect each other. Second, there must be complete confidence, throughout, that decision makers will be fully supported. And third, there must be internal mechanisms for resolving conflict, mechanisms that will be accepted by everyone in the organization. These in turn require management processes which will anticipate and define problems and discipline their solutions. The organization itself must be highly sophisticated and mature to withstand the stress of continual tension, especially if it operates in an environment of unusual external pressures. Those within it — from janitor to president — must be highly skilled interpersonally to deal with organizational conflicts that are, for the most part, resolved on a personal basis.

In the Columbia organization, the parameters define *where* and *when* an action would occur. They do not prescribe *how* a conflict should be resolved or who should win it. As one in the thick of daily action put it, "There is a collective, tribal spirit in which each does his own thing with a consciousness of codes and taboos." Put another way, the organization's widely felt and deeply infused value system allows individual action to be taken within the parameters of the Columbia concept. The planners particularly seem to have personalized this to as great a degree as Rouse himself. And this style of operating has marked the work of the project team from the beginning.

However, some people who are effective executives and understand the organizational philosophy do not like an operational style with so much flexibility that independent action can produce crises. Others view it as a burden because uncertainty in organizational relationships and norms is an inevitable result. This uncertainty, coupled with emphasis on individual performance, has made such individual freedom a constraint for them. Those with a strong need for organizational identity — in clearly defined roles and responsibilities — are frustrated by the lack of an explicit, formal information flow and shifting patterns of influence. They either are unable or, more often, do not wish to perceive and deal with the power relationships which exist within the free-form structure and processes which are claimed for the organization. Their problem is common in organizations which require political sensitivity in addition to professional competence, for they are made increasingly aware that "doing a job well" is more than executing a series of specific functions; but they often have not developed the talents or the understanding required to work well in such an environment. As in the development process itself, success in decision making may depend more on political judgment (or suffer more from political ineptitude) than on analytic or professional ability.

Uncertainties also have been heightened because the second premise of creative tension — confidence in the support one receives for decision making — has been difficult to apply. Executives have suffered from personality clashes and "wrong" decisions which they made. While the executives have remained in the organization, their influence within it has diminished. Those whose influence is technical and knowledge-based have been anguished, not at harsh reactions, but at indifference or ignorance of their functions or capacities. At the same time, the unusual style of the organization has resulted in greater opportunities for individual impact, occasionally from unlikely sources. In one sense, the inherent art and entrepreneurship of the project itself have reinforced the atmosphere of flexibility and freedom encouraged by Rouse, and have created a belief in these values which can and do conflict with the systematic, methods orientation of the engineering staff.

The limitations of the systems approach in Columbia were reflected in the decision-making process. That process included: *gathering* information, at first on an ad hoc basis and then systematically; *discussing* the data and the opinions in interdisciplinary groups; *sifting* the output of those discussions further, usually on the basis of implicit criteria; *negotiating* differences in judgment or opinion; and *making* the decision. While Rouse was unquestionably the prime decision maker, he encouraged as many inputs from a variety of sources as time would permit. However, a number of decisions had to be made because of financial constraints or engineering requirements. Other decisions, such as proceeding with a village center or a specific golf course layout, were made during the planning process, without either a technique or any time to examine their long-range impact. When pressure for these decisions would intensify, the project group and the creative process would break down. "It got to the point where somebody *had* to say, 'Go with what you've got,'" recalls one manager.

The greatest immediate hurdle for systems applications to over-

come is the identification of system with paper work. In a recent
conference for senior and middle management, led by Peter
Drucker[17] and Chris Argyris,[18] this view was repeated continually.
Drucker told them:

> There has always been a general resistance here to management
> systems as impositions, not as tools. "Loose-leaf books, budget and
> expense account procedures — I wish you'd get them off and let
> me go to work" has been a typical reaction. The initial systems
> tried to convert managers to clerks. But you are now living in an
> increasingly complex managerial environment. The whole world
> is that way, but you have not changed. You are not going to find
> an alternatively simple solution to that complex situation. This
> is the price you have to pay. However, paper work must be
> minimized and managers not burdened by trivial diversion.

While the limitations of systems applications in the Columbia
project arise from many unique characteristics of TRC, the organization has responded to the challenges of building a new city
with significant innovations in analytic approaches. These confirm the supposition that new methods of management may result from, as well as assist, the deliberate development of new
urban environments. The acceptance and use of these techniques
in the project are beginning to lead the company as a whole into
a new era of management technology, which should enable it to
enhance its capabilities and more fully realize its potential.
Columbia has indeed created a new vision of what might be
achieved in community development. Its management processes
suggest that a systems approach and related techniques, tailored
to the subjective needs of an "optimum" human environment, will
be essential in realizing that vision.

To those seeking to apply systems analysis in city building,
Columbia also suggests an important caveat, for the most distinctive qualities of the emerging new city *are* subjective and unpredictable. From initial planning to each detail of execution,
the organizational characteristics of creativity, flexibility, and
sensitivity in understanding human needs have been more important to the reality of Columbia than analytic capability.

Clearly, this does not imply that creativity and analysis are mutually exclusive. But it does establish an extraordinary requirement for analysts who have such qualities if they are to be accepted and effective in a creative interdisciplinary project group. With rare exceptions, today's systems analyst has neither the breadth nor depth of understanding to temper the rigor of his craft with sensitivity to the subjective, emotional, often chaotic nature of a human community. Moreover, his training and inclinations lead him to view the proponents of humanistic approaches to managing the community development process as opponents or "antiplanners." [19] The result is an atmosphere of conflict within which the analyst's primary role of problem solving is clouded by a difference in philosophy and in operating style.

In order to produce an environment that is responsive to human needs, the Columbia experience argues strongly for a systems approach that is interpreted by organizations whose skills in objective management and analysis are complemented by the creative and sensitive qualities of the humanist. Indeed, if a "new city technology" is evoked through public policy, as Rubel suggests, the technology-based organizations which respond may have to undergo considerable transformations in attitudes, structure, and processes in order to comfortably meld the artists with engineers and analysts. If they respond only with the art of analysis, the cities that are created may be ideal problem "solutions" but unlivable environments.

FOOTNOTES

CHAPTER 5

1. See Wolf von Eckhardt, "The Case for Building 350 New Towns," *Harpers,* May 1964; Donald Canty, ed., *The New City* (New York, Frederick W. Praeger, 1969); Committee on Science and Astronautics, U.S. House of Representatives, *Science and Technology and the Cities* (Washington, D.C., U.S. Government Printing Office, 1969).

2. By comparison, Manhattan Island is 14,286 acres, with 17 percent devoted to open space.

3. John Rubel, *Systems in Cities* (Washington, D.C., Urban America, Inc., 1968). Rubel is Senior Vice President, Litton Industries, Inc.

4. Among many accolades which TRC has received, one of the most significant was *Business Week's* First Annual Business Citizenship Award, announced on November 1, 1969, for "contributions to the physical environment."

5. The nature of these characteristics and their implications for private development of new towns are discussed in detail in Mahlon Apgar's "New Business from New Towns?" (*Harvard Business Review,* January–February 1971, pp. 90–109). See especially the Appendix on the economics of community development.

6. These are compounded rates. The original debt service range was $6\frac{1}{12}$ to $8\frac{1}{4}$ percent.

7. Since this investment was refinanced, TRC has almost no invested capital in the project.

8. The Columbia Association serves as the city's "private government" during the development process. All new residents automatically belong to the Association, which is financed by levying assessments against all taxable property. Its primary responsibility is to provide community facilities and services to supplement those which are the local government's responsibility. Among other activities, it owns and operates the neighborhood centers, nursery schools, golf courses, tennis courts, swimming pools, lakefront parks and marinas, and the minibus system.

9. Throughout this chapter, "project" refers to Columbia as a whole, and "subproject" refers to individual elements such as buildings, roads, sewers, etc.

10. As one member put it, "Nothing but 14,000 acres and a herd of cows out there."

11. Land "sales" to subsidiaries are recorded at full market value, and

working capital requirements for subsidiaries are included in determining total debt requirements.

12. An engineering consultant calculated that 65 percent of the project elements scheduled for that date would be late by an average of approximately 20 percent. These included the lake, sewerage system, gas and electric, water main, access roads and bridges, industrial park, shopping center, neighborhood center, and model homes. "Columbia CPM Control Program," Meridian Engineering, Inc., June 10, 1965.

13. The extent of this effort was visible in sheer volume: The charts consumed 50 rolls measuring 20 feet by 5 feet each.

14. One anecdote, perhaps apocryphal, illustrates his method of expediting. Upon discovering that there were no detailed plans to permit full-scale engineering work to begin, he contracted for "most of the heavy grading and earth-moving equipment in Baltimore," walked into the planning department and said, "That stuff is costing us $6,000 a day. We're ready to begin as soon as you give us working drawings." Several project executives claim that without his manner and method, implementation would have been delayed much longer.

15. This officer was the second in TRC history to be hired at vice presidential level.

16. John W. Gardner, *Excellence: Can We Be Equal and Excellent Too?* (New York, Harper & Row, 1961), p. 28.

17. Management consultant, noted author, and Professor of Management, New York University.

18. Behavioral scientist and Professor of Industiral Administration, Yale University.

19. C. West Churchman offers an incisive description of this conflict in Chapter 13 of *The Systems Approach* (New York, Delacorte Press, 1968).

CHAPTER 6

THE ROLE OF ANALYSIS

NOW THAT WE HAVE LOOKED AT THE RECORD, what can be said? What is the promise of these new tools, and what are their limitations? In this chapter we try to formulate some general statements about the possible role of analysis in urban management and about the ways in which its potentialities can be realized and enlarged. Thus, two questions are to be addressed. First, to what extent and within what bounds can these new tools be put to practical use in cities? The answer to this defines the *domain of innovation;* its limits are set both by factors inherent in the technology and by characteristics of the situations in which the technology is to be used. The second question is: How can *innovation be managed* effectively? Whatever the inherent potential for innovation in analysis, an organization's ability to introduce change and to cope with its consequences will be an important determinant of the actual role of analysis in decision making.

The second question warrants further emphasis. As we said earlier, new methods of analysis must be coupled to the choices that shape an institution's behavior if they are to have a real effect.[1] In our opinion, it is not sufficient for the new methods merely to provide more sophisticated justification for a status quo (although this may sometimes result); they must lead to worthwhile changes in the level and char-

acter of services, the nature and degree of incentives and
limits defined by public authority, or the distribution of
power among competing interests. If the results of analysis
are to justify their cost, they must contribute to change that
helps resolve the imperfections in the status quo that constitute the "urban problem."

The Limits of Innovation

To assess the limits of innovation, we need to take into
account both those factors that limit the analyst's ability to
produce results of satisfactory quality and those that limit
the practical application of analytical results whatever their
quality. Limits of the first type are *technical;* their significance is a function of the adequacy of the analytical technique in relation to the difficulty of the problem to be
analyzed. Those of the second type are *institutional;* they are
found in the social context in which analysis is done. The
effect of the two types is cumulative; that is, it is necessary to
overcome both in order to introduce change.

Technical Limitations

Modern methods of analysis can assist decision makers in
choosing better courses of action to deal with many problems
on the urban scene but, like all tools, they are more useful
in some situations than in others. There are evident technical
limits to the use of analysis in cities. As Charles Lindblom
points out, analysis is inapplicable to issues of public policy
"to the degree that clarification of objectives founders on
social conflict, that required information is either not available or available only at prohibitive cost, or that the problem
is simply too complex for man's finite intellectual capacities. . . ."[2]

In practice, however, these limitations are less severe than might be expected. To the decision maker who must make a choice, the utility of analytical results does not hinge on whether the results are "right" but rather on whether they are better than any alternatives. Decisions are made anyway on the basis of inadequate analysis, implicit or explicit, resting on incomplete or inaccurate statements of facts and faulty understandings of functional relationships. The analyst can be useful by improving the basis for choice, even though he cannot wholly resolve these problems.

The proper criterion, then, for the technical feasibility of analysis is one of "credibility" rather than correctness. Can the analyst's findings command sufficient confidence on the part of the decision maker to lead him to take them into account in his future actions? It follows that there are no absolute or objective measures, a priori, to judge whether a particular analysis can produce credible results. An analysis that inspires confidence in one administrator may be rejected completely by another. Moreover, the same administrator's attitude toward a particular analysis may change, depending upon the magnitude and implications of the decisions involved.

For his results to be credible, the analyst must first demonstrate an adequate grasp of the present status of the system under consideration. Otherwise, the decision maker cannot be sure that the analyst understands the problem or even that a problem exists. In addition, the analyst must comprehend the dynamics of the system; he must understand how the system will respond to changes in certain of its constitutents or in the environment in order to evaluate alternative policies or actions designed to deal with a given problem.

Almost every urban analysis must cope with inadequacies of data and an inability to deal systematically with the real complexities of urban systems. These factors limit the extent

to which the present state of the system can be understood
and its future behavior predicted. But the effects of these
limits vary according to the problem at hand. The limits
are less severe for analyses intended to produce tools, rather
than advice, for problems that can be treated as matters of
pure efficiency in technical and economic terms, and for
lower levels of systems scope. In other words, technical
limitations will tend to encourage the introduction of new
methods of urban analysis within the more modest bounds
of *operational analysis*, rather than through the conduct of
what we have defined as *systems analysis*.

Consider, for example, the introduction of new analytical
techniques in the New Jersey Housing Finance Agency, as
described in Chapter 4. The Agency's primary goal was "to
provide a great deal more housing primarily for low-income
and moderate-income groups, as quickly as possible. . . ."
The mandate given to Robert O'Block, the analyst, was very
broad: to use his skills in ways that would help achieve the
Agency's goal. O'Block began by working with Agency executives to define the "housing system" in New Jersey. As
O'Block's case study makes clear, that system is extremely
complex and its structure impossible to delineate. The supply
of low-rent housing, the Agency's prime concern, is affected
by myriad private interests and public agencies, by economic, social, and political forces, by varied local conditions
in numerous communities in the state, and by changes in
technology, national economic conditions, and other forces
beyond the control of any single state government. Although
a *study* of this complex system might have been feasible, a
more limited scope seemed necessary for any analysis that
could provide useful assistance to Agency executives in the
near term. The result was an operational analysis — judged
to be highly successful — that produced a computer program
for routine evaluation of the financial aspects of specific
projects proposed for Agency financing. Thus the very broad

initial parameters for analysis were limited in several ways. The objective was narrowed to one of creating an operational tool, the scope was narrowed to a financial subsystem and focused on single projects, and the definition of the problem limited to one of pure efficiency.

The experience of New York City's government in introducing analysis in recent years, as described in Chapter 3 by Carter Bales, also illustrates the effect of technical limitations on the feasibility of significant application of new approaches. In New York, the initiation of change in an agency was conditioned explicitly by the adequacy of its information system and expectations about the probable success in quantifying casual relationships between resources and results. The most cautious approach was taken and the least progress made in those agencies dealing with such concerns as education and human resources.

There is a further implication of this finding. In general, given the present state of the analyst's arts, the most useful results will be obtained in relation to systems whose central functions are technical and economic, rather than social and political. In the case of "hard" systems, like housing, or firefighting, for example, analysis defined within the bounds of available data and manageable complexity can still address a meaningful problem. This was so in the New Jersey case, just cited, and was also true in the analysis of firehouse location in East Lansing, Michigan (see Chapter 2). In East Lansing, given data about the structures in the city, the history of occurrences of fires, and travel times along a network of pathways in the city, the effects of alternative firehouse locations could be assessed. In "soft" fields such as manpower or education, where essential functions and relationships depend on human factors, the analyst often faces a dilemma: whether to concentrate on the tractable technical issues that are of low significance in relation to the overall system or to tackle the primary issues for which there is little chance that he can produce credible results. The analysts in Dayton, Ohio, chose the latter path, and failed.

In Dayton, as Chapter 2 describes, the subemployment analysis failed to uncover adequate information about the state of the system (particularly the subemployed population) or about the way it could be expected to respond to changes such as the initiation of new subemployment programs. It is understandable of course, that such "soft" systems are difficult for analysis. Efforts by governments to deal with them analytically are relatively new. But added effort and experience may not go very far toward alleviating the present difficulties. For example, when the prime concern of the analyst in a social system is a group that remains hidden or uncommunicative as a matter of conscious policy (for example, the "undercount" males in the subemployment study, or a criminal population), it may be virtually impossible to make an accurate assessment of the present state of the system. Similarly, if the effectiveness of a social program is heavily contingent on the idiosyncrasies of local conditions and participants, as seemed to be true of Dayton's CEP, the ability to predict its effectiveness may never improve very much.

Therefore, it can be said that almost every important issue facing an urban administrator contains elements that are beyond the grasp of the analyst who would help him resolve that issue. For some issues, largely those arising in connection with "hard" systems, credible *systems* analyses are still feasible because the analyst can focus on central factors for which data are available and the level of complexity is manageable. For other issues, where complexity is greater or data less reliable, credible outcomes can be attained only for *operational* analyses. But for many other issues — and particularly the "soft" systems of such great importance — even limitations of scope and purpose will not suffice to keep the requirements of analysis within the bounds of practicality.

Thus, in manpower, education, health, and selected fields, progress will be slow and disappointing to enthusiasts.

This finding may disappoint those who hope to find analytic "cures" for the "chaos" of the city, but it will not surprise those who have been dealing with the real problems of urban government. The recognition of limits to the applicability of present analystic tools, however, should not justify their rejection as useless. On the contrary, their effective use, within the bounds of technical feasibility, can be an important aid to government, as shown by the benefits realized in East Lansing, New York City, New Jersey HFA, and Columbia. To realize any benefits however, an urban administrator must forge an additional link so that the results of a credible analysis can be translated into effective action.

The link between analysis and action is provided by the *client for analysis*. Each analysis must address a particular client who is an actor in the situation being analyzed. In many cases he has provided the initiative to introduce analysis; in all cases, his active support will be needed to implement the recommendations of the analysis.

The client for analysis has a limited agenda and a set of priorities that evolve slowly. Thus, if analysis is to be relevant to him, it must, at a minimum, be able either to speak credibly to the issues that he considers important, or to lead him to revise his priorities. In financially autonomous organizations, a tool that can help assure the economic feasibility of a number of commitments has evident appeal to the chief executive. The Columbia Economic Model and the computer-based system in New Jersey thus were immediately attractive to Rouse and Seessel, respectively, and gained their continuing support. In East Lansing, the question of firehouse location was high on the city manager's agenda, while in New York an issue like sanitation began to rise among the Mayor's priorities because of political factors. The salience of all these issues, combined with the technical feasibility of analysis, contributed to the successes achieved. In Dayton, subemployment was a salient issue, but the kinds of guidance needed by decision makers could not be provided at the time they were needed because of technical limits in analysis.

Institutional Limits

Having gained his client's attention, the analyst may still fail to influence his actions. Despite the obvious relevance of explicit and objective evaluation of the costs and benefits of alternative policies and courses of action, the decision maker must also weigh the bureaucratic and political consequences of his actions. However credible and germane the results of analysis, they cannot be translated into action unless the client is capable of acting in the situation. *Institutional* forces limit both the client's propensity to act on the results of analysis and the effectiveness of his actions. How important are these forces?

The client's ability to effect change (and, by implication, that of analysis) is limited by those factors that limit his influence in an executive or political role. To understand those limits we must attend to the more general nature of the process by which individuals and organizations can introduce change in urban management.

How are the actions of urban governments determined? Obviously, that question has no simple answer. Some would argue that administrators and policy makers ought to deal "rationally" with the issues before them. Goals should be clarified, alternatives defined, costs and benefits compared, and the "best" plan "implemented." Indeed, the objective assessment of the technical aspects of issues does have an important role in many decisions. This is the role of analysis and the area in which new methods can contribute. But other factors must be taken into account in any attempt to understand the decision-making process.[3] As Graham Allison has demonstrated in an insightful analysis of the policy process in the federal government, there is an important organizational dimension as well. As Allison puts it:

> For some purposes, governmental behavior can be usefully summarized as choice of a unitary, rational decision-maker: centrally controlled, completely informed, and value maximizing. But this abstraction must not be allowed to conceal the fact that "governments" consist of a conglomerate of semifeudal, loosely allied organizations, each with a substantial life of its own. . . . governments perceive problems as organizations feel pinched.[4]

The definitions of issues and the data needed to develop rational policy choices are produced by organizational units whose goals, history, and inner workings color their outputs. Analysis is not something apart from these organizational processes; it is intertwined with and affected by them.

A government comprises numerous quasi-independent entities with specific responsibilities and limited powers. These organizational subunits develop unique perceptions of reality; define subgoals and recognize constraints in ways suitable to their narrowed roles; and employ a repertoire of routines to deal with their tasks. For example, a junk car abandoned on a street may properly be reported to "the city" as a problem. Whether and how it will be attended to will differ depending upon whether it is reported to the police, the traffic department, or the sanitation department. The contributions of those departments to analysis of alternative policies to deal with the existence of thousands of cars on the street will be similarly varied.

The sharing of power and the different perceptions of means and ends held by leaders within organizations necessitate that politics within the organization enter into the resolution of issues. This is a further limitation on the role of analysis. Although some would deplore it, few would deny that the resourcefulness and influence of particular advocates carry weight beyond the measure of the objective merits of the arguments they advance. Allison notes the relevance of "bureaucratic politics" on decisions:

> . . . the "leaders" who sit on top of organizations are not a monolithic group. Rather, each of the individuals in this group is, in his own right, a player in a central, competitive game. The name of the game is bureaucratic politics: bargaining along regularized circuits among players . . . who focus not on a single strategic issue but on many diverse [intragovernmental] problems as well, in terms of no consistent set of strategic goals and objectives but rather various conceptions of national, organizational, and personal goals, making government decisions not by rational choice but by the pulling and hauling that is politics.[5]

Almost all the actions of local governments impinge directly on some outside individuals and organizations. City politics thus comes into play, as those who are affected attempt to preserve their interests as an issue is resolved. Politics also helps to define the issues worth attention in a city. When the inadequacy of snow removal operations threatens to become an electoral issue, it reaches the Mayor's agenda, whatever its "objective" significance. Local governments provide essential services to a community, services whose operations should, in some views, be "free of political influence." But, as Banfield and Wilson put it: "Whether one likes it or not, politics, like sex, cannot be abolished." [6]

Some of the institutional limits to the effectiveness of urban analysis derive from these very fundamental forces: the dynamics of large organizations and the politics of cities. Yet it is part of the myth of organizations that decisions are made rationally. Except occasionally, when a blatant example of organizational myopia, bureaucratic maneuvering, or political pressure will surface, these forces are so subtle that they often go unnoticed, and it is considered bad form to acknowledge the influence of politics, even in government.[7] Thus, the myth survives, and advocates of analysis are led to speak of "implementing" the results of an analysis as if a simple executive mandate were all that was needed in most situations. To be sure, an executive within a hierarchical organization is presumed to have the authority to impose his will on subordinates. An urban administrator's ability to act in this mode is severely restricted, however, by the limited jurisdiction of executive authority in the complex institutional structure and process of urban government.

Within urban institutions, an administrator's authority is limited territorially, functionally, and organizationally. This can be illustrated by the problem of subemployment in Dayton. That problem might have been viewed most logically in terms of the entire metropolitan area, but the authority of the city manager did not extend to the suburbs. Moreover, by the nature of the Concentrated Employment and Model Cities Programs, his appointees directing those programs had jurisdiction over only a limited territory within the city. Similarly, although the educational function is clearly related to the subemployment problem, the city manager's jurisdiction did not extend to the schools. In large cities, the complexity of organizational structures within the municipal government may add further limits to action by departmental administrators. For example, in New York, the head of the Housing and Development Administration — a "super agency" — lacks authority over the city planning and public housing agencies.

Furthermore, even within the range of executive authority, there remain limits to its efficacy in introducing change.[8] Even within private enterprise, the ability of a senior executive to bring about change in the far reaches of a large organization is limited by the dynamics of the organizational process. Inertia is a fact of life, and established subunits will often cling to existing ways unless forcefully dislodged. Thus, fundamental change often requires that its initiators play the game of "organizational politics." These considerations apply to public bureaucracies, with a further complication. Almost any significant action by a city government affects some people so directly that it induces political opposition. So "city politics" becomes a factor, sometimes intertwined with power relationships within the organization.[9]

If the client for urban analysis is to be an initiator of important change, he must be able, almost invariably, to extend the influence of executive authority by political means. In some cases this may mean only an ability to play "organizational politics." In most cases, "city politics" must be added to the mix. In many instances, the scope of the relevant system should be viewed as extending beyond the limits of his executive jurisdiction, thus calling for the assumption of yet another kind of political role. We shall call this "system politics."

The nature of system politics can be defined in terms of Norton Long's notion of the city as an ecology of games.[10] For each aspect of city life — housing, employment, education, public safety — there is an established set of players, each having carved out a de facto role and each having some interests to protect. Some games are relatively simple, like those centered around municipal services, such as police or sanitation. These typically involve only an agency of the municipality and private citizens, usually represented through political clubs, neighborhood organizations and similar groups. Other games are crowded and complex, engaging many competing public and private interests, as is true for housing or transportation. To the extent that the progress of a game meets the interests of the most powerful players, change may be very difficult to introduce, no matter how poorly the "public interest" is being served. Changes which can be introduced within the existing structure of the game are likely to be more readily implemented than actions which envision a fundamental change in that structure, such as the introduction of a major new participant (e.g., community controlled school boards).

Although it is common to point to the deadening effect of institutional complexity on change, that is not the whole story. The players operate in relationships of mutual influence which also create certain opportunities for implementing change. Thus if a new entity, like the Housing Finance Agency (in Chapter 4) can establish itself in the game, it can begin to effect behavior of developers, federal agencies, and municipalities.

All this implies that analysis can be effective beyond the bounds of the client's formal jurisdiction. Even when it cannot be translated into directives for executive action, the results of analysis can form the basis for an influential position to be taken by a political actor. Although the Howard County commissioners retained the authority to control land development in Columbia, the astute political behavior and imaginative ideas of James Rouse brought about a revision of zoning ordinances and achieved for the Rouse Company a considerable degree of flexibility in development decisions. The New Jersey Housing Finance Agency's computer model has become a factor in its negotiations with independent parties — federal agencies, municipal agencies, and private developers. It has a subtle, but real effect on the actions of the other players. In New York City, although the existence of multiple political jurisdictions has an important impact on the city's ability to deal analytically with its major problems, a creative and forceful mayor is capable of influencing behavior beyond his own jurisdiction and thereby of expanding the impact of analysis done for and by the municipal government.

Interacting Limits

Finally, the political character of urban action, in the context of fragmented urban institutions, produces an interaction between technical and institutional limits. For example, jurisdictional definitions determine who controls access to the data for analysis. As the Dayton case points out, if an agency is dependent on other players in the game to provide necessary data, it must be careful about the actions taken as a consequence of analysis. Information is power; one cannot long continue both to threaten another player and to rely on him for data.

Conversely, technical aspects of the analysis may determine the feasibility of action based on its results. Consider the effects of variations in the definition of system scope. At the low end of the range, an operating subsystem usually will fall entirely within the jurisdiction of the client's executive role. Thus, an analysis limited to the jurisdiction of a Concentrated Employment Program or another defined in terms of police patrol operations can be more readily acted upon than similar analyses defined at a higher level in terms of the "natural" boundaries of subemployment or criminal justice systems. At higher levels action must deal with the "game" of "system politics" (as implied, for example, by the third alternative suggested by the analysts in Dayton).[11] This is likely to be more difficult than coping with the political effects within an organization or constituency of an executive change. While the analyst may feel that everyone "ought" to recognize the wisdom of his findings, rational arguments are of limited effect in situations of multiple goals and conflicting interests.[12]

The problems of inherent institutional complexity are aggravated if the scope of analysis is defined at a still higher level, for example, in terms of a problem such as "delinquency and unemployment." At that level of system scope, the analysis overlaps several "games" (schooling, police, employment). The analytical impulse to seek "total efficiency" by changing the bounds and structure of the existing games is commendable, but carries with it certain evident problems in implementation.

THE LIMITS OF ANALYSIS

In sum, although we can draw no final conclusion about the proper domain for innovation in analysis, it seems clear that that domain is limited to a considerable extent by the technical and institutional obstacles that are present in the urban setting. Both sets of obstacles may become less serious with time. It is inconceivable that we have reached the point where our ability to gather information about the state of social systems and to predict the consequences of actions taken to influence these systems cannot be improved. Indeed, if there is one common thing that the Dayton and New York City cases suggest, it is that progress along these paths is possible. Equally important, however, both studies suggest that the progress will be slow and difficult. The same can be said with regard to institutional obstacles. Regional cooperation on such problems as air and water pollution, transportation design, and education has begun; a number of core cities are pursuing active programs of annexation of surrounding communities. Both kinds of activity are eroding traditional jurisdictional boundaries and reestablishing them in such a way that stronger executive direction is possible over larger parts of the urban system. Similarly, there is considerable discussion of returning to the cities a greater measure of self-direction through such measures as the substitution of unrestricted block grants for the more traditional policy of federal support and control of specific programs in carefully delineated areas. Such changes are bound to proceed slowly, the more so since there is a countervailing trend toward the return of greater autonomy to communities within the major urban centers. We cannot hope to predict the final balance that will be struck between these opposing trends. We can simply conclude that the eventual domain for analysis will be in no small measure dependent on the pace of change that results from either trend.

Within the foreseeable future, innovation in analysis occurring in the urban environment will probably have to take place within the limits of present technical and institutional constraints. On the other hand, in aggregate the opportunities within that domain constitute a significant opportunity for useful change in urban management. At the same time that we note the force of existing limits, we must acknowledge the present nearly infinitesimal utilization of the potential that lies within those limits. The extent to which that potential is realized, and its boundaries pushed back, will depend, in part, upon the skill of urban governments in the management of innovation.

THE MANAGEMENT OF INNOVATION

Men bring about change. The use of modern methods of analysis in urban management will be shaped by the ways in which administrators and analysts carry out the recommendations of analysts. No autonomous process insures the adoption of new practices; men must provide the impetus for the use of new methods of analysis and guide the activities connected with their implementation. In each instance, urban administrators responsible for the introduction of new methods face a problem in the *management of innovation*. Those responsible for innovation in analysis must cope not only with the normal resistance of an organization faced by change but also with unique pressures implied by the technical and institutional constraints discussed above.

First, there is an inevitable tension between the capabilities of analysis and the needs of the client. The urban administrator wants timely advice on the most salient issues. The analyst, on the other hand, is very limited as to the kinds of problems he can deal with and the rate at which he can produce results. He will resist being put in a position where he must reach rapid conclusions on complex and poorly defined problems for which he has little valid and pertinent data. The tension thus created may be said to result from the *limits of analysis* in relation to the *demands of the client*.

A second set of tensions arises out of the limits on urban action and the demands of analytic "solutions." The analyst defines his role as one of identifying needs and opportunities, comparing the costs and benefits of alternative policies, and determining what "ought" to be done. But will the client *do* it? In a situation in which analysis can produce a conclusive result, the analyst will feel frustrated to find that the urban administrator cannot, or will not, act as he "should." Yet, as we have noted, the logic of analysis may produce a "solution" whose realization requires action beyond the scope of the client's jurisdiction or influence. Moreover, even when the administrator can act, it may not be in his interest to do so.[13] He will take into account the effects of the proposed action on the inner workings of his organization, its power in relation to others, and so forth. While the analyst exhorts him to exercise "leadership," the leader may be inclined to protect his constituency, preserving the sources of influence that energize his leadership.

The two sorts of tensions described above are at the root of the stereotyped views that analysts and public officials have come to believe about each other. Officials who resist analysis — and some who have been burned by experiments with it — will point out the analyst's propensity to work on the wrong questions, in the wrong way, and produce the wrong kind of answers. It is alleged that the analyst is insufficiently responsive to the decision-maker's needs and priorities, choosing problems because they are "interesting" or "tractable." Lacking a practical understanding of the operational details of a field, the analyst tends to take a "top down" approach, to seek "optimum" answers when anything "good" would suffice, and to overlook the inadequacies in the data on which his conclusions are based. Those who take this view will argue, furthermore, that the analyst's technical virtuosity seldom extends to consideration of the parameters of implementation. He does not utilize available feedback when proposals are implemented, and generally fails to couple his work effectively to the battlefield of urban action. Like every stereotype, this one has some basis in fact; each of the criticisms, no doubt, has been true in some cases.

The analyst, on the other hand, perceives the low level of effectiveness of most municipal programs and services and marvels at the resistance of responsible officials to advice that could produce improvement. The officials, somehow, cannot reach any clearcut decision. Policy is formulated diffusely — sometimes not at all. Decisions that are obviously going to lead to "improvement" are often reversed because of the parochial interests of some bureaucracy or the narrow interests of a pressure group. A consulting analyst, with considerable experience in one city, speaks of municipal employees as "imprisoned in a pervasive conventional wisdom that won't change."

To repeat briefly, innovation in analysis is blocked by conventional resistance to change, the inherent tensions related to changes in analysis for urban government, and the unfavorable perceptions that analysts and urban administrators have of each other. Yet, those blockages can be overcome if the effort is properly managed. What is needed is sufficient impetus for change and wise guidance of its course. Inadequacy on either count will probably mean that no practical results are attained, and probably will reinforce the stereotypes already discussed.

The Impetus for Change

In matters of organizational change, the sine qua non is leadership at the top. This is a common generalization about innovation in business corporations.[14] We find it equally true here; we know of no urban situations in which meaningful use of analysis has been possible without the visible and continuing support of the chief executive. In New York City, John Lindsay has identified himself closely with the introduction of PPB and analysis and has given consistent support to the efforts of Budget Director Frederick Hayes. In Columbia, James Rouse was instrumental in the creation of the work group and the Columbia Economic Model. Apgar's analysis shows that the use of analytic tools throughout the organization was conditioned by his interests. To the extent that Rouse demanded use of those tools — or subordinates viewed them as helpful in meeting goals that were important to Rouse — they took hold; lacking his interest and support, other innovations went unused. In New Jersey, the Executive Director, Tom Seessel, had a continuing personal involvement in the development of the computer model, in a setting in which Paul Ylvisaker's initiative in engaging the efforts of a university team had already signaled a commitment to seek and promote the application of new ideas and techniques.

Under what circumstances will the head of a government or agency provide the impetus for change? In general, the need for change seems to arise most strongly from change itself. Administrators in novel settings seem most likely to be receptive to experimentation with new modes of analysis. Both the Columbia Project and the New Jersey Housing

Finance Agency were new organizations, unfettered by established procedures and bureaucratic rigidities, relatively free of outside political pressures, and lacking useful precedents to guide their policies and operations. Each organization had a clear financial measure of success. In those cases, the situation itself tended to create a keener awareness of the need for analytic assistance and a greater opportunity to implement its results. It is also likely that administrators who commit themselves to so risky a situation are likely to have a greater tolerance for change.

Urban government is buffeted by cross currents tending toward greater centralization of some functions and decentralization of others. As noted earlier, there are pressures — and there have been some changes — leading to institutional and administrative reforms that would insure a metropolitan or regional perspective for important functions. Metropolitan governments, like Dade County's, and novel ventures like New York's statewide Urban Development Corporation are outgrowths of the desire to provide more appropriate structures within which policies can be formulated and implemented. A more general expression of this tendency, albeit with far less real impact on action so far, has been the emergence of metropolitan planning agencies, Councils of Governments, and the like. A stimulus to increased attention to planning on the metropolitan level has been the increasing pressure of the federal agencies, seeking to insure that their support for housing, manpower, and other local programs makes sense for the metropolitan area, and not just for the isolated municipality.

With the rise of participative politics in the 1960s has come a contrary pressure for decentralization, to return power to the neighborhoods. If Scarsdale can elect its own school board, why not Ocean Hill-Brownsville? Self-determination has become a rallying cry for the political leadership in many inner-city communities. Federal Community Action and Model Cities Programs, providing the form if not always the substance of participation, have raised expectations among the poor that they, too, can get a piece of the action.

Meanwhile, back at City Hall, and in the myriad centers and outposts of state and local government, the bureaucratic system — comprising, now, nearly 10 million men and women — continues to do business each day, pretty much as usual. The visions of reformers, whatever their stripe, ultimately confront the reality of the established system. The setting varies, and so do the outcomes, but the lesson is pretty much the same. Whether it is an attempt to consolidate police departments into a metro agency, or to decentralize an ossifying school bureaucracy, the interests of the staff become a major force in the essential political process.

Changes in the leadership and in the environment of cities may yet provide the impetus for change within the established entities of government. Innovation obviously is not an inevitable consequence of change or crisis. The annals of business, for example, offer ample testimony to the ability of an organization to cling tenaciously to old ways to the bitter end.[15] But, especially in large cities, changes in the environment make the gap between the resources available and what is expected of the city's leadership more serious every day. As one analyst commented: "When the rate of fire alarms triples in ten years, even firemen notice, and even firemen may come to feel that instinctive response, perfectly adequate in prior times, may no longer be adequate." The fiscal crisis of the cities is real to every mayor and budget director; in New York revenues have grown annually at a rate of 5% while costs rise at a 15% rate. The manager responsible for allocating resources under such conditions will inevitably grow skeptical of the demands emanating from the various agencies. Within the context of a PPB system, analysis grows attractive as a means of enforcing "objective" criteria on funding requests, restoring to the chief executive some measure of control over his "subordinates." [16]

The economic pressures for change are growing. As governments come to command a greater share of national resources and as their functions become increasingly visible and important to the citizenry at large, their shortcomings also gain in visibility. In 1929, one out of fourteen members of the civilian labor force was employed by government; by 1965 the ratio was one out of six; by 1975 it will be slightly less than one out of five. Almost all of the annual increase in public employment is now accounted for by state and local governments; the number of people in their payrolls, according to BLS projections, will have increased by 50% between 1966 and 1975, while manufacturing employment gains less than 3% and federal employment rises by 8%. To put it another way, according to these projections, more than one out of every four new jobs during the period 1966–75 will have occurred in state and local governments.[17]

Environmental stress, in other words, creates an opportunity. A leader who is so inclined may seize it to articulate a direction for change, using the evidence of troubled times to bolster his argument. Thus it is possible that recent developments in the cities may ease the way for future innovation in analysis. James Q. Wilson has suggested that the nation may be entering a new era in city politics.[18] The behavior of a "new breed" of mayors in the cities — Wilson cites John Lindsay as the archetype — now reflects fundamental shifts in the distribution of urban power. Wilson argues that to an increasing extent the Mayor's *audience* has become separate from his *constituency*. The audience has power, since it includes the media, federal officials who control an increasing share of the Mayor's discretionary funds, and the suburban elite, who dominate the city's power structure and may control the Mayor's chances of election to higher office.

The new breed has no easy time striving to meet the aggravated problems of the big city. The mayor is hampered by a decline in authority, the city is perpetually strapped for funds, and the bureaucracy yields grudgingly to direction from above. Yet both the aura and the substance of more modern methods of management and analysis can be of value to a man in that situation. To the extent that change leads to better use of limited resources or better performance by underperforming agencies, and to the extent that it solidifies his image as a "modern" man, innovation in analysis can meet his needs.

Guiding the Innovation

Given the impetus for change, the management of analysis will affect the degree of actual accomplishment. The first task is the definition of issues for analysis. In any organization, problems abound while resources for analysis are limited. Analysis must be focused, especially in its early days in the organization. The question is: on what? The choice of issues must reflect a balanced evaluation of their salience to the responsible administrators, the feasibility of producing credible analytical results, and the likelihood that useful results could be acted upon.

The definition of an issue implies a certain client for the analysis. Thus a second managerial task involves structuring the relationship between the analyst and the client. The cases repeatedly demonstrate that the efficacy of analysis is enhanced when it is conducted in an interactive mode in which analyst and client share in shaping its contents and direction. The least impact on action can be expected when the task is defined as producing a "report" to be delivered to a client who is expected to "implement" it. This occurs for two reasons. First, the client's perception of the validity of the results — the subjective component of their credibility —

is affected by his participation. More important, the analyst's understanding of the structure of the problem, the relevance of various aspects of it, and the feasibility of certain kinds of action are greatly enhanced by such interaction.

Given a problem and a client, the analyst still has considerable latitude for choice. The time horizon for his work (with its implications for the availability of data and the subtleties of analysis) and the choice of purpose and scope for the analysis are within the range of his discretion. For example, in East Lansing, a study of the "fire protection system" might have been defined to include such factors as methods of fire prevention or the varying human propensities to cause fire. No real progress could have been made on these questions with the information and time available. The scope of the study was narrowed to a subsystem of fire protection, and the analysis focused on an issue of considerable importance to the client: the location of fire stations. While "suboptimum," the results were of greater actual impact than those that could have been achieved by studying the "whole system."

Finding a focus for analysis that reconciles the limits of analytic capabilities and the needs of urban administrators is not as easy in practice as it may sound in principle. The administrator who is willing to work with an analyst is likely to press hard for definitive advice, on a fixed timetable, directed to the issues of greatest concern to him, which are likely to be those least amenable to the analyst's art. If the latter demurs, he risks giving the impression of sidestepping the "real problems," which leads naturally to a loss of interest on the part of the administrator. To accept the challenge is to risk reducing the potential contribution of analysis to zero, either because the results lack substance or are achieved after the important commitments have been made. In the Dayton case, the analysts yielded to what they perceived as a demand for advice on resource allocations and policy direction for the entire model city subemployment system. The unhappy result was a product of uncertain technical credibility, completed too late for use.

The successful introduction of analysis in a government requires both energy and guidance to overcome these obstacles. The energy is imparted by the initiation and support of the process by a man at the top: he energizes and sustains a process of organizational adaptation. His function is entrepreneurial; he perceives and articulates an opportunity and brings together the resources needed to exploit it. He must have sufficient influence within the organization to create an effective demand for analysis and to sustain its practice in the face of disinterest or opposition on the part of agency or departmental chiefs. The man fulfilling this role becomes a "champion" for innovation, in the sense that Donald Schon uses that term.[19]

But a champion is not enough. Although he may bring together the necessary resources, it is important that they be assembled in proper relation to each other and to the existing governmental organization in order to produce results. The process of change must be guided in a way that will resolve the several tensions and other obstacles in a manner that is appropriate in that time and place. No universal blueprint for analysis can be acquired to do this job; the effort in each setting must be managed on its own terms. Thus there is a role for a "manager of analysis." He is not simply the "head analyst"; more likely he may be a deputy to the mayor or city manager, or a budget director, or chief of an agency.

To be able to resolve the various tensions impinging on the direction of analysis, the manager must be perceived by the principals (analysts and clients) as qualified to participate in its direction. This requires a *balanced competence*. He must have sufficient grasp of the technical aspects of analysis to understand the limits of its feasibility in specific applications. He must also have sufficient understanding of administrative and political priorities to know what applications are worth undertaking. Furthermore, he must have a sensitivity to bureaucratic and political forces that might aid or impede action on an issue.

The task of the urban manager of analysis corresponds to that facing anyone in an integrative role in a situation comprising specialized competences, environmental uncertainty, and a certain degree of goal conflict. Lawrence and Lorsch, in their study of problems of differentiation and integration in business organizations, define the integrator's role in very similar terms.[20] Such men, they found, exhibited relatively balanced orientations and ways of thinking, in relation to those of specialists in research, marketing, or production, whose work they had to influence. Their influence with others tended to be based on competence or expertise, and they usually chose to resolve conflict by relatively open modes of confrontation. Furthermore, the effective integrators felt that they were rewarded — and they were perceived by others as being rewarded — on the basis of unified measures of organizational performance, rather than on the achievements of any part.

A Strategy for Innovation in Analysis

In some circumstances, analysis can be designed to provide significant advice for a specific nonrecurring decision of some consequence. This was the case in East Lansing, and was exemplified by several efforts in New York, such as the initiation of an air pollution abatement program. In other cases, the absence of such an opportunity does not mean that useful analysis cannot be done. It may be possible to develop analytic tools for continuing use in connection with recurrent decisions: as in Columbia's economic model or the financial analysis of applications for the NJHFA. Operational analysis, in other words, may also be of strategic significance to a senior administrator.

In some settings, however, isolated accomplishments are insufficient. What if the leader's goal is nothing less than a fundamental alteration in the spirit and methods of the government? One aim of the Lindsay/Hayes strategy in New York is said to be to effect a pervasive and lasting change in the structure, attitudes, and procedures of the main organizational entities. If this sort of long-term, broad-based change is sought, the management of analysis must be backed by a *strategy* for change and must be given force by the establishment of a permanent staff.

New York provides the only example, at present, of such a strategy in an American city. Because of its size and other unique characteristics, New York's experience probably cannot be reproduced elsewhere, but the principles on which its efforts have been based have wider relevance and are worth reviewing here. First, the Lindsay administration has created a demand for analysis as a part of the regular business of government. Although the record there shows few striking victories, there is solid evidence of progress on what Bales characterizes as "probably a 10-year Odyssey." Second, the unwavering nature of Lindsay's commitment is emphasized by the energies and resources mobilized for the task. At the core is a group of new analysts in the Budget Bureau and growing staffs in the agencies. For example, in the Housing and Development Administration a central research group that recently numbered six or seven was expanded to more than forty. The in-house staff provides a necessary coupling for the outside talents that have also been recruited. In addition to the work by McKinsey & Company, New York has made major use of the services of the Systems Development Corporation and several smaller private organizations and has contributed to the founding of the New York City — RAND Institute.[21]

Variety and managerial relevance have been the dominant characteristics of the strategy for analysis in New York. As Bales shows, there has been a deliberate effort to cover a wide range of agencies and problems, all the while seeking high-priority targets of opportunity and issues that had high payoff to the agency administrators. Peter Szanton, who heads the New York City — RAND Institute, has described how his organization has rapidly become engaged in studies that are enormously varied in purpose, intensity, significance, and method. As he describes them:

Some are quick operational analyses produced by one person over a two-week or three-week period: for example, an analysis of the varying number of telephone operators required to handle the shifting pattern of calls for police service. Others, like an analysis of the economic and demographic forces at work on the city's housing stock, have occupied four or five researchers for eighteen months. Some employ new technology, as did the experiments showing that the addition of long-chain polymers to the waterstream in a firehose could, without any change in pumping pressure, increase by more than half both the amount of water discharged and the distance the stream would travel on leaving the hose. Some attempt to extend the boundaries of an analytic art, such as the work which produced a mathematical model able to specify in detail how, at various points in Jamaica Bay, water quality is affected by polluting discharges of changing composition, timing, and location. Some merely establish basic information, like the analytic catalogue that describes in compatible terms the various housing programs at work in New York; or a count of how many patients seek mental health services within their own neighborhoods, and how many go elsewhere, and where. Some try to estimate the probable costs of future programs; others design new operating policies, such as a method of routinely augmenting the police patrol force during high-crime hours.[22]

The style, as well as the substance, of the work in New York has been significant. Again, Szanton's description reiterates the themes sounded by Bales. He emphasizes their concern, in adapting to the environment in New York, that they do so "in such a way as not only to be able to do research, but to enlarge the chances of it being useful."

By working at various levels, on varied issues, to develop basic understandings and immediate operational results, the New York effort holds the possibility of transforming the infrastructure of analysis and decision in the government.

Few other cities will be willing or able to mobilize hundreds of analysts and commit millions of dollars annually to their work. But meaningful efforts are possible on a smaller scale. Whatever its size, such a staff is likely to be effective only if it comes into the government supported by a champion at the top, motivated by a strategy that makes sense in the particular local circumstances, and guided by a manager of analysis[23] able to meet the demanding requirements of that task. To make use of their talents, the government will have to be able to develop a sensible strategy for analysis — one that suits particular local circumstances — and must be prepared to work toward a longer (3- to 5-year) time horizon. Whether this sort of commitment is likely to be worthwhile, and how the cities can be helped to raise the money, attract the talent, and develop the know-how to exploit it, are issues addressed in Chapter 7.

FOOTNOTES

CHAPTER 6

1. Chapter 1, p. 15.

2. Albert O. Hirschman and Charles E. Lindblom, "Economic Development, Research and Development, Policy Making: Some Converging Views," *Behavioral Science* (April, 1962).

3. For an excellent comprehensive survey, see Joseph L. Bower, "Descriptive Decision Theory from the 'Administrative' Viewpoint," Chapter 3 in *The Study of Policy Formation*, Raymond A. Bauer and Kenneth J. Gergen, Eds. (New York, The Free Press, 1968).

4. Graham T. Allison, "Conceptual Models and the Urban Missile Crisis: Rational Policy, Organization Process and Bureaucratic Politics" (RAND Corporation, P3919, August 1968), p. 15.

5. *Ibid.*

6. Edward C. Banfield and James Q. Wilson, *City Politics* (Cambridge, Harvard University Press and the M.I.T. Press, 1963), p. 20.

7. Thus, the New York City capital budget released shortly after Mayor Lindsay's reelection in 1969 was believed by the press to include a number of changes that were closely related to the pattern of votes for Mayor. Projects serving districts which had supported him gained new prominence, while those where he ran poorly lost facilities that had previously been planned. The suggestion that "political considerations" might have entered into these decisions was, of course, fervently denied by the Lindsay staff.

8. President John F. Kennedy became uncomfortably aware of the limits of the "chief executive's" control over the agencies of government. For example, Roger Hilsman reports that Kennedy ordered in August, 1962, that steps be taken immediately to remove American Jupiter missiles from their bases in Turkey. The State and Defense Departments, not entirely in sympathy with the President and his Secretary of Defense, responded slowly. According to Hilsman, the President was angry to find that no action had been taken when those bases became a key issue in the Cuban missile crisis that Fall. (*To Move a Nation*, New York, Doubleday, 1967, pp. 202–203.) Schlesinger comments that under an activist leader, the Presidency becomes a "fourth branch of government" (p. 680) and quotes Kennedy's wry remark that "The President can't administer a department, but at least he can be a stimulant" (p. 685, Arthur M. Schlesinger, Jr., *A Thousand Days*, Boston, Houghton Mifflin, 1965).

9. A senior career administrator may flout the will of an elected or politically appointed "superior" because of his concern for the maintenance or enhancement of his organization, or for the standards and ideology of a professional calling to which he gives first allegiance. If necessary, he will marshal outside political support, all the while accusing the Mayor or the Commissioner of "playing politics" with the public interest (cf. Banfield and Wilson, *op. cit.*, p. 218).

10. Norton E. Long, *The Polity* (Chicago, Rand McNally, 1962), Chapter 10, pp. 139–155.

11. See Chapter 2, p. 45.

12. This is related to a phenomenon observed in the relationship between client and analyst. The interactive mode is best; yet when analysis is used after the fact to "persuade" other players, it seldom is preceded by the kind of interaction that lends validity to the analysis and credibility to its results.

13. Although an oversimplification, there is truth to the notion that the analyst cares primarily about the method by which an action is evaluated, whereas the politician cares primarily about the nature of the action itself. It is said that an economist and a political chieftain were sitting together listening to a public speech by a Mayor, who commented that he thought it would snow tomorrow. The economist's first thought was to wonder whether or not that was true; the politician wondered why the Mayor said it.

14. See Donald A. Schon, *Technology and Change* (New York, Delacorte Press, 1967), pp. 125–133.

15. Witness the demise of the steam locomotive manufacturers.

16. The value of analysis as objective justification is illustrated also by the rather special circumstances in East Lansing.

17. U.S. Bureau of Labor Statistics, *Tomorrow's Manpower Needs*, Vol. IV, Bulletin No. 1606, February 1969, Appendix B (Washington, D.C.: U.S. Government Printing Office).

18. "The Mayors vs. the Cities," *The Public Interest*, No. 16, Summer 1969, pp. 25–37.

19. Schon, *Technology and Change.*

20. Paul R. Lawrence and Jay W. Lorsch, *Organization and Environment* (Boston, Harvard Business School, Division of Research, 1967), cf. pp. 124–127, p. 158.

21. An independent nonprofit organization founded in 1969 as a joint venture of the city and the RAND Corporation, the Institute is an outgrowth of the New York office opened by RAND in January 1968. By October 1969, with a staff of some 85 professional analysts, the Institute was engaged in nearly 50 separate studies for nine municipal agencies. The city pays approximately $2.5 million annually to support the Institute, thus providing more than 80% of its budget.

22. Peter L. Szanton, "Working with a City Government: RAND's Expe-

rience in New York," paper presented to National Academy of Engineering, Washington, D.C., October 22, 1969, p. 3.

23. By this we refer to the role discussed above, not to a formal position, such as that of "chief analyst." The "manager" must be able to perform the integrative function we have described, and must have the power to act.

CHAPTER 7

TAPPING THE POTENTIAL

THE METHODS BY WHICH urban governments develop policies and reach decisions are changing; they will continue to do so. Changes in the force and character of organizational, political, and analytic processes in decision making emerge and interact as the urban scene itself undergoes fundamental change. Organizational change is stimulated by changes in the tasks and shifts in the politics of local government. Formerly passive groups, such as the minority poor and public employees, organize and develop a new political clout; seemingly simple and minor public functions, like sanitation, grow in scale, complexity, and significance. Powerful external forces impact on local governments, sometimes retarding, at other times accelerating these changes. The big city mayor's job may be affected by such disparate events as an increase in interest rates, a Congressional mandate for "maximum feasible participation of the poor," or a fall in cotton support prices.

Changes in the role of analysis are but one thread in the matrix of ongoing change in urban management. There is a strong dynamic behind many of the other changes; these changes will continue whether or not urban managers choose to acknowledge them. Changes in analysis, on the other hand, are not "self-propelled" in the same way; they will not be introduced unless there is an explicit directive to do so. Un-

less the political and executive leadership in urban governments sees advantage in innovation in analysis, it will not
take place.

What potential advantage does innovation in analysis
offer to the urban executive? How much effort should a local
government make to introduce new methods of analysis?
Should others emulate the very sizable commitment of New
York City? Should the national government be concerned
about the fact that few local governments are making a comparable commitment to innovation in analysis?

In specific instances, as shown in the East Lansing case,
analysis may lead to important cost savings or enhanced
levels of performance. Greater efficiency, in any task, is not
to be taken lightly, especially in view of the perilous fiscal
condition of most local governments. Doing a better job can
also earn political dividends, as the performance of urban
functions becomes increasingly of concern to the electorate.
More generally, as governments become bigger and their
work more complicated, public executives are likely to seek
increasing "rationalization" of methods and controls. Even
the appearance of more modern management may provide
political benefits to a mayor or commissioner.

But abstract rationalizations, such as the desirability of
"modernity," are insufficient to sway local executives when
significant costs are involved. From the viewpoint of the
local decision maker, while better analysis may seem like a
good thing, it may not be good enough to warrant the commitment of time, energy, and money needed to achieve it.

In the first place, the fiscal crisis endemic to local government engenders an understandable caution about new commitments. While government funds have always seemed
extremely limited to those who administer them, the gap between needs and resources in our cities is especially great at
present and promises to increase in the decade of the 1970s.
One can argue that the rationalization of operations and a

critical examination of policy should become increasingly desirable as pressures build up for increased performance and greater efficiency. But as a practical matter, when discretionary funds are at a premium, opportunities that offer an absolute gain may be discarded in favor of even more attractive competing uses, or in favor of no action at all.

A commitment to analysis, moreover, implies a significant risk. There is a real chance of failure arising, in part, from the differential expectations and capabilities on each side of the relationship between analyst and client. While an effective entrepreneur can help resolve those tensions by the way he arranges for the management of analysis, he cannot eliminate the risk of failure. The cost of a failure, furthermore, can be greater than just the dollar amount involved; in the political arena other penalties may be incurred as well.

Even if the "success" of analysis could be taken for granted, an objective evaluation of its worth would remain difficult to obtain. Reasonable men may disagree, even well after the fact, about the real nature of the consequences of an analysis, the dollar value of any benefit, or the likely course that events would have taken had there been no analysis. These uncertainties in evaluation are, of course, many times greater when the question has to be considered before the fact. Thus, any assessment of the economic returns to analysis, intended to justify such an undertaking, is inevitably an arguable one. A fair presentation of costs and benefits must be hedged about with considerable uncertainty.

For a new piece of cost-saving machinery, specific economic returns can be demonstrated to justify the initial resource expenditure; utilization of the "intellectual technology" of analysis can rarely be so justified. While general arguments can be offered to justify new commitments to analysis in urban government, in any given situation a valid and objective justification for any particular analytic undertaking can rarely be developed. Even though the consequences of such a commitment may often be interpreted in dollars and cents terms, the decision itself, given the present state of the art, more often than not boils down to "a matter of faith."

Reasonable and knowledgeable men will continue, no doubt, to disagree about the degree of commitment that local governments should make to bring about innovation in analysis. Some degree of modernization will occur as a matter of course in most organizations. For example, new entrants to planning and administrative ranks often bring with them the skills and disposition to employ new methods. But the kind of change illustrated by our case studies demands a commitment beyond that underlying more gradual change. And the importance of making such a commitment within local government remains open to question.

Scholars are divided on the issues. Some are optimistic about the possibility of systems analysis for social decisions; others are pessimistic.[1] We can provide no conclusive evidence for either side of such a debate. Our purpose was a different one: to document some early experiences with innovation in analysis at the local level in order to illuminate the limits and potential contribution of new ways, to suggest methods and strategies by which their potential value might be realized, and to provide a record of experience against which more abstract arguments could be evaluated. We hoped that even a limited record of experience could suggest a few simple truths and, perhaps, contribute to the demise of some unhelpful myths.

The evidence does demonstrate that, in particular instances, analysis can yield benefits worth many times its cost. The examples from East Lansing and the New Jersey Housing Finance Agency illustrate the possibilities. While it is difficult to produce a specific measure of the benefits received by New York for its large investment, it is clear that a number of specific analyses, particularly in housing, environmental quality, and the uniformed services, have produced worthwhile returns. We see little reason to doubt that many comparable opportunities for highly productive ventures in analysis exist in other metropolitan areas across the country.

On the other hand, the available evidence suggests that the most reliable payoff lies outside the areas of highest priority to urban executives and political leaders. The analyst's ability to produce credible results diminishes as he confronts broader or "softer" systems. Moreover, his client's ability to take action diminishes as the analyst's conclusions extend beyond the geographic, bureaucratic, or political boundaries of the client's influence. The factors which impose these limits are deeply rooted in the nature of urban problems, and there is no easy path to development of the analytic competence that will make it possible to overcome them. The principal opportunities to expand the uses of analysis seem to lie in operational analysis of well-structured functions or in systems analysis applied to issues in which social factors are not of central importance. Meanwhile, it is welfare reform, educational enrichment, and economic development, rather than fire engine and police car dispatching or garbage truck routing, that are of greatest salience to those whose commitment is needed to increase the level of effort for analysis.

Thus, the advocate of urban analysis is caught in a bind. To capture the attention of prospective clients he may yield to the temptation to overstate currently realizable capabilities, offering "a cure for chaos," or to oversimplify the effort needed to realize this cure. While the intent is understandable, the practice is ultimately self-defeating. Innovation in analysis is subject to the harsh test of reality, and word gets around. Attempts to overreach the limits of analysis, or failure to make appropriate arrangements for the management of analysis, will lead to failures that will tend to discourage further efforts.

It is not necessary to exaggerate the contribution of analysis in order to justify a greater effort in local governments. A limited opportunity may be substantial by absolute standards. Because of the large scale of local government operations, taken in the aggregate, minor increases in efficiency or effectiveness would represent sizable gains for the nation. Expenditures by local government were $64 billion in 1968. While education is the largest single activity, accounting for nearly half of expenditures, the remaining $34 billion is still of great consequence. Municipalities alone spent $18 billion in 1968 on functions other than education. Police, fire, and sanitation expenditures by cities amounted to $5¾ billion that year.[2] Annual expenditures by local governments will begin to exceed $100 billion early in the 1970s.[3] If an additional $100 million were spent annually on analysis by cities, the expenditure would be more than repaid by an improvement of a fraction of 1% in the cost or output of their operations.

Some skeptics are concerned that a government's commitment to innovation in analysis would detract from efforts to cope with pressing issues that are not presently susceptible to extensive analysis. This need not be so. The expenditures required for a program of analysis certainly do not measurably detract from the resources available for these other needs. The sums needed to support programs in welfare, education, employment, or housing are many times greater than can be invested in analysis, even if done on a comparatively large scale. In 1970, reallocation of New York's $8 million expenditure for analysis, for example, could hardly have been noticed in the context of its $8 billion budget. The argument, in fact, runs the other way. The dollar savings which should result from effective use of new analytic capabilities could begin to augment the resources available for those programs.

Others are concerned about the impact that analysis may have if it *is* directed toward "critical" social problems. They see two dangers. First, analysis may tend to postpone action when decisive steps are urgently needed. To be sure, analysts need time to probe the structure and function of social systems in order to develop understandings of currently obscure interrelationships, and to acquire the means for measuring both status and change within these systems. They cannot provide administrators with advice and guidance regarding the design and selection of alternative courses of action until this initial research has been performed. Yet, taking *some* action now may often be more important than taking more *rational* action later. Indeed, the potential effectiveness of later action may rest on whether or not some earlier ameliorative effort was undertaken. To the extent, then, that a carefully phased program of analysis is either the reason or the excuse for the postponement of rapid response to urgent crises, analysis is likely to prove painfully counterproductive.

The second danger stems from the possibility that analysis may cause a short-sighted approach to the formulation of social policy. It is often said that one attribute of a good analyst is the capability to suggest and evaluate new and imaginative alternatives for action. On the other hand, the analyst relies heavily on his ability to compare and justify alternatives on the basis of criteria that are measurable and that have firm objective foundations. At best, this concern with quantification is bound to constrict his ability to be the catalyst behind radical departures in social programs and policies. The more innovative the program or policy, the less he will be able to be "analytic." At worst, it may leave him impotent to do anything more than to reexamine or embellish old approaches.

Like the benefits of analysis, the dangers outlined above are, perhaps, implicit in the new tools. But their occurrence is not inevitable. The opportunity for innovation in analysis cannot be subjected to a generalized evaluation; it is inherently neither good nor bad. The extent to which innovation will yield either benefits or disadvantages depends upon the social system in which it takes place and not on the technological basis alone. To say that greater effort for analysis is desirable, then, is not to imply that it is a panacea, nor that all attempts to increase the effort will be successful (or have been). But it can be said that realistic expectations of improvement can be fulfilled if prudent attention is paid to the management of analysis.

Promoting Innovation in Analysis

What are the prospects for a significant increase in the use of analysis in local governments? History shows that the widespread diffusion of technological innovation among numerous autonomous potential adopters, such as business firms, households, or farmers, may take an extended period of time, even when the economic benefits of adoption are significant and when the principal criterion of relevance to the adopter is economic.[4] The "need" for urban analysis is, of course, widely distributed throughout the country, rather than centralized. Its costs are very real, while its benefits are more difficult to specify, and the potential adopters, i.e., municipalities and other public or quasi-public agencies, are essentially political entities for whom economic calculations are seldom the whole answer to a problem of resource allocation. Widespread adoption of new approaches to urban analysis will occur only when mayors, commissioners, city managers, and other urban executives are prepared to make the necessary commitment of resources for analysis.

So far, few local governments have shown themselves ready to commit more of their resources to analysis as a function. We have tried to show that their failure to do so on any significant scale may be quite justifiable. The apparent economic justifications for investment in analysis are offset by the necessary fiscal conservatism of local executives and by the inevitable uncertainty and subjectivity in an assessment of the payoff from the investment. Thus, while there may be a need for analysis, there is no effective demand. That is, there are few "customers" able and willing to spend the money necessary to meet that need.

Stimulation of demand is the first step toward realization of the potential value of analysis for local government. The economic deterrents to local demand can be offset by economic incentives. For example, subsidies provided by state or federal governments could encourage greater resource commitments by local governments. But, financial incentives are not sufficient to bring about the utilization of new technological possibilities. To be sure, they can promote expenditures for that purpose. As federal aid to education has convincingly demonstrated, categorical aid programs can bring about sizable expenditures by local units for the conduct of studies and the acquisition of hardware. But, financial aid, per se, does not assure that studies will lead to action or that hardware will be used.[5] Innovation in an "intellectual" technology cannot be readily introduced by commissioning studies by outsiders and "implementing" their results. As the case studies demonstrate, analysis cannot be introduced as simply as a city might commission the design of a novel incinerator and contract for its installation. A more subtle process of change is implied.

The essence of the new technology for analysis is embodied in people, rather than in objective methods or tangible equipment. Innovation in analysis results from the introduction to an organization of new skills, acquired by bringing in new people and educating existing staff. This also means that innovation in analysis — to a greater extent, perhaps, than innovation in hardware — will affect the functions of an organization and its relationship with its environment in many ways, not all of which are predictable, and some of which may not be desirable. Change will occur to the extent that people in the organization begin to think and act differently about problems and issues. The acquisition of new skills will cost money, thus governments must make additional resources available for analysis. The full utilization of those skills will require the development of a relevant strategy for analysis and the assignment (to an appropriate executive)[6] of responsibility for management of that strategy.

The key variable determining the adoption of innovation in analysis will be the deployment of people. As P.M.S. Blackett advised the British government in 1941:

> In general, one might conclude that relatively too much scientific effort has been expended hitherto in the production of new devices and too little in the proper use of what we have got. Thus, there is a strong general case for moving many of the best scientists from the technical establishments to the operational Commands, at any rate for a time. If, and when, they return to technical work, they will be often much more useful by reason of their new knowledge of real operational needs.[7]

The operational commands for the urban battlefield are to be found in the city halls of this nation. Circumstances in which large numbers of scientifically trained personnel can work in continuing relationship to the executives in those "commands" will help more than anything else to bring about the utilization of new approaches to urban analysis.

Two tasks are implied: First, to insure the buildup and maintenance of a flow of resources sufficient to support the work of many analysts newly engaged in urban issues. Second, to design organizations that will employ these analysts and the funding system that will support them in such a way that meaningful utilization of their services is likely to ensue.

How can these tasks be accomplished in the near future

in the United States? To answer this question, it will be useful to be able to employ specific terms for the magnitudes of both expenditures and employment. Our discussion will assume an aggregate national expenditure of $100 million annually. Some readers may feel that this is too modest an aspiration; others, no doubt, will feel that we are too ambitious. We do not claim to know what level of effort would be "best"; our purpose here is to define a specific attainable goal in order to simplify and clarify subsequent discussion of the steps necessary to attain any increase in the role of analysis. We believe that the main considerations will be valid across a wide range of possible increases in effort.

To be practical, a specific goal should be small enough to be attainable and large enough to make a difference. The proposed level of effort is *large* enough to represent a significant departure from the status quo and to reach enough governments to affect the lives of a majority of the population. On the other hand, the goal is *small* enough not to strain the availability of skilled personnel and funds for their work, and not to exceed a level at which the probable economic returns from analysis would readily repay its cost.

If a $100 million expenditure were to be taken as a target to be reached, on a national basis, over four years, it would mean that by 1975 the full-time work of some 2,000 professionals would be directed to the analysis of issues confronting local governments.[8] If assistance were limited to the 100 largest metropolitan areas, and if the effort were distributed among areas on a per capita basis, $100 million would support the work of four analysts in a metropolitan area the size of Lancaster, Pennsylvania (in 1967, the 100th in size, pop. 300,000), and as many as 120 in metropolitan Chicago.[9] In 1975, the dollar cost per capita in each of these areas, would be less than that expended by New York City (from its own resources) in 1970.[10]

The employment of 2,000 analysts in 100 metropolitan

areas would represent a fivefold to tenfold increase, in manpower terms, over the present nationwide level of effort for analysis within urban governments[11] and a much greater increase in the number of urban jurisdictions affected by the analysts' work. By providing for at least four full-time professionals in the smallest areas, and considerably larger commitments in most areas, this standard permits the attainment of a "critical mass" and the continuity of effort necessary to have an impact on the administrative process. It also would have sufficient breadth to have a national impact.

Granting that such a program would be large enough, are the men and money available, and is their use for this purpose desirable? We have already discussed the arguments for and against significant expansion of analytic efforts for local government. A national program on the scale under discussion, i.e., $100 million, would certainly be within the bounds of the limited commitment we find justified. As noted above, it will amount to a fraction of 1% of the relevant annual expenditures of local governments.

The availability of skilled personnel and the ability of local governments to bid for their services are the most significant factors determining the feasibility of a $100 million program. The manpower should be readily available, although it appears that local governments currently have relatively few persons with relevant skills and may have difficulty hiring a great many more.

It is difficult to assess the magnitude of efforts presently devoted to analysis in urban governments, and even more difficult to identify specific sources of skilled manpower to augment these efforts.[12] Analysis is a function, not an occupation or a single discipline; those now performing the function have been trained or employed as engineers, administrators, planners, and so forth. However, there are some indirect measures of the size of the relevant manpower pool and of the fraction employed by local government. Thus, it can be noted that scientifically trained personnel in general are substantially underrepresented in the ranks of those employed by local government. For example, in 1968 about one in 45 professionals in the quantitative sciences was employed by state and local governments in work other than teaching,[13] a fraction roughly one-third the proportion of all wage and salary workers employed by those governments (exclusive of educational functions).[14] Systems analysts are also underrepresented in local government. In an analysis of the number of systems analysts employed in all sectors of the economy, Robert Krueger of the Planning Research Corporation concluded that there were approximately 18,000 in the United States in 1967.[15] His estimate was based on a functional definition of analysis consistent with the one used in this study.[16] Even if Krueger's result were a moderate over-estimate for 1967 (in the context of his analysis a very large error seems unlikely), normal growth would mean that by 1975 the total number of systems analysts ought to be at least 20,000 and the supply of quantitative scientists three times that number. To plan for a reallocation of manpower so that 2,000 of them might be occupied with the problems of local government seems a modest objective.

How should those 2,000 people be employed? They need not all work in City Hall; it is possible to have many professional analysts occupied by the analysis of local issues while few are employed directly by local governments. Institutes, consulting firms, and other private organizations providing services by contract could, conceivably, supply the skilled manpower that would be needed by many governments.

To what extent should governments employ analysts within their organizations, as opposed to purchasing analytical services from other organizations? Local governments will face substantial difficulty if they attempt to meet all their needs for analytical skills by direct employment. Private organizations are better able to compete for talented people and can more readily provide a professional milieu for their work. A pilot study of the employment of planning and administrative personnel in five cities, published in 1969 by the Bureau of Labor Statistics, illustrates the problem.[17] All five cities reported difficulty in hiring such personnel. Among the specific obstacles cited were low salaries, lack of clear promotion opportunities, low prestige, civil service impediments, residency requirements, and lengthy delays in reaching hiring decisions. Differentials in salaries can be substantial (even though starting salaries are being made competitive now in some places). A recent comparison of salaries for scientists shows that those employed in the federal government, nonprofit institutions, and business firms commonly earn one-third more than those employed in local government. (See Table 7-I.)

TABLE 7-I

SCIENTISTS' MEDIAN SALARIES, 1968

Type of Employer	All Degree Levels		Doctorate
	All fields	Mathematics	Mathematics
Nonprofit Organizations*	14,700	18,000	20,000
Business and Industry	14,700	16,800	19,600
Federal Government	13,500	15,300	19,500
Other Government	11,200	13,100	15,000

* Excludes educational institutions.

SOURCE: *American Science Manpower 1968*, Appendix Table A-14.

New York, of course, has succeeded in building up a staff of analysts and a nucleus of executives drawn, in many cases, from outside municipal government. The Lindsay administration has been deliberately eclectic, seeking men and women of diverse training and experience. The élan of the administration, the pioneering atmosphere engendered by Frederick Hayes, and the unique challenge of New York have probably helped in the task of recruitment. Since those factors will be hard to reproduce in most other settings, many cities will have to draw upon the services of outside institutions.

In addition to its advantages in recruiting staff, an independent institute or similar organization can attain important economies of scale. It can build up a critical mass of professionals, provide them with continuity of employment, and establish better linkages to universities and other sources of fundamental knowledge. For example, a group highly competent in fire department operations could be supported by an institute serving many governments within a region, while most municipalities would be hard-pressed to sustain even one professional in that field. Such a group would be more visible to other professionals engaged in applied research and would be better able to devote some of its own effort to work lacking in immediate payoff. In serving a particular city, furthermore, it would have a broader background of experience and could serve as a channel for transfer of operational information between cities.

On the other hand, a staff of analysts *within* government enjoys a decisive advantage with respect to two characteristics that are important in insuring the effective utilization of analysis. The analysts can gain a greater familiarity with the informal mechanisms of government in the particular setting and can provide continuity of attention to a problem over an extended period of time, and even beyond the conclusion of the period of analysis, per se. Both abilities can increase the analysts' opportunity to bring about appropriate action. In addition, an in-house group can become keenly aware of the priorities given to various issues, the feasibility of action on those issues, and the identity of those people whose commitment is likely to be essential to action. An internal staff may not do better analysis, but it is better structured to bring analysis to bear on the actions of govern-

ment.[18] Any sizable government intending to build a larger
role for analysis will find it necessary, then, to build a small
in-house staff of analysts and to develop the skills needed by
executives who will be working with them as well as drawing on outside sources of expertise.

So far, our discussion of a national program for urban
analysis has been couched in very general terms. We have
argued for a much greater effort overall, but have not specified how that effort should be financed or precisely where
the analysts should be employed. A detailed specification of
those matters would be beyond the scope of this book. But
a statement of general goals and criteria for program design
can be offered. It is implicit in the foregoing discussion that
any program of financial assistance and institutional development should:

1. Attract into government and related organizations a substantially greater number of talented specialists.
2. Provide market-like controls of the allocation of analytical
   efforts, so that the energies of analysts are directed toward
   areas of high payoff to local government.
3. Facilitate a process of mutual adaptation and learning, so that
   both the intrinsic capabilities of analytical tools and the capacity for social utilization are enlarged over time.

The major share of the financial support, at least for the
first decade, should come from the federal government.
Federal oversight can help bring about a coherent national
system for urban analysis in a way that would facilitate the
transfer of knowledge and experience between states and
regions. State and local governments should share in the
cost of developing this system and should be prepared to
assume its operational costs at some time in the future.

The direction of the analysts' work should remain securely

in the hands of the local government. We have argued that successful utilization seldom results unless the local organization follows an appropriate strategy for analysis and has an effective manager to oversee it. These are unlikely to occur if control of resources rests outside the local government. Thus, whatever their source, funds should flow to a substantial degree through the local executive. Unless an expenditure makes sense to him, it probably will not be useful.

A federal program of financial support should be designed to meet two other needs. First, it must provide impetus to and guidelines for the establishment of local and regional institutes for urban analysis.[19] Second, through the mechanism of these institutes, with the assistance of universities and similar organizations, it should provide a stimulus to the education of local government executives in the management and utilization of analysis.

In summary, to expand the role of analysis in urban government, administrators must engage many more analysts in the issues confronting those governments and create within the governments conditions necessary to the effective utilization of analysis. The underlying notion, then, is that the transfer of people is the most effective means to accomplish the transfer of technology to the urban sector. To do this successfully within any locality it is necessary to:

1. Increase the *level* and choose carefully the *allocation* of effort; i.e., augment the amount of money and manpower invested in analysis and develop a strategy for their distribution among various problem areas, organizational units, and tasks.
2. Establish a *capacity for social utilization* of analysis, i.e., improve the abilities of local organizations to manage and sustain the work of analysts so that the analysts can realize the intrinsic capabilities of their tools and so that the organizations can comprehend, assimilate, and act on their conclusions.

Epilogue

We have argued that the intrinsic capability of analytical methods, i.e., the extent to which analysts are capable now of producing meaningful results on significant issues, is sufficient to justify a much higher level of effort. We expect that an increase in the level of activity will also lead over time to enhancement of those intrinsic capabilities. Employment of substantial numbers of analysts should set in motion a process of mutual adaptation in which the organizations' capability to use analysis will grow, as budgetary systems and organization structures are realigned and data bases accumulated, and as the capabilities of the analysts and their tools are refined and adapted through a continuing process of application and review. The extent to which this actually occurs will depend, to a great degree, on developing new relationships between the professional analysts and the executives who will be their clients. Both will have to learn from the experience if analysis is to be effective. Lacking theory, urban analysts will have to build their generalizations primarily on induction from experience. Lacking simple pathways to implementation of results, analysts will have to conduct their work in continuing interaction with executive clients and with due regard for idiosyncrasies of local situations.

Thus we have conceived of the task as being one of changing the managerial competence of local government rather than one of introducing a specific technology. Industry began a managerial revolution more than a century ago. Local government is becoming too important to be left to unchanging bureaucracy. It is our hope that the kinds of changes suggested here in only the most general outline, if put into effect, could create the spark for a comparable revolution in government. What is needed is a process of calculated incrementalism, leading hopefully to a process of change which will be self-sustaining. It would be presumptuous at this point to pretend to forecast the final results of such development.

FOOTNOTES

CHAPTER 7

1. See, for example, the review of research on "Technology and Governing," in *Technology and the Polity*, Research Review No. 4, Program on Technology and Society, Summer 1969, especially pp. 44–52.

2. U.S. Bureau of the Census, *Statistical Abstract of the United States: 1970* (91st Edition, Washington, D.C., 1970), Tables 607 and 625. Significant opportunities for the analyst are to be found in police, fire, sewerage, and sanitation operations, which, in 1969, accounted for 39% of municipal employment, exclusive of education, in medium and large cities (those greater than 50,000 population). (1970 Stat. Abs. Table No. 637.)

3. Most projections assume that the rate of growth of state and local government expenditures will decline from the peak rates of the early 1960s. There is disagreement as to the extent of that decline. See "Revenue Sharing and Its Alternatives: What Future for Fiscal Federalism," Volume III, prepared for the Subcommittee on Fiscal Policy, Joint Economics Committee of the Congress, July 1967.

4. See Everett Rogers, *The Diffusion of Innovation* (New York, The Free Press, 1962); and Edwin Mansfield, *The Economics of Technological Change* (New York, W. W. Norton & Co., 1968), Chapter IV.

5. See, for example, Anthony G. Oettinger, *Run, Computer, Run* (Cambridge, Harvard University Press, 1969), and especially Appendix A: "A Visit to a Small City."

6. See discussion of the management of analysis in Chapter 6, above.

7. P.M.S. Blackett, *Studies of War* (New York, Hill and Wang, 1962), p. 176.

8. Assuming an average support cost (salaries, nonprofessional assistance, expenses, etc.) of $50,000 per professional man-year.

9. To illustrate this further, Tulsa would have 8, Atlanta 25 and Boston 55. Based on projected population in 1975, from the U.S. Bureau of the Census, *Pocket Data Book, U.S.A. 1969*, Table 9.

10. The 100 largest metropolitan areas contained 56% of the U.S. population in 1966; if they hold that share in 1975, they will include 120 million persons out of the projected national population of 214 million. The indicated expenditure for analysis would amount to 85¢ per capita; New York City's expenditure was approximately $1 per capita in 1970.

11. See manpower discussion below.

12. A pilot study of the employment of planning and administration personnel in five cities, published in 1969 by the Bureau of Labor Statistics, illustrates the difficulty of obtaining more precise estimates of current employment in this function. That study encompassed several hundred professional, administrative, and technical job titles, ranging from engineering technicians and planning assistants to city manager and commissioner. These were condensed into 40 occupational groups, one of which was called "systems analyst." That occupation, as defined by the BLS, however, describes a data processing or "systems and procedures" expert, and not someone who would perform the function of analysis as we have defined it. *Planning and Administration Personnel in Local Governments: A Pilot Study,* Bureau of Labor Statistics Bulletin No. 1631 (Washington, D.C., Government Printing Office, June 1969).

13. National Science Foundation, *American Science Manpower 1968,* NSF 69–38, December 1969 (USGPO). Appendix A. Table 9A. Data are drawn from the National Register of Scientific and Technical Personnel, which is intended to be inclusive of all professionals in the specified technical fields currently engaged in professional activity. We have aggregated data for mathematics, computer sciences, statistics, and economics under the term "quantitative sciences." For 1968 the register records 45,000 professionals having at least a bachelor's degree and some professional experience in those fields. Of these, 1,003 were employed in work other than teaching and by governments other than the federal government.

14. U.S. Bureau of Labor Statistics, *Tomorrow's Manpower Needs,* Bulletin No. 1606, February 1969 (USGPO), Appendix B. The data are for wage and salary workers in nonagricultural employment.

15. Krueger's estimate indicates that in 1967 an almost negligible fraction of systems analysts were engaged in the problems of local government. Only 250 were thought to be employed by all governments other than the federal government. In contrast an estimated 11,000 were employed by business firms and there were 1,620 systems analysts employed in 1967 in six defense-related, nonprofit corporations. Both the Aerospace Corporation and the RAND Corporation employed more systems analysts (350 and 400 respectively) than the estimate for all state and local governments in the nation. See statement prepared for the Special Senate Subcommittee on the Utilization of Scientific Manpower in *Scientific Manpower Utilization,* 1967, *Hearings,* printed for the Senate Committee on Labor and Public Welfare, Washington, D.C., Government Printing Office, 1967, pp. 289–297.

16. Krueger defined "systems analysts" as: those scientists and engineers who are concerned with a search for preferred designs of systems by logical comparison of a variety of combinations and uses of the equipment, personnel, and procedures that comprise the alternative systems. The systems analysis includes the investigation necessary to determine the criteria by which the system may be judged. The functions of these systems analysts include:

Identifying functional and operational performance requirements for new systems from analyses of defined goals, objectives, policies, and potential operational environments.

Synthesizing alternative systems and operational concepts capable of meeting the identified systems requirements.

Analyzing the alternative systems and operations to provide the decision with comparative data on the consequences, benefits, and penalties associated with the implementation of each alternative.

Deriving and evaluating initial design requirements for the preferred system to provide basic systems engineering criteria for subsystem performance selection.

17. BLS Bulletin #1631, *Planning and Administration Personnel in Local Governments*.

18. Unlike some later exponents of operations research, P.M.S. Blackett, a British scientist who was intimately involved in early applications of operational research to military affairs in World War II, places great emphasis on the need for a close and continuing relationship between executives and operational research specialists. In an internal memorandum written in 1941 he stated, for example, "An operational research section should be an integral part of a Command and should work in the closest cooperation with the various departments at the Command." (P. M. S. Blackett, *Studies of War*, New York, Hill and Wang, 1962, p. 175. See also his article, "The Scope of Operational Research," *Operational Research Quarterly*, Volume 1, No. 1, March 1950, reprinted in *Studies of War*, pp. 199–204.)

19. The New York City—RAND Institute is, in our view, an appropriate model for such organizations. Most, however, should be designed to serve a multicity region rather than a single municipality or metropolitan area.

APPENDIX

APPENDIX

Analyzing Urban Problems[1]

ANALYSIS IS THE WEIGHTY WORD for the thinking process that every man uses in every decision he makes — although more often than not he makes his decision without consciously analyzing the problem. For most problems, explicit analysis is unnecessary. For most urban problems, which by their nature are difficult and complex, the search for solutions, for adequate policy, for adequate programs is so crucial that anything short of careful, thorough, and systematic analysis must be considered totally inadequate.

That analysis is often ignored in the process of reaching many important urban government decisions testifies to a widespread misunderstanding of both the value and the workings of analysis. We do not argue the value of analysis applied to urban problems in this paper.[2] Our concern is with the misunderstanding of how analysis works and with the inability of most bureaucrats to work with analytical tools. Though often viewed as an esoteric

---

[1] This Appendix describes a methodological approach to the analysis of urban issues. It was written by Carter Bales and Edward Massey of McKinsey & Co., based on their experiences in New York City, as described in Chapter 3 of this book.

[2] For the reader relatively new to the task of applying analysis to urban problems, *Public Administration Review*, March/April 1969, devoted its entire issue to a reexamination of PPBS, but with a latitude that included much good argument over analysis.

rite performed only by initiates or as a mechanistic, inhuman way of approaching a problem, analysis is neither of these. Never intended, much less able, to replace the judgment required of a good decision maker, the purpose of analysis is to help the decision maker formulate and then sharpen his judgment. Stated more analytically, its purpose is to explicitly identify and, where possible, adequately quantify the objectives sought, the alternatives available, and the cost and the effectiveness of each alternative.

While analysis is not a difficult process, it does require understanding of the concepts and training in the techniques used in analysis. When Frederick O'R. Hayes, the director of the Bureau of the Budget for New York City, began to introduce analysis of problems as a basis for making important budgetary decisions, the need to work with analysis comfortably, quickly, and pragmatically led to the discovery of a further need: the need for helpful, succinct ways to develop, sharpen, or refresh analytical skills. Yet job demands left little time for classroom training sessions; and in the available reading material, the analytical method was neither worked out completely enough nor stated simply enough to help the person sitting behind a desk who needed quickly to learn more about formal analysis.

Our concern for the development of analytical method at all levels of municipal government led us to write this paper.[3] While this treatment remains far from exhaustive, it does follow the analytical process, step by step, from beginning to end by explaining a number of techniques that have proved useful to others. Our goal is nevertheless ambitious: We want to help working city employees, within the context of their already harried and full days, to learn to use analysis and, perhaps more important, to be comfortable with its use.

---

[3] An earlier version of the paper was distributed as part of the yearly instruction concerning planning, programming, budgeting systems development from the Bureau of the Budget, City of New York, to the various agencies.

THE ANALYTICAL PROCESS

The analytical process is a simple 4-stage approach in which the analyst's task is to:

Stage 1: *Define the problem* precisely enough to provide a framework, a structure, for the analysis.

Stage 2: *Develop a statement of objectives* to show what the solution must do and ways to measure the objectives to show how nearly the various alternatives achieve what they must.

Stage 3: *Develop alternative actions* to achieve the objectives.

Stage 4: *Evaluate the alternatives and make recommendations* in terms of how effectively each alternative meets the performance objectives and how much each will cost.

Although formal analysis requires explicit consideration of each of the four stages, no two analyses are the same. Lack of time and insufficient staff resources often dictate that an analysis be "quick and dirty" rather than lengthy and comprehensive. Also, the effort, time, and resources devoted to each stage within any particular analysis cannot be assigned by rule of thumb, but must be tailored to the problem under study:

Some problems require the greatest effort in *defining objectives*. Normally, these problems have never been tackled before, largely because old policies and old shibboleths have kept decision makers from thinking in terms of exactly what results should be achieved. Once objectives are determined, the rest of the analysis often follows quite easily.

Some problems require most effort in *developing alternative solutions*. If the problem has been studied before and objectives are clearly established, then the major part of the work has to be devoted to coming up with fresh approaches.

Some problems require heaviest concentration on the *evaluation of alternatives*. The difficulty here is that methods for projecting and measuring the results of possible actions may be lacking.

And even when projecting and measuring alternatives proves easy, any two alternatives are apt to perform differently against any two objectives.

Stage 1:
Defining the Problem

Only the most successful analysts have sufficient respect for problem definition. Most analysts, regardless of experience, get off to a bad start by defining the problem too hastily — perhaps because the problem seems so obvious and simple. Later on, they are likely to discover that much of their time was wasted in racing down blind alleys.

Although it varies from problem to problem, the analyst with a good healthy respect for problem definition will devote as much as one-quarter of his effort to this stage. Good problem definition saves time because it sharpens understanding, improves perspective, and points toward a broad outline that helps determine what to include in and exclude from the work that remains. Thus, the main function of problem definition is to develop sufficient understanding of the "real" problem to provide a beacon for all later work. We found the following steps helpful in achieving this substantive precision and breadth:

Identify the Specific "Need" to Be Satisfied and Indicate its Magnitude.

Identifying the kind and amount of goods or services required takes the analyst to the core of the problem. It forces him to go beyond general propositions like "we need better housing." The specific need, say, for "standard quality renter housing units" might be to "replace those that will be demolished or withdrawn from the market"; or it might be to "replace those units that are deteriorated or deteriorating." The question of magnitude or "universe-of-need" requires asking how widespread the need is now and how large it is likely to become in the future. For example, "16,500 housing units per year are currently demolished or removed from the market. We have no indication that future loss will be any less."

Isolate the Causes of, or Major Contributors, to, the Problem.

This is by far the most difficult and time-consuming task in defining a problem. Its importance lies in helping the analyst distinguish between symptoms and the problem itself, as well as providing him with a general idea of what broad changes may be required. For example, a drop in the supply of housing is usually blamed on unavailability of financing. To stop here in defining the problem is to focus on a potentially false symptom and to omit examination of very important contributors like the availability of sites or the possibility that costs are rising faster than incomes.

Identify the Specific Population Group Most Affected.

Few programs are really aimed at the entire general public; rather they are directed to specific groups that are identifiable by geography, income, race, age, or special need.

The following brief definition of a problem demonstrates the usefulness of the above steps:

The Board of Education is legally responsible for providing kindergarten classes for all eligible children, with special emphasis placed on reaching children in poverty areas. During the last school year, approximately 95,000 children were accommodated. The estimated total number of eligible children is 150,000 (universe of need), leaving a gap of about 55,000 children not served by the existing program. Of these 55,000, approximately one-half are located in poverty areas (population group affected). Primarily, the gap is the result of limited facilities, although even if they were adequate, we have only enough teachers to accommodate 35,000 more children (major contributors to problem). The Board's goals during the budget year are to advance toward the long-term objective of accommodating all eligible children as rapidly as available facilities permit and to give priority attention to poverty areas.

After defining the substance of the problem, one usually has gained enough understanding to attempt to "presolve" it. Presolving often saves time and energy by helping the analyst refine the framework, thereby building more direction into his analysis. However, presolved problems are not solved problems. The analyst must guard against the danger of becoming so enamored of his initial solution that he is unable to revise his thinking as new facts come to light.

The presolving process simply involves jotting down first impressions, as hypotheses, about possible ways (i.e., alternatives) to solve the problem. These hypotheses become the analyst's first attempt, however broad, to look at the course of the entire analysis. Even hastily developed hypothetical alternatives will require the analyst to make some tentative, rough statements about appropriate objectives (these can be used in the next stage as starting points for the task of establishing clear and explicit objectives). Because this effort is designed only to point the way to selective fact-gathering and analysis, the analyst should not worry about the number of "ifs" he has to use. Consider the following hypotheses that might be used in attempting to "presolve" the problem of too few kindergarten classes for the number of eligible children.

> Even *if* we could secure funding for all facilities required, we would probably have land, labor, and scheduling constraints that would make it impossible to produce the needed facilities within, say, 5 years. *If* we are producing facilities less rapidly than other cities, we could probably develop a "facilities delivery system" to acquire land more systematically and coordinate and schedule the production more rationally. However, *if* "delivery" is at the core of the problem, a workable system will probably still not have any appreciable effect for the next 2 or 3 years, so short-term hypotheses will be required. *If* physical problems are solved, we may still have a labor (teacher) problem, which will probably require a program to recruit, train, and place more teachers, let's say 10 percent a year more, than we presently can.

Short-term hypotheses are:

- Extra shifts can be added in some districts.
- Temporary facilities can be found, especially in poverty areas.

- Class size can be increased in some districts, either where the average class size is lower than the city average or where the average absenteeism is higher than the city average.

Although he will automatically hypothesize conditions or opportunities that he believes true, the analyst could just as fruitfully hypothesize the opposite, for the hypotheses are used to guide his work, to be proved or disproved and in that way to construct the true picture in a mosaic of collected-as-needed facts.

Stage 2:
Stating Objectives and
Evaluation Criteria

From problem definition, the analyst moves on to a description of the end to be achieved — both what it is (objectives) and what tests will tell him that it has been achieved (evaluation criteria).

Stating Objectives

Initially, to set tentative objectives, the analyst searches his own experience, knowledge, and attitudes, and talks with decision makers, experts, other analysts or anyone connected with the problem. How the objectives will be reached can be determined later and should not be confused with the objectives themselves. To provide a certain supply of housing, for example, is an objective that can be set before one considers how to achieve the supply — e.g., the mix between building new or renovating old buildings.

From the beginning, the analyst should state whatever objectives he can in terms of tangible results: 10,000 more living units, 6 fewer pupils per teacher, 10 percent less refuse accumulation in the streets. For those objectives not easily and not reliably quantified (increased reading comprehension for 8 to 14 year olds might be one), the analyst defines the qualitative objectives as precisely as possible.

To go beyond tentative to specific, tight objectives, the analyst can:

State goals in relation to the universe of need. Level of program output is stated in absolute numbers or as the percentage increase necessary to provide the good or service to all eligible recipients.

Isolate the factors that limit the agency's ability to satisfy the need. Some of these, such as interest rate for financing housing, are totally outside the agency's control. Others, say level of funding, might be partially responsive to the agency's influence. Constraints beyond, or even only partially beyond, the agency's control set limits on what is "doable." Although frustrating, they must be worked within.

Consider the degree of past progress. Look at historical program output in relation to the universe of need and ask these two questions: "Have we ever come close?" and "Why not?" The answers may shed light on the agency's administrative ability to carry out a program as well as turn up other constraints not found earlier.

Often the scope of the problem is so broad that the analyst can identify many specific objectives that a solution should achieve. Most of these are likely to be compatible, but some may conflict or compete with each other. While the following hypothetical objectives, which relate to the preschool education problem, are compatible under most circumstances, conflicts could arise.

Objectives

1. Upgrade quality of preschool education.
   a. Reduce average class size 25 percent to achieve optimum load.
   b. Hire teachers who have at least certain minimum skills.
2. Obtain additional facilities to handle 5,000 children this year.
3. Start 5-year building program for additional preschool centers.
4. Fully utilize existing preschool classroom facilities.

Objective 1 is ostensibly compatible with all other objectives, while 1.a may conflict with 2. and 4., because reducing class size may create need for facilities to handle 6,250 more children (5,000 known, plus 1,250 extra children, owing to 25 percent reduction) or reduced classes may not fully utilize existing preschool classroom facilities. Objective 2 is compatible with 1.b unless the Board needs so many teachers that the skills requirement must be waived.

The existence of conflicting objectives should not greatly concern us because most city agencies develop policies within an implicit or explicit hierarchy of objectives. If conflicts do arise, the agency's priorities will help determine which objective should be satisfied and in what sequence, although the analyst's task may be complicated by the need to review the agency's priorities with decision makers as he tries to define objectives. Priorities should be carefully examined each year (sometimes more often) because they may have been set in response to a situation that has since changed. Budgetary constraints, provisions of the law, the administration's commitments, all are subject to change, which then affects priorities, and sometimes vice-versa.

Establishing Evaluation Criteria

While defining objectives, the analyst actually works back and forth between the statement of the objectives and the measurement scales or criteria that allow him to determine the degree to which each alternative meets the objectives. Most urban decision makers think in terms of four broad criteria: (1) How effective will the alternative be in reaching the objectives (i.e., solve the problem)? (2) How much will it cost? (3) How long will it take to bring results? (4) How likely is it that the chosen alternative can be implemented?

The first major criterion, the effectiveness of the program in meeting each objective, requires the analyst to decide both what to measure and how to quantify the measure. He must also recognize that an effectiveness measure is not a theoretical monkey bar, not a place to do intellectual exercises. It will aid the analysis only if it is real, only if the decision maker accepts it as a good basis for taking action. To insure that effectiveness meas-

ures will be useful to the decision maker, we have found it helpful, at some early stage, to discuss the choice of measures with
him. The three listed below are ranked in order of the decision
maker's normal preference:

1. *Use the direct measure,* when possible, by reducing the objective
   to its basic unit of measurement. Direct measures are normally obvious, e.g., the measure for housing construction would be the
   number of housing units constructed. If there are no direct measures, consider alternative 2.
2. *Measure the effect on the causes of the problem.* The objective
   is to improve the quality of the air. However, we may not be able
   to test the air's pollution directly because of the cost of such tests.
   Since we must somehow rid the air of dirt and noxious gases to
   achieve our objective, performance could be measured in terms of
   the effluents emitted (e.g., tons of soot or cubic feet of sulphur
   dioxide) rather than pollutant concentration. If this is impossible,
   consider a third kind of measure.
3. *Develop a proxy measurement.* Proxy measures are used for the
   most difficult objectives, such as seeking to increase family stability,
   where measures may be known (number of divorces, illegitimate
   children, etc.) but determinants are likely unknown or undocu-
   mented. Also, some objectives can only be measured by proxy
   even though the causes of the problem are known and measurable.
   In comparing fire-protection alternatives, since we cannot measure the prevented loss directly, we assume that loss is proportional
   to the time it takes fire-fighting equipment to reach the fire and
   measure that instead.

Measurement of cost, the second criterion, is easily understood.
The physical use of resources (i.e., personnel and equipment required over time) can generally be related to dollar cost quite
simply. However, it is sometimes difficult to know what are the
relevant costs that should be charged (and what are the irrelevant
costs that should not be charged) to an alternative. In figuring out
the cost of an alternative, six basic guidelines are helpful:

Separate capital expenditures from expenses. The one-time cost
for goods with value or use to the agency extending beyond a
single year (e.g., buildings and equipment) is not comparable

to the cost, usually recurring, for goods and services whose value or use does not extend beyond a single year. (The only way to make them comparable is to consider the pattern of the cost over time, using a discounting technique which is not discussed in this paper.) A further difference between capital and expense funds is that, in some cities, they are provided from different budgets.

Identify both direct and indirect expenses in deriving total cost. All significant costs that might affect the choice of alternatives must be included. Consider indirect and supporting costs (staff support, fringe benefits, maintenance) as well as obvious direct costs (line personnel, trucks, offices) where a reasonable basis exists for allocation.

Omit "sunk" costs. Although direct and indirect cost should be identified and charged to the program, costs that have already occurred should not be allocated. These sunk costs are omitted because they have already been paid and accounted for and cannot be recovered. In this respect, analysis differs from strict cost accounting. For example, if a new sanitation program required 10 trucks, 3 of which would be purchased and 7 of which would be transferred from other uses where they required no replacement, the 7 transferred trucks represent a "sunk" cost and should not initially be included in the program's cost.

Consider future funds commitments in a multiyear projection in cases where current municipal activities that have resource requirements and revenue availabilities in future years are expected to change. These changes should be charted to obtain a full picture of an alternative's cost commitment.

Indicate sources of funds that will be used to pay for alternatives. A program's total cost may be paid out of several identifiable sources — i.e., tax levy, state, federal, capital or private; some of these sources may be more restricted or more expensive than others.

Show private cost as well as public cost where applicable. Most programs have some private costs that should be shown — e.g., the cost to the builder resulting from a change in building codes or to the factory from changes in pollution-control laws. Technically, these costs do not affect the city budget; but since the true cost of an alternative is met by both public and private funds, the importance attached to these private costs is one of the key judgments that have to be made in the final stage of the analysis.

Evaluating alternative solutions based on the two criteria of cost and effectiveness taken together yield the concept of cost/effectiveness analysis. Thus, cost/effectiveness analysis is merely a method for trying to achieve either of the following:

Maximum results for given cost: Given a cost constraint of $200,-000, Alternative 1 can provide 1,000 spaces for preschool children, 70 percent of them in poverty areas; Alternative 2 can provide 1,100 spaces, 65 percent of them in poverty areas.

Minimum cost for given results: Given an objective of processing the city's 4 million income tax returns, to contract out for the service (Alternative 1) will cost $1.4 million, and to do it ourselves (Alternative 2) will cost $1.2 million in expense funds and $0.3 million in capital costs for required new facilities.

Two other criteria, time and feasibility, are used in evaluating alternatives. Time is most often considered as it affects the total cost of the program. But it should be remembered, also, that alternatives fulfill the need at varying rates. Some produce a lower total level of results at an earlier point in time, while others produce a higher total level of results later. And if we believe that the same level of results achieved next year is not as valuable as the same level of results achieved this year, time affects the total effectiveness of the program.

A surprisingly common mistake, especially in analyzing capital projects, is to consider time only in terms of how long it takes to implement the project. Actually, the analyst should be concerned with three time factors: (1) the time required to implement the decision, (2) the time required to bring the first results, and (3) the time required to achieve the objectives.

Feasibility is the final general criterion used in evaluating alternatives. Even though an alternative may meet all other criteria, the actions required to change a recommended alternative from a paper exercise in analysis to a physical reality may not be possible or acceptable. Feasibility boils down to: "Can I get the action required?" Usually, some form of action is required at various levels within an agency, from the top administrator to the personnel in the field. Also, feasibility changes over time; what was possible last year may be impossible today because of political ramifications. And, what is impossible today may be done next year.

To test for feasibility, the analyst has to ask several questions: Who has to say "yes"? What does it take to get agreement? What if the answer is "no"? How can we overcome or design around a "no"? Can we muster the necessary broad support? By asking these questions, the analyst tries to protect himself from naïve recommendations as well as to ferret out possible blockages so that if necessary he can devise ways to overcome them.

Stage 3:
Generating Alternatives

By now, the analyst has a reasonably complete picture of what he wants to achieve. He knows what the problem is, what the objectives are, and in what ways he will measure the performance of the various alternatives against objectives. Even though he has not yet tried to make use of it, he is likely to know quite a bit about what it will take to get an acceptable solution.

The next stage, generating alternatives, is the creative core of the analytical process. It is hard work, requiring effort, imagination and leg-work. It also requires breaking the shackles of pattern and habit that burden one's thinking. All too often the analyst who has worked for a long time in a given area finds it particularly difficult to come up with fresh ideas. His intimate knowledge of current methods tends to blind him to more innovative alternatives.

Because criticism interferes with the creative process, the analyst should concentrate on creating or generating alternatives in this stage and leave the critical task of screening and evaluation until later.

By definition, every decision situation presents at least two alternatives; most have many more. But how does the analyst generate them? He looks for ideas. The best way to look for ideas is to talk with operating personnel, other analysts, experts, bosses. In general, he should talk with the same people he talked to about objectives and perhaps at the same time. A very efficient way of generating alternatives is to meet with a knowledgeable group and record all the ideas that come out of a two-hour or three-hour session.[4] Another good place to find ideas is reference sources. What have other cities done about the problem? What do the professional journals say? What is the latest theory? What did the city try to do 5 years ago? What ideas have been considered in the past and rejected without analysis?

The analyst may also get ideas by searching for ways to affect cost criteria. Some of these are:

Investigate cost-savings economies. Opportunities to reduce cost exist even when the output level is fixed by external factors, e.g., the number of income-tax returns filed. Such alternatives are particularly important with a tight expense budget. Specific possibilities include:

- Using labor-saving capital investments that can reduce both total costs and, to an even greater extent, expense budget costs. Automatic elevators, larger sanitation trucks requiring fewer trips to transfer stations, computers, and automatic office machinery are all good examples.
- Reducing indirect costs. If these costs have not been reexamined recently, they may offer the analyst possible alternatives. Overall ratios should be examined first — e.g., is total number of men per total number of trucks the same in each firehouse and how do these figures compare with the overall department? Does the department maintain a higher ratio than its most efficient firehouses?
- Contracting out for goods and services. It may be more economical to contract out for goods or services — e.g., battery manu-

---

[4] In a brainstorming session, participants defer criticism and evaluation of ideas to encourage freewheeling thinking. The more ideas, the better the session, and "wild" ideas are sought in order to increase the probability of uncovering creative ideas. Later in the session, further ideas are generated by combining and improving the ideas already before the group.

facturing or paint mixing — than have the agency itself provide them.

Examine alternatives to city financing. Are there opportunities to increase federal, state, or private participation? Can user charges or fees be employed? Example:

During a recent year, the use of an optional federal welfare formula, the transfer of certain operations from family court to probation, and several other similar moves provided an additional $25 million in state and federal aid for the city.

Examine opportunities to fund activities out of capital appropriations, rather than tax levy funds. This can be done where consistent with the provisions of the city's local finance law. For instance, in some cities, books for grammar and high schools can be paid for out of capital appropriation funds even though they are not capital projects.

Consider alternatives to direct city operation such as might be created by regulatory measures, tax incentives, and other approaches. Example:

Waste collection from nonprofit institutions such as voluntary hospitals now costs an estimated $X million annually. City service could be discontinued since it is not required by law and, under the requirements of the sanitary code, the institutions would have to make other arrangements for the disposal of their refuse. This approach could provide the resources necessary to extend the manual sweeping program to Y additional miles of street.

Generating alternatives by focusing on effectiveness, as opposed to cost, is much more difficult, but a few techniques have proved helpful.

Examine trade-offs between quality and quantity of service. Example:

An increase from 25 children to 30 children in the maximum kindergarten class size, where facilities permit and where there are eligible youngsters not currently served, would add an estimated 6,300 spaces at negligible additional cost. On the other hand, this increase may be undesirable in terms of program quality. Average class size is already 25 percent over the maximum level suggested by recent research as appropriate for effective child development. Moreover, only 700 of the spaces would be in poverty areas.

Look for ways to eliminate unnecessary tasks or simplify needlessly complex routines. The analyst is not an efficiency expert, but if he feels that different methods could prove more effective, he should look into them. Especially in problems that have important time elements, like construction delays, the reduction of unnecessary tasks is important. One of the most useful ways to ferret out the unnecessary and needlessly complex is to develop a simplified but complete flow of the entire process (like the process of applying for welfare), noting how much time, how many participants, what activities, and what motives are involved from beginning to end. The analyst then seeks to simplify or streamline the process.

Look for more efficient deployment of existing resources. If work load is heaviest or reaches a peak in a few hours per day or days per week, the service offered can generally be improved by rescheduling.

Examine new technologies and radically different systems for achieving long-term objectives. Some examples would be: the substitution of electronic surveillance systems and automatic alarm equipment for a small increase in the number of regular police patrol; disposable packaging as a means of cutting back on waste disposal needs; Methodone clinics to deter criminal behavior resulting from the need for drugs.

Stage 4:
Evaluating Alternatives and
Developing Recommendations

The analyst's final analytical task is to develop recommendations based on an evaluation of the alternatives he has generated.

Our experience with analysis in the City of New York suggests that it is very hard for people to evaluate alternatives objectively when they are convinced at the outset that the current way of doing things is the best way. Even analysts themselves — who should be open minded, objective, and critical — often reject out of hand all but the most common and tired alternatives. To combat this all-too-human tendency, every alternative should be given a thorough preliminary examination in light of the criteria discussed earlier. Early rejects should be discussed and the reasons for rejection documented in the write-up supporting the recommendations. Obviously, the alternatives that are carried through the full evaluation stage should be treated objectively and thoroughly. After all, the existence of a problem in itself indicates that present policies or practices leave room for improvement.

Evaluation involves two normally quite easy and straightforward steps: (1) projecting forward each alternative's probable performance against each criterion, and (2) comparing the alternatives with each other on the basis of performance against criteria.

Projecting Probable Performance

To project each alternative's probable performance against each criterion, the analyst generally needs to use nothing more than straight arithmetic calculations tied in with some obvious judgments. More complex alternatives may require equations from basic algebra or other branches of mathematics. Very few will call for a computer model since such models are generally built because of the need for manipulating vast quantities of data, not because of the complexity of the problem. For example, in analyzing housing programs, a computer model often proves helpful because up to 7,000 variables and combinations of variables are affected by program changes.

When the analyst has trouble making these calculations, he can usually trace his difficulties back to one of two sources. Either he does not know what the cause-and-effect relationship is (e.g., will increased welfare payments really insure adequate care for the child?); or he does not know how the cause-and-effect relationship works (e.g., how much can we reduce the number of robberies if we double the size of the police force?). When faced with this, he has to find better data or better assumptions, not better formulas.

Projections require a consideration of time. Primarily, the analyst looks at time only as it affects cost. Less complex, but perhaps more important, is consideration of time as expressed in the question "How many years will we be committed to this policy?" Cost aside, future-year commitments to present programs require explicit consideration of future sources of funds (to see if the city can pay for the program) and future objectives and priorities (to see whether the city should pursue this program as intensively some years out).

Before comparing alternatives, the analyst should explicitly identify major uncertainties in his analysis. Uncertainty is to be expected in any realistic analysis since final proof of any alternative's cost/effectiveness lies only in future performance, and projected costs and results most of the time have to be based on inadequate data, inadequate experience, and inadequate knowledge. The fact that analysis does not treat uncertainty — and inadequate data — in traditional ways to some extent accounts for the opposition to it still found in urban government. Some managers will try to ignore or rationalize away the problem of uncertainty rather than face it squarely.

The rational and proved way of handling uncertainty is for the analyst to make explicit assumptions. Assumptions are best guesses based on what is known. Thus, they allow gaps in the data to be filled in temporarily. Because these assumptions are visible, they can later be challenged.

Once the analyst has finished his first evaluation of an alternative, he may test the importance of any assumption he made by means of a "sensitivity analysis." To do this, he first alters the assumption by some reasonable amount — say 5 percent to 50 percent — normally determined by asking, "If I'm wrong, how far off am I likely to be?" Second, he uses exactly the same calculations and judgments he used before. Third, he compares the new projection of the alternative with the original projection. Finally, he compares the change of projected results with the change of assumptions. Thus, he finds out how sensitive the performance of the alternative is to the assumption he has made.

He goes through this process with each major assumption he has used and for all likely values of the assumption.

Because the analyst has automatically made the original assumption as close to reality as he possibly can, he will normally find that a change in the assumption brings a much smaller change in output, as the following illustration shows:

The need for new housing units to shelter families that will form in the decade of the 1970s has been estimated as follows:

	1970	1980	Net change
Population	7,810,000	7,850,000	40,000
Household size	2.66	2.45	(0.21)
Number of households	2,940,000	3,200,000	260,000

1. If population change is wrong by 100 percent, i.e., net change of 80,000 or zero, number-of-households change is overstated or understated 0.5 percent, i.e., 16,300.
2. If household-size change is wrong by 50 percent, i.e., 0.105 persons per household, number-of-households change is overstated or understated 46 percent, i.e., 120,000.
   The household-size estimate must be justified because it is very sensitive.

Comparing Alternatives

After developing projections, the analyst's next step is to compare all of the alternatives to each other on the basis of how well they perform against the criteria. In many analyses, one alternative clearly outperforms all others, thus making the recommendations simple. However, when the analyst is faced with two or three alternatives with similar performance, comparison requires more effort. In the no-clear-choice situation, the analyst should examine the "trade-offs" he will have to make in recommending one alternative over another. The most common usage of the term trade-offs is in decision situations where Alternative 1 fulfills Objective A better than Alternative 2, but Alternative 2 fulfills Objective B better. Viewed schematically:

	Objective A	*Objective B*
Alternative 1	High	Low
Alternative 2	Low	High

Trade-off analysis in this situation requires first a reexamination of all objectives and priorities. If no changes in priorities are acceptable, the analyst examines the ramifications and foregone results (known as opportunity costs) of choosing one alternative over others. Following are four trade-offs likely to arise:

Cost versus effectiveness. Alternative 1 costs less, while Alternative 2 is more effective. For example, one pollution-control alternative employs baffles or cyclones, both of which are low cost and about 50 percent effective; another alternative employs higher-cost precipitators or scrubbers that are 70 to 90 percent effective.

Effectiveness versus effectiveness. Both alternatives meet the cost objective, but differ in ability to meet multiple effectiveness objectives. Consider the following hypothetical fire truck:

Alternative	*Cost Objective* ($120,000)	*Objective 1* (Capacity to transport at least 12 men)	*Objective 2* (Respond in 60 seconds)
Model A	118,000	10 men	50 seconds
Model B	118,000	14 men	70 seconds

Quality versus quantity. Alternative 1 produces more direct results than Alternative 2, but at a lower quality. For example, larger class sizes at the expense of lower reading scores.

Short term versus long term. Alternative 1 is effective immediately, but cannot remain effective as long as Alternative 2, which does not become effective for a year. The decision becomes more difficult if Alternative 2 is the correct long-term approach, but action must be taken now and Alternative 1 may not only be wrong long term but also acting on Alternative 1 now may make it impossible to act later on Alternative 2.

Trade-offs are not analytically complex, although they do make decisions very difficult. Once the analyst has reexamined the objectives and priorities and, if necessary, reprojected the results for each alternative, he can do no more than display the trade-off clearly, showing the decision maker the ramifications of each possible decision.

DOCUMENTING FINDINGS

The analysis is not formally complete until it has been communicated to the decision maker and a decision is made. Especially in municipal government, the analyst and the decision maker are rarely the same person. The analyst should keep the decision maker informed of his progress throughout the analysis. He also is responsible for carefully documenting his findings to help the decision maker understand the flow of logic leading to conclusions and recommendations. Even when the decision maker is doing his own analysis, he is likely to need documentation to gain support and understanding from other audiences — the community, elected officials, or other agencies.

The documentation format will, of course, vary by agency and decision maker. However, a general format with a few comments on what might be included in each section may be helpful.

Statement of the Issue: Very briefly define the issue with the same explicitness used in the problem definition (Stage 1) of the analysis.

Summary of Conclusions and Recommendations: If the recommendations are not clear cut, the analyst should point out the trade-offs and his judgment, if any, of which alternative seems preferable.

List of Objectives Used: List each objective and briefly state its importance relative to other objectives. Also list the criteria used to measure performance against each objective.

Key Background Data on the Issue: Provide the essential descriptive quantitative and qualitative data that will be necessary for the decision maker. If data are missing, the decision maker must know what assumptions the analyst has used and why.

The Alternatives: List all alternatives, including those not fully developed. Justify early eliminations.

Conclusions and Recommendations: Concisely show the evaluation
of alternatives that led to the recommendations appearing at the
beginning of the memorandum. Implementation considerations
should also be discussed and detailed implementation plans are
often included.

Selected Bibliography

Black, Guy. "Systems Analysis in Government Operations," *Management Science,* XIV, II (October 1967), B41–B58.

Churchman, C. West. *The Systems Approach.* New York: Delacorte Press, 1968.

Enke, Stephen, ed. *Defense Management.* Englewood Cliffs, New Jersey: Prentice-Hall, Inc., 1967.

Heymont, I., et al. *Guide for Reviewers of Studies Containing Cost-Effectiveness Analysis.* Research Analysis Corporation, October, 1965. Economics and Costing Department Study, 63.2.

Kepner, Charles H., and Benjamin B. Tregoe. *The Rational Manager.* New York: McGraw-Hill, 1965.

McKean, Roland N. *Efficiency in Government Through Systems Analysis.* New York: John Wiley & Sons, Inc., 1967.

Office of the Assistant Secretary of Defense (SA). "Costing Guidelines for Department of Defense Cost-Effectiveness Studies," *Resource Analysis* (May 1, 1966).

Osborne, Alex F. *Applied Imagination: Principles and Procedures of Creative Thinking.* Revised edition. New York: Charles Scribner & Sons, 1957.

Roger, E. M. *The Diffusion of Innovations.* New York: Free Press of Glencoe, 1962.

Schnick, Allen. "The Road to PPB: The Stages of Budget Reform," *Public Administration Review* (December 1966), pp. 243–258.

Schultze, Charles L. *The Politics and Economics of Public Spending.* Washington, D.C.: The Brookings Institution, 1969.